Harnessing Professio
Development for Edu

Harnessing Professional Development for Educators

A global toolkit

Alison Fox, Helen Hendry and Deborah Cooper

 Open University Press

Open University Press
McGraw Hill
Unit 4
Foundation Park
Roxborough Way
Maidenhead
SL6 3UD

email: emea_uk_ireland@mheducation.com
world wide web: www.mheducation.co.uk

First edition published 2022

A catalogue record of this book is available from the British Library

ISBN-13: 9780335251407
ISBN-10: 0335251404
eISBN: 9780335251414

Library of Congress Cataloging-in-Publication Data
CIP data applied for

Typeset by Transforma Pvt. Ltd., Chennai, India

Praise page

"As well as being a valuable contribution to professional knowledge in this field, this resource can be thoroughly recommended to educational professionals as a guide to practice. In Wales where we have a strong focus on tackling the impact of poverty on attainment, the section on Equity will have particular relevance."

Professor David Egan, Emeritus Professor of Education, Cardiff Metropolitan University, UK

"Alison Fox, Helen Henry and Deborah Cooper should be congratulated for bringing out of the shadows and into our consciousness the need for and importance of professional development for educators. At a time when much more is demanded and required from educators in terms of cultural competence and cultural responsiveness, this book is a timely reminder that educators too need to be supported and challenged in their own development. The authors examine a range of issues that are important to enhancing practice (e.g., equity, agency, crises), some of which also present challenges to their practice. The tension is skilfully mediated in chapters 2 and 11, both of which articulates the importance of lifelong learning for educators whilst also providing guidance on how learning can and should lead to improvements in practice through increased understandings, knowledge and agency. This book is well written and is crucial for any educator at any stage of the education landscape. Well done."

Paul Miller, PhD, Professor of Educational Leadership & Social Justice

Contents

List of figures and tables

Figures

Tables

PDP tables

Acknowledgements

Chapter 1

Vignette 1: Helen would like to thank everyone involved in producing and contributing to the *Innovate* journal, which is freely available online and shares teachers' research

Vignette 3: Deborah and Alison would like to thank the members of the CPD-State of the Nation project team and all the school staff who fed into this project their experience of PD

Vignette 4: Alison would like to thank Terese Bird, University of Leicester Medical School for her collaboration in building the evidence for this vignette

Figure 1.1 (and The authors would like to thank Adrian Fox for his help in
Figure 11.1): adapting this diagram for the purposes of this book.

Chapter 2

Vignette 5: with thanks to Moortooza Puttarroo, Aston University and The Open University

Vignette 6: with thanks to Anna Richards and Kate Sida-Nicholls, both programme directors at the Suffolk and Norfolk SCITT who commissioned the project on which this vignette is based, and also to Dr Rob Loe of Relational Schools, who led the research, Lyn Dale for leading the Cambridge Assessment Admissions Testing contribution, and Eido Research for handling and analysing the database

Vignette 7: with thanks to Dr Martina Emke, Bielefeld University of Applied Sciences, Germany and The Open University. To all participants in the study who shared their Twitter experiences with me, Martina says: Herzlichen Dank!

Vignette 8: with thanks to Professor Alan Pence, UNESCO Co-Chair in Early Childhood Education, Care and Development, School of Child and Youth Care, University of Victoria, BC; Director, Early Childhood Development Virtual University (ECDVU), and member of the Centre for Global Studies, University of Victoria. Acknowledging, with respect, the University of Victoria stands on the unceded territories of the Lekwungen Peoples

Chapter 3

Deborah would like to thank Dr Jacqueline Baxter, Associate Professor in Public Policy and Management, The Open University for discussions on educational leadership during the COVID-19 pandemic

Vignette 9: Deborah would like to thank the authors Dr Liz Chamberlain, SAGE Academic Director, The Open University; Charlotte Chishava, National Programme Coordinator, PLAN International, Zimbabwe, and Claire Hedges, Senior Programmes Manager, The Open University

Vignette 10: Deborah would like to thank Dr Lauryn Oates, Executive Director, Canadian Women for Women, Afghanistan

Vignette 11: Deborah would like to acknowledge the work of AdvanceHE

Chapter 4

Case study 1: with thanks to Dr Patrina Law, The Open University

Vignette 13: with thanks to Sarah Stewart, The Open University in Wales. Sarah wishes to give thanks to the OU ITE Partnership staff and schools

Vignette 14: with thanks to Dr Kris Stutchbury, The Open University

Chapter 5

Case study 2: with thanks to Professor Freda Wolfenden, The Open University and the TESS India team

Chapter 6

Vignette 16: with thanks to Dr Esinam Avornyo, Research Fellow, University of Cape Coast, Ghana

Vignette 17: with thanks to Dr Alison Buckler, Senior Research Fellow in International Education at The Open University. Alison would like to thank the 39 tutors in Uganda who gave up their time to share their stories with the research team. Thank you also to the co-authors of the publication from which the ideas in this cameo have been drawn: Dr Kris Stutchbury, Dr George Kasule, Dr Jane Cullen, and Ms Doris Kaiije

Vignette 18: with thanks to Dr Ghulam Behlol, Fatima Jinnah Women University, Rawalpindi, Pakistan. Ghulam and Alison wish to thank leaders, tutors, and prospective teachers at Fatima Jinnah

Women University, International Islamic University Islamabad, and Government College for Elementary Teachers for their work on the project activities, facilitation, and hospitality, together with Khalid Kiani on behalf of the Federal Directorate of Education. We wish sincere thanks to both the British Council Pakistan and the Higher Education Council, Pakistan for funding the 'Promoting Inquiry Informed Practice: Bridging the gap between theory and practice for participants of pre-service teacher education program' (2014–2017)

Vignette 19: with thanks to Dr Jackie Musgrave, Associate Head of School for Education Childhood, Youth and Sport at The Open University. Jackie would like to thank her co-researcher, Karen Neal, for teaching her so much about the value of good relationships in working with parents. And thank you to all of the staff and children at the nursery for their generous sharing of their knowledge and time during the period this research was carried out

Chapter 7

Case study 3: with thanks to Jonathan (Jonty) Rix, Professor of Participation and Learning Support at The Open University and the Inland Norway University of Applied Sciences

Case study 4: with thanks to Dr Fiona Maine and the partners in the DIALLS project. The DIALLS project received funding from the European Union's Horizon 2020 research and innovation programme under grant agreement no. 770045. The sole responsibility for publication lies with the author. The European Union is not responsible for any use that may be made of the information contained therein. We are grateful to all teachers and children who took part in the project

Chapter 8

Case study 5: with thanks to Dr Claire Tyson, Paul Hanson and the Homewood School and Sixth Form Centre, Kent. Claire and Paul would like to thank Yvette Robinson and Rebecca Bennett for their feedback on their staff training

Vignette 20: with thanks to Kathy Chandler. Kathy would like to thank the students and tutors who contributed to the research

Vignette 21: with thanks to Professor Teresa Cremin. Teresa would like to thank colleagues in the partnership between Arvon, The Open University, and Exeter University, as well as all teachers who participated in the residential week

Chapter 9

Case study 6: with thanks to Anna-Marie Norden, Swavesey County Primary School, Cambridgeshire

Vignette 22: with thanks to Sarah Badger, Notre Dame High School, Kent. Sarah would like to offer her thanks to Notre Dame School, Cobham, for their support whilst she was studying for her master's and to Alison Fox and her team at The Open University for engaging her in the PDP process and helping her to see its benefits beyond the realms of academic study

Vignette 23: with thanks to Dr Tom Power, The Open University. Tom would like to offer thanks to Professors Robert McCormick and Rama Mathew for their contributions to the EIA RME, and to all of the EIA programme team and participants

Chapter 11

The book authors would like to thank alumni of the Master's in Education programme Charlotte Lord (Vignette 24), Elizabeth Edwards (Vignette 25), Anne Kagoya (Vignette 26), and Susannah Burrell (Vignette 27) who worked together to create the body of the content for this chapter collaboratively

0 **How to use this book**

This book has been designed to be of interest and use to multiple audiences. Depending on your role, career experience, and aspirations, you might find different parts of the book of more interest than others. We have signposted you to which chapters might be good ways into the book. Look for the hashtags under the chapter headings:

> #early career professional; #middle leader; #senior or executive leader; #teacher/professional educator, abbreviated to #EC #ML #SL #TE respectively.

More than one of these categories might suit you. Early career professionals often find themselves quickly taking on what might be considered middle leadership positions. In smaller settings, a divide between middle and senior leadership might not be clear. Teacher educators might also hold leadership roles in practice settings.

Whilst we have suggested that you can access the book at multiple points, it is recommended that you refer to Chapters 10 and 11 after the other chapters. We imagined the readership of this book as educators and educational leaders in a range of educational settings such as schools, colleges, and Higher Education Institutes. We have deliberately taken a broad view of professional development (PD) and illustrated the key ideas and issues through references and examples in international and a range of practice settings. We hope you will find the diverse reference list for the book a resource in itself.

Underpinning this book is a personal development planning (PDP) toolkit to support you in reflecting on the significance of what you read now and in the future. By focusing on personal, academic, and professional/career/employability dimensions separately and in combination, this book alerts you to opportunities to identify how issues covered here might stimulate you to take actions, record your progress, and review your next steps.

If you see a box like this, it is a point for reflection:

Reflection point 0:1

This will be generally a question provoking reflection. You might use your reflections for your own self-development individually or as a stimulus for collaborative discussion.

These reflection points, which are included in all chapters, are relevant to the issues covered in the surrounding text. They build to further questions and suggested actions in a table at the end of each chapter by focusing on dimensions of PDP. One implication is that, by using this book as a form of PDP with these reflection points and tables, you might find that other parts of the book become more relevant to your context.

PD involves reading widely, like you are doing now. To support you in this, we have committed to pointing you towards open access materials wherever possible. You will find recommended readings towards the end of each chapter, selected of relevance for different roles available to the public with no fee.

Reflection point 0:2

You could gather together your responses to reflection points to see how your thinking has developed and what implications this has for developing your practice. This will support you in being a reflexive practitioner.

If you are a master's student, teacher educator or, increasingly, a member of a school trust or alliance, you can check which references you can source from the book's bibliography through your library's subscriptions, for anything which has piqued your interest. We note that there is a movement towards opening access to academic publications and so it is worth searching to see whether any journal article is also available that way. If you are interested in a particular academic's publications, you can search to see whether their institution has an open repository to help you track down any open access copies of the publications you are interested in. There are also social networking platforms such as LinkedIn, ResearchGate, and Academia.edu which you can join to contact or search for academics who have opened access to pre-print copies of their publications. We have included some doctoral theses in our recommended reading. We hope you will find these in-depth studies of interest, even though you might not necessarily read the whole of any thesis. The thesis introductions and conclusions are likely to guide you as to whether you want to read more about the evidence collected.

Reflection point 0:3

If you are planning to take advantage of the ideas for wider reading, think about where you will store the information you will gain so you can find it again or pass it on to someone else.

---

1 Professional skills and professional knowledge

#EC #ML #SL #TE

The why and what of professional development

You might pick up this book and wonder why you should spend time thinking about professional development (PD). Perhaps the most important reason is that PD is an essential tool for improving educators'[1] skills and knowledge, so crucial to improving student outcomes (Opfer and Pedder, 2011; Sancar et al., 2021). The relationship between the key elements of PD are conceptualised in Figure 1.1.

The arrow in Figure 1.1 illustrates the journey of contexts for PD, acting as opportunities for learning throughout an educator's career. On joining the profession, an educator is entering a landscape of reforms and policies driving their

Figure 1.1 A conceptual framework for educator PD

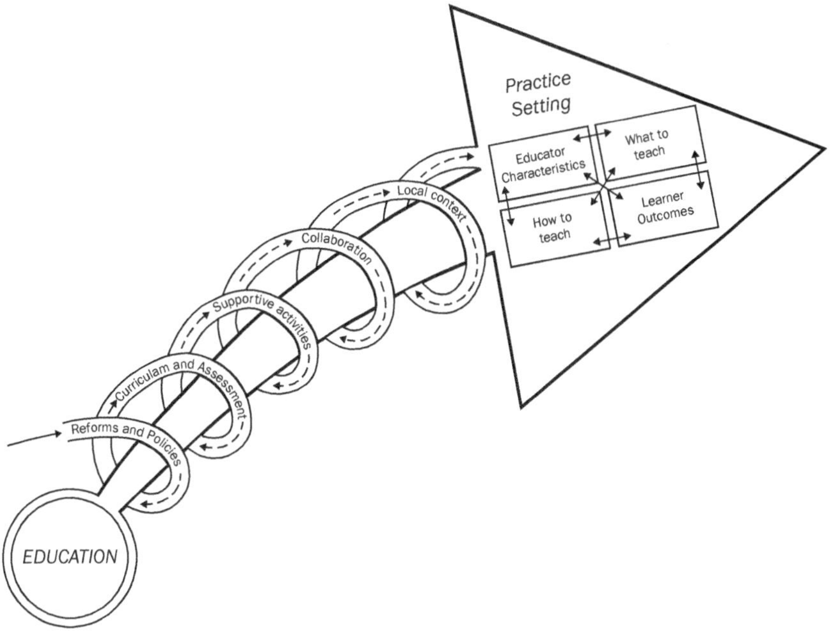

Adapted from figure 2 in Sancar et al. (2021: 8).

work. They need to learn about how to enact these through their implementation of the curriculum, associated assessment, standards, and pedagogies, in ways which can be supported through collaboration. This needs to be set in the local context to allow each educator, through continuing professional development (CPD), to constantly adapt their support of teaching and learning in their practice setting to maximise learner outcomes. However, there is debate about what models of PD might be most effective or appropriate in different circumstances. This chapter introduces key ideas from the book: characteristics of effective PD, collaboration and inquiry, research literacy, global and digital PD.

More than ever before, teacher professional skills and knowledge are subject to increasing standardisation, measurement, and accountability (D.H. Hargreaves, 2019). Effective approaches to PD are needed. However, PD is constantly evolving and recent responses to the coronavirus pandemic have highlighted new ways of networking and online opportunities for PD. As explored further in Chapter 3, these responses have also emphasised the wider professional role of teachers in the heart of their communities (e.g. Allan, 2020; Gill, 2021). Responses to the pandemic offer optimism for educators' ability to rapidly adapt and work together in new, outward-looking ways.

Ideas about educator PD have changed with changing perspectives on the role of educators and educational leaders. For the first half of the twentieth century, the teacher role was perceived as managing classes and transmitting knowledge skills; requiring limited PD (Hargreaves, 2000). However, in the 1980s, individual PD came to the fore based on a more complex concept of teaching aiming to examine and build on educators' deep internalised understanding or tacit 'craft knowledge' to apply to teaching in different contexts (Hagger and McIntyre, 2006; Zeichner et al., 1987). PD began to focus on teachers developing individual strategies to communicate subject matter knowledge in the classroom (Shulman and Shulman, 2009).

The next shift took account of context and working in communities. PD that focused on individual development was criticised as problematic if it did not acknowledge the role of contexts, school communities, and workplace environments. These social environments have an important influence on an educator and, in turn, educators can influence and shape the community through their practice (Cochran-Smith and Lytle, 1999). The early twenty-first century might be termed the 'age of the collegial professional' (Hargreaves, 2000: 151). PD became connected to the needs of the community through a culture of whole-school professional development and collaborative inquiry.

Reflection point 1:1

- *Is your experience of PD focused more on you as an individual or organised at a school/organisational level?*
- *What are the benefits and challenges of these different types of PD in your experience?*

The principles behind collaborative learning and professional learning communities

Collaboration can be within and across organisations. Organised forms of this have been termed professional learning communities, an idea which has travelled globally from the United States (Lieberman, 2007), through Africa (e.g. Botha, 2012) to Asia (e.g. Chen, 2020; Lee and Kim, 2016). This might see, for example, groups of schools working together around hubs or in consortia (Nelson et al., 2015). Within an organisation, this might be through forms of what have been termed joint practice development (Sebba et al., 2012), for example through lesson study (Dudley, 2012).

Lesson study originated in Asia, and travelled via the USA to Europe (Hadfield and Jopling, 2016; Xu, 2020). It differs from previous models of classroom action research by having a focus on, 'How can we teach x to y (even) more effectively?' (Dudley, 2012: 87). If lesson study is used as a whole- or inter-school approach, it can examine teacher beliefs, teacher knowledge, professional learning, student learning, classroom tools and routines (Dudley et al., 2019). Lesson study has been shown to be versatile for adaptation to higher education and initial teacher education (Larssen et al., 2018), and its potential for supporting teacher agency (examined in Chapter 10) is exemplified further in Chapter 8.

Whatever the format, key principles include care and concern for the children, trust and reciprocity between staff, and opportunities for evaluation and challenge (Sebba et al., 2012). Single institutions offering PD can be at a disadvantage compared with those collaborating across a cluster, network or alliance and have been reported as more likely to lose momentum due to external competition, funding, external curriculum changes, and pressures of testing (Giles and Hargreaves, 2006). Collaboration between schools has been seen as offering a 'self-improving' school system (Hargreaves, 2014) of networked schools (Katz and Earl, 2010).

Working collaboratively across 'self-improving' schools might be a goal, but you will probably appreciate that changing culture and proposing new ways of working might meet resistance. It requires more than sharing good practice, especially when it is felt possible that poor practice might be exposed. Staff at all levels might not wish to work beyond their comfort zones and take on these additional expectations (Fullan, 2007), especially as they seek to balance work/life responsibilities (Gronn, 2003). The success of PD involves adequate support and individual commitment. Staff need to work in a culture in which it becomes usual to have a range of opportunities to expand their experiences beyond their current role, team, and organisational setting. This has been termed an 'expansive environment' for PD (Fuller and Unwin, 2004) and its role is reiterated in Chapters 2 and 9. Deep partnerships (Hargreaves, 2014) can contribute to such an 'expansive' environment, using joint PD to help adapt practices to the needs of those in their setting.

Reflection point 1:2

In relation to the strategy for PD in your organisation:

* *In what ways does this include opportunities for collaboration, either internally or beyond your organisation?*
* *Are these opportunities always welcomed and embraced by others, or can you identify factors affecting engagement in collaborative PD?*

The challenge of research-informed teaching

Educators are regularly presented with new initiatives: from consultants, training events or transferred through practitioner networks. It is not always clear on what these initiatives are based. Part of leadership is encouraging interest in examining the evidence basis for recommendations. A key problem is accessing research published by academics in higher education settings, so often hidden behind subscription walls. Luckily, more and more open access literature is becoming publicly available and some leaders organise subscriptions to targeted publications. Accessing research evidence is important but is not a straightforward solution. 'What works' in different situations with different learners, interpreted by different staff members, varies. As well as access, educators require 'research literacy' skills and an ability to critically filter and evaluate (Addae-Kyeremeh, 2020). Cain (2018) suggests teachers need to consider their prior assumptions about an issue, identify and discuss different evidence, and use this to inform their teaching decisions. Criticality is needed to navigate conflicting research evidence and gain the most from educators' own enquiries and others' research.

School-based journals and websites (acting as teacher 'hubs') are emerging to support teachers' research literacy. Vignette 1 describes a platform encouraging teachers to read research and conduct their own small-scale studies.

Reflection point 1:3

* *Identify a source of published work which has inspired your practice. Reflect on how you came across this.*
* *Were you convinced about the evidence on which it was based? Did you feel confident in evaluating the evidence?*

Vignette 1: Innovate Journal – 'By teachers for teachers' (Helen Hendry)

Innovate Journal publishes teacher-led research inquiries with the aim of helping to build a research-informed community. It began in its current form in 2017 and is a publicly accessible online journal linked to the Innovate Teaching School Partnership in Northamptonshire, England. The publication began by offering a structure to support teachers to conduct their own small-scale inquiries over an academic year with three issues taking them through the context and aims of their research, the data collection process and rationale, followed by their findings and impact on their teaching practice.

In the third year of publishing, the journal moved away from this structure as more content came in from teachers who were already familiar with the process of conducting a small-scale inquiry. The journal Editor, Meera Chudasama, an English teacher with a master's degree in education, wanted to create a teacher-research journal that encouraged teachers to read research in a format that was 'easily digestible and applicable to the classroom'. The focus was making a connection between research and practice that she felt was missing in traditional academic journals.

Whose knowledge counts?

Education systems around the world have an embedded focus on performance and accountability, which can present a tension for staff teams and school leaders. This focus can lead to a 'top-down' view of PD where teachers are told what they need to learn. An emphasis on government priorities and curricula initiatives may result in PD that focuses on training teachers to 'teach to the test' (Isaacs et al., 2019; Sachs, 2016) and sometimes has limited impact on educator understanding (Isaacs at al., 2019). More authentic PD can be based around staff concerns, questions and issues experienced within a school or cluster of schools. PD based on a shared understanding of local priorities can be transformative for teachers, enabling them to effect change, critique policy, and question taken-for-granted assumptions thus contributing to the social endeavour of schools (Sachs, 2016). Whilst covered further in Chapters 6 and 7, a recent example of this can be seen in PD developed for Early Years practitioners in Malawi. The starting point for educators' PD was interviews with parents of Early Years children with disabilities enrolled in the centres in the region. These revealed details of their experiences and expectations for their children which were used to shape the PD, stimulating staff discussion from the perspectives of families that they were working with (Soni et al., 2020).

PD for teachers is big business. Vignette 2 reflects on the marketisation and globalisation of PD and outlines concerns in these approaches.

> **Vignette 2: Globalisation of CPD (Deborah Cooper)**
>
> Teachers collect resources for their classes like magpies; shiny practices to bring learning to life. They can fine-tune curricula for the learners in front of them: changing an assessment here, selecting a poignant story there, varying the pace of delivery on the spot through tacit knowledge.
>
> After a busy day at work, a pre-prepared meal can be a welcome, time-saving relief. But the education 'ready meal' equivalent in the form of commercially produced learning packages raises several critical questions for leaders. Ball (2012) refers to this as 'Edu business' in relation to globalisation.
>
> In the US, there has been fierce debate around the use of scripted lesson plans for teaching schemes in New York, California, and other states (Papanastasiou, 2017; Rooney, 2018). One rationale for giving everyone the same intervention is fairness in developing quality teaching towards core standards that can be measured in tests. Others see teaching to high stake tests as unhelpful for equity, furthering the privatisation of education and undermining teacher professionalism.
>
> Whilst schools may need to buy in software or curricula, rather than design their own, this global marketplace of educational commercial training products blurs lines between a product and required PD (Crowley, 2017). Critics have, for example, questioned the evidence basis and misconceptions of 'neuromyths' seen in commercial products and ineffective teaching (Howard-Jones, 2014).
>
> These debates show that PD is not neutral and reflects what is going on in national and international arenas. As leaders, we need to examine if what works in one context will work in our own.
>
> Similar debates surround private schools in Africa, which have used lesson scripts and headphone technology to guide teachers in the classrooms. Teacher unions have protested this use of underqualified teachers as a form of colonialism (Ravitch, 2015). Others have raised equity and moral issues of the need for philanthropy and new solutions to meet chronic teacher and resource shortages.

Choices about what and how to teach, as exemplified in Vignette 2, are at the heart of whose knowledge counts in PD. At a regional level, marketisation can lead to inter-school competition (Outhwaite, 2021). Where schools train others, they develop new PD offers and engage in the marketisation of these to others (Elliott, 2018). Scaling up PD is the focus of Chapter 5.

Caution is needed as with any PD programme, particularly when transported internationally. PD created in one country may be underpinned by a view of education that does not represent the context, culture or social norms and values in another. There are alternative, locally-driven approaches. Soni and colleagues' (2020) study in Malawi shows the potential for a more participatory 'bottom-up' and situated approach to PD that includes the voices of children and families. This is based on the assertion that '… consulting pupils can enhance the effectiveness of CPD because pupils tend to provide feedback that is practical and lesson specific' (Opfer and Pedder, 2010: 426).

Creating an expansive culture for PD with opportunities to investigate areas meaningful to staff is clearly important. In addition, the form that PD takes can influence the impact, as discussed in Vignette 3. Who decides if CPD is funded or not, who can access it, what form it takes, and whether or not it is accredited? The answers to these questions will vary according to where you work, your role, and the local and government priorities. This variety might be positive, allowing a local focus on different needs in the workforce (Jones, 2011) or local issues (Outhwaite, 2021). Alternatively, the differences might be seen as inconsistent gaps reflecting unfair lack of access to quality PD.

Vignette 3: State of the Nations – nothing has changed (Deborah Cooper and Alison Fox)

To map the differences in PD practice, large-scale reviews of teacher CPD were commissioned in the late 2000s both in England (McCormick et al., 2008) and Wales (Jones, 2011). The English study consisted of a survey and literature review (McCormick et al., 2008) designed to understand the benefits and impact of CPD, how it was organised, and what the most and least effective strategies were.

It showed that, although a range of CPD practices was possible – from observation, mentoring, collaboration, and team teaching and networks – many were ineffective in having an impact on school improvement. This was generally because the conditions for CPD were not prioritised (Opfer and Pedder, 2011). Both reviews found that CPD was often too short, not supported, not tied into collaboration, and not evaluated beyond perceptions. Despite national studies such as these, little has changed (Teacher Toolkit, 2019).

The implication for leaders of CPD is to take a strategic approach to organising CPD around school improvement priorities. Leaders can create conditions for developing social capital and balance the needs of individuals or they will find that they are hindering these conditions, for example through the negative, punitive impacts of performance management.

The who and how of PD

As evidenced in the 'State of the Nation' reviews outlined in Vignette 3, in-school PD has often been concentrated on 'event-delivery' through whole-school staff 'training days' or a succession of twilight sessions amounting to less than a week of PD (Opfer and Pedder, 2011). The limitation with this method of PD is that there may be inadequate staff connection or ongoing support to implement and evaluate any changes to practice. Event delivery of PD tends to offer fewer opportunities for hands-on 'active learning'. Teachers need to try new ideas in practice in collaboration with staff teams over a sustained period (Cordingley, 2009; Opfer and Pedder, 2011).

These findings are globally relevant. For example, a doctoral study of teachers in Nigeria and England found agreement about aspects of effective PD. In both cases, PD was sought that offered new ideas to improve teacher knowledge and enhance skills for practice, offering practical strategies based on evidence. PD was agreed to be clearly linked to improving students' learning and outcomes (Adagiri, 2014).

Teachers can offer resources to one another whether in formal or non-formal roles. This might involve coaching or mentoring relationships. Coaching involves the facilitation of dialogue and thinking, resulting in equal contributions rather than a hierarchical relationship. Mentors are generally more experienced in a particular area and can provide a role model or share advice. Both approaches commonly include reflection and sharing, agreed outcomes, a focus on learning and teaching, mutual benefit, support, and challenge. Often the coached or mentored peer raises the agendas driving the associated PD activities. Successful mentoring strategies might include team teaching with mentees so that both teachers can construct teaching solutions through dialogue, in planning, during and after a lesson. Alternatively, mentors may lead a reflective discussion after teaching (Cuenca, 2011; Kane and Francis, 2013). In a collective case study of pre-service teachers and newly qualified teachers learning to teach early reading in England, the participants most valued:

- support in the classroom through team teaching and follow-up dialogue about the next steps in pupil learning;
- daily informal discussion about teaching and learning;
- opportunities to observe teaching in different classes and discuss the teaching strategies observed (Hendry, 2016).

In any mentoring relationship, problems can be caused by over-reliance on an observation–feedback loop that can make teachers feel particularly vulnerable. Studies of pre-service and early career primary and secondary teachers in England found that many mentors focused on 'judgementoring', which involved concentrating on giving, often negative, feedback (Hobson and Malderez, 2013). As important as the organisation of coaching and mentoring opportunities might be, it is the supportive relationship and open dialogue that characterises effectiveness.

Key features of effective PD discussed throughout the chapter have been based on supportive environments, collaboration, contextual relevance, practitioner inquiry and research. Access to PD at different levels is further expanding through digitalisation, including massive open online courses (MOOCs), badged open courses (BOCs), and the use of social media platforms. These offer unique opportunities to access at any time and complete at a teacher's own pace.

Vignette 4: What do we know about social media use for professional learning? (Alison Fox)

Social media use in the 'caring' professions has sparked international media attention. Rather than highlighting its value as a vehicle for professional development, attention has been drawn to negative aspects of inappropriate behaviour and reputational damage. In response, both professions have developed national or state-wide codes of conduct (e.g. Victoria State Government, 2013) with guidance to protect professionals from detrimental implications of 'unprofessional conduct' through social media (Department for Education, 2014). In the UK, social media risk avoidance training is now built into the first weeks of initial teacher and medical training courses and compliance is expected (e.g. The King's School, 2015). The same is true for schools, colleges, general practice surgeries, and healthcare trusts, with individual organisations setting advice, usually guided by professional associations and unions (e.g. Association for School and College Leaders, 2016).

A scoping review of literature published between 2009 and 2016 about teachers' and doctors' use of social media (Fox and Bird, 2017a) concluded that, as a consequence, research was not taking place which focused on professional learning. This is needed by professionals to provide an evidence base to evaluate their social media use. The main similarities across the two literatures is that most research is taking place in higher education, rather than other contexts for teaching and learning. The high number of empirical studies in these settings provide evidence about how training teachers and doctors use and wish to use social media for their learning. A body of knowledge is being gathered about the use of, attitudes to, concerns about, and reported benefits of social media use by such professionals. Since this review, which noted useful studies with teachers (Aaen, 2015; Goodyear et al., 2014; Luehmann and Tinelli, 2008; Rutherford, 2013; Wood, 2012), evidence is now being generated, often focusing on the affordances of certain tools; with most attention being paid whilst this book was being written to Twitter and Facebook.

Vignette 4 highlights that teachers engaging in digital opportunities for PD need to feel safe from repercussions. This is not so different from moving from individual to collaborative practice development covered earlier in the chapter. However, it involves the new dimension of negotiating personal and professional identities online (Fox and Bird, 2017b). This might mean some participate peripherally in networked communities (Kontopoulou, 2019). To move this engagement to impact on an educator's practice requires opportunities to reflect and discuss with other teachers (Parsons et al., 2019). For isolated educators in geographical locations without local expertise, or when like-minded colleagues are disparately located or distanced by a pandemic, online PD can offer such opportunities and the chance to become part of one or multiple professional learning communities. The potential and challenges of offering and receiving PD at a distance are covered further in Chapter 4 and reiterated as a concern throughout the professional career in Chapter 2.

In conclusion

This chapter has shown that views of PD opportunities have changed over time and are still a subject of some tension and debate. PD is influenced by policy directives, market forces, and changing technology. However, there is consensus that educators need to be empowered by PD. The danger is to avoid schools being overly driven by accountability agendas in the educational sector leading to an overt focus on policy implementation or mandated improvement (Hadfield and Jopling, 2016). Explored further in Chapter 8, a genuine culture of professional learning, with leadership is needed '… to encourage, engage and empower teachers in the collaborative quest' (A. Hargreaves, 2019: 618). PD should offer practical connections to educators' real-life concerns, whilst also helping them to look beyond their own teaching and learning settings with sustained opportunities to learn from and with one another. They also need to develop the critical skills to respond to and create research relevant to their own circumstances.

Personal Development Planning Table 1 Focus: Academic

Question	What can I do?	What do I need from others?
	Short-term action	Medium-term action
1.What do I know about different models of PD?	Note down some different ways of organising PD that you have experienced and anything you would like to find out more about	Find out about other models of PD from colleagues. Follow up on reading about selected PD approaches
2. How do I engage critically with research literature?	Think of an area of research that would support your PD. Look for ways to access reports and articles online. Explore whether sites such as LinkedIn (https://gb.linkedin.com), ResearchGate (https://www.researchgate.net/), and Academia.edu (https://www.academia.edu) look worthy of signing up to	Compare readings with a colleague or team. Discuss any alternative perspectives and possible bias, and reflect on application in your context
3. What online PD is relevant to my needs?	Note down any area that you would like to pursue. Investigate open education resources on platforms such as OpenLearn	Ask if others have engaged in online PD and have recommendations

NB: Recommended Open Access Readings are highlighted below, using asterisks as follows: *Leaders and Teacher Educators, **Practitioners, ***Early Career Professionals.

Recommended reading

* British Educational Research Association (BERA) (2014) *Research and the teaching profession: Building the capacity for a self-improving education system.* Final report of the BERA-RSA Inquiry into the role of research in teacher education [https://www.thersa.org/globalassets/pdfs/bera-rsa-research-teaching-profession-full-report-for-web-2.pdf].
* Hendry, H. (2016). *Becoming a teacher of early reading: An activity systems analysis of the journey from student to newly qualified teacher.* Doctoral dissertation, University of Leicester [https://ethos.bl.uk/OrderDetails.do?uin=uk.bl.ethos.696132].
* Sebba, J., Kent, P. and Tregenza, J. (2012) *Joint practice development: What does the evidence suggest are effective approaches.* Nottingham: National College of School Leadership (NCSL) [https://assets.publishing.service.gov.uk/government/uploads/system/uploads/attachment_data/file/335729/jpd-what-does-the-evidence-suggest-are-effective-approaches-long.pdf].
** Adagiri, S.O. (2014) *A comparative study of teachers' continuing professional development (CPD) in Nigeria and England: A study of primary schools in Abuja and Portsmouth.* Doctoral dissertation, University of Portsmouth [https://researchportal.port.ac.uk/en/theses/a-comparative-study-of-teachers-continuing-professional-development-cpd-in-nigeria-and-england(92d3e1df-fcce-40bd-a774-b9cfbb25da26).html].
** Nelson, R., Spence-Thomas, K. and Taylor, C. (2015) *What makes great pedagogy and great professional development. Final report: Teaching schools R&D network national themes projects 2012–14* [https://core.ac.uk/download/pdf/74377321.pdf].
*** Rutherford, C. (2013) Facebook as a source of informal teacher professional development, *E in Education*, 16 (1): 60–74 [https://ourspace.uregina.ca/handle/10294/3101].

Note

1 Educator is generally used in the book for more inclusivity of the range of language used to cover 'teaching' roles. Teacher is used when the evidence specifically refers to a role in schools and classrooms.

2 PD through the professional career

#EC #ML #SL #TE

This chapter examines the need for professional development (PD) in preparation for and within a professional career linked to education. Different stages of developing a career bring with them different needs for support. Therefore, PD is sometimes referred to as CPD, or continuing professional development, to highlight the need for ongoing professional learning throughout a career in education. In terms of implications for leadership of PD, five key issues are identified: recognising personal histories, accepting its social nature, enacting inclusivity, providing opportunities for collaboration, and allowing for educator agency.

The importance of personal histories

It is important to recognise that where you are now in terms of your role, interests, and practice has its roots in the life you had before you became involved with education. It is beyond the remit of this book to cover how childhood and adolescent identity development, and familial, educational, and wider life experiences influence routes into educational roles (e.g. Chang-Kredl and Kingsley, 2014). However, we believe it is worth reflecting on.

Reflection point 2:1

- *What or who have affected your route into your current educational role?*
- *How have these influences shaped you as a professional?*

Leaders need to recognise how the personal histories of those joining the profession impact on a professional's identity development. We start by considering the significance of pre-service PD, the roles of pre-service training, and acknowledging the range of routes into teaching and educational roles (e.g. Akinbote, 2009; Robertson and Brott, 2013). These might include career changing from other sectors, taking educational roles within other sectors than primary, secondary, tertiary or higher education (such as healthcare or the military), and recognising international contexts for teacher recruitment.

Professional identity can be considered both an individual construct of self and a collective representation of a profession (Wiles, 2013). It is not fixed and is context dependent. Developing a professional identity therefore connects with forming an impression of a chosen profession and socialising into that profession (Browne et al., 2018). This socialisation process occurs through education and experience (Nuttman-Schwartz, 2017). Shaping professional identities therefore starts before undergraduate study, with students potentially arriving with a preconceived idea (pre-professional identity) of their chosen future profession (Jackson, 2016). Vignette 5 illustrates that it can be useful to explore perceptions of a profession before joining it, which might affect someone's interest in and expectations from that profession.

Vignette 5: New opportunities for recruiting professionals through open courses – nursing (Moortooza Puttaroo)

Around the world, nursing baccalaureate, master, and doctoral degree programmes prepare nurses for a variety of nursing roles. Nurses are educated to develop nursing theories and conceptual models, conduct nursing research, and test nursing theories (Lee et al., 2013). As a result, nursing is becoming more scholarly and thus transforming the professional identity of nursing (Cronenwett et al., 2011). Prospective nursing students need to become aware that the professional identity of nursing has evolved. This awareness, in turn, can have a positive effect on prospective nursing students to be motivated to embrace the nursing profession.

Massive Open online courses (MOOCs) are also being used by several universities to enable participants to engage with university-level study, to explore a new subject area, and to prepare them for higher education more generally. Recent examples of UK-based MOOC courses in nursing are: *Introduction to Nursing: The Role of Nurses Around the World* (King's College London – FutureLearn platform) and *Introduction to Nursing: The application of bioscience, psychology and sociology* (York University – FutureLearn platform). Increasing numbers of universities are using MOOCs as a taster of different courses to raise aspiration for further study. Beyond recruitment there is an educational potential from such courses. Open courses can reach out to a wide audience and, prior to making decisions to start formal training, explore and support the development of future professional identities towards embracing a career, for example, in nursing.

Vignette 5 illustrates how professional identity development can be supported by those already in the profession, inviting potential new entrants into a conversation about the purpose, values, and practices existing in the profession. Such a welcome could open a door to starting peripheral engagement in existing communities of practice (Lave and Wenger, 1991) even before taking on an official role. This might lead those interested to take volunteering roles, ask to shadow experienced practitioners, or talk to those already in the profession about the realities and possibilities of becoming an education professional.

PD is social

As highlighted in Chapter 1, the role of others in PD cannot be overemphasised, particularly when joining a profession. This might involve formal induction, coaching, and mentoring as part of training and early career PD programmes (e.g. Ehrich et al., 2004), or the more informal support embedded in relationships built when joining the education workforce (e.g. Le Cornu, 2013). Others can help overcome the potential danger of professional isolation when working with discrete groups of learners and enable socialisation into different teams and communities within an organisation and/or beyond.

Reflection point 2:2

- *Identify who helped you as you joined the profession or who you have supported in a new position or role. What help was needed/useful?*
- *What do you think about the role of digital networking in supporting a sense of belonging to education as a profession?*

Relationships influence the ways in which people cope with stress, access advice, learn, collaborate, and find fulfilment in their work. The significance of considering wellbeing in PD provision is picked up in Chapter 3. The affective support gained from others is particularly so in professions which rely on positive relationship-building, such as in education. Teaching involves relationship-building with a wide range of others: students, colleagues, leaders, parents, and agency workers supporting students (e.g. Fox and Wilson, 2015). In many Global North contexts, there is a crisis in teacher retention that is particularly acute during teachers' early careers (e.g. Hughes, 2012). Vignette 6 reflects on a teacher education provider in England that wished to maximise its relational support for trainees. The trainees came to recognise that support could come from anyone and anywhere and did not need to be limited to formal support provided.

Vignette 6: Support for training teachers (Alison Fox)

It is not fully understood as to who stays and who leaves teacher training and why. The Suffolk and Norfolk School-Centred Initial Teacher Training (SCITT) programme wanted to gain an understanding of the relational factors that help explain why some people do not complete their training (Hobson et al.,

2009), and to use this evidence to inform earlier and effective interventions for their early career teachers (Joiner and Edwards, 2008). They commissioned a social start-up company Relational Schools, in partnership with the established Cambridge Assessment Admissions Testing and the Open University, to carry out a five-year research and development project focused on relationally-focused diagnostic tools.

A dataset built from a demographic survey, socio-mapping of trainees' personal and professional networks, Cambridge Assessment's Cambridge Personal Styles Questionnaire, and Relational Schools' Relational Proximity Framework was correlated against performance both mid-year and on course completion. The project found empowerment potential from using these tools with trainees to reveal and explore the value and challenges of their existing and emerging relationships. This project also gave the training provider clues about relational protective and risk factors related to trainee retention. Protective factors included:

- using friends and family for relaxation and, if they have children, practical help;
- having friends and family who also help professionally;
- strong relationships with mentor(s);
- strong relationship with tutor(s);
- strong relationships with other staff in schools, in particular teaching assistants;
- positive experiences of using social media with peers;
- a high total number of others in their network.

It was important to be welcomed into and develop a sense of belonging in schools as workplaces. However, recognising that work relationships are not always constructive and supportive, but may also be challenging, requires a relational resilience. Sufficient support is needed in a network to be able to deal with situations, whether challenges arise personally or professionally (Fox et al., 2021).

A need for inclusivity

The diversity of educators (and, as discussed in Vignette 5, potential educators) brings us on to the need for an inclusive approach to PD. Whilst planning to offer inclusive PD, it is important to avoid systematic or inadvertent exclusion. Factors to consider include: age, educational background, gender, as well as any of the protected characteristics which underpin rights in UK society (HM Government, 2010).

Education is often a non-linear career, characterised by career changers both on entry into the profession (e.g. Tigchelaar et al., 2008) and within it (e.g. Wilkins and Comber, 2015). Age and the different life experiences new professionals bring is one factor to consider when planning PD. Just over half (54 per cent) of the trainees joining the programmes discussed in Vignette 5 for both primary and secondary school teaching were under the age of 25. Conversely, some trainees each year exceed the age of 50 (Fox et al., 2021). Although these are postgraduate trainees, even the under 25s usually have experience other than academic study, typically working with or volunteering in roles involving children and young people. The implication is that courses inviting, welcoming, and supporting new trainees should not adopt a deficit model of PD needs. Instead, they should build on the life experience which all, but especially older trainees from other careers, bring into the profession (Fox and Wilson, 2008). A second factor to inclusive approaches to PD is to consider different educational histories. Teaching and educational roles are not a graduate profession internationally and new teachers or early years workers might join without any formal qualification, such as based on the number of years they have completed schooling. The issue of teacher recruitment internationally is covered further in Chapter 5. In South Africa, the Project for Inclusive Early Childhood Care and Education consortium created a framework for higher education provision for early childhood practitioners that takes into account these different starting points (PIECCE, 2020).

Reflection point 2:3

What expertise do you bring into your current educational role from beyond your workplace or previous experiences?

Support for professionals continues to be needed once in-service in ways that might depend on their particular setting (e.g. Newmann et al., 2000) or discipline (e.g. Fiorentini et al., 2011). This should continue into recognising the needs of established professionals, who are likely to have developed multiple identities in the course of their career (Iwaniec-Thompson, 2022) and will benefit from PD in relation to these. Further factors to consider include gender (e.g. Baker et al., 2003), ethnicity or disability (e.g. Nishimura, 2014). In some settings, PD needs to take 'account of the vulnerability of [early childhood education and care] settings such as food shortages and lack of buildings and play materials' (Soni et al., 2020, p. 20) to ensure not only that the training is locally appropriate in terms of using easily sourced resources, but also that the physical needs of the educators are looked after. Culturally relevant PD is the focus of Chapter 6.

The value of collaboration

If PD is social and is to be inclusive, it is no surprise that effective PD is usually collaborative, as introduced in Chapter 1 and explored further in Chapter 8 (Stoll et al., 2012). As noted earlier, informal community support to teachers joining the profession (Izadinia, 2016) is important. Enacting inclusivity will involve reflecting on contemporary evidence about the constraints on career progression, such as those related to gender – for example, girls' access to education (e.g. Chamberlain et al., 2021) and experience of 'glass ceilings' to careers (e.g. Runhare and Gordon, 2004), and men joining from military backgrounds or feeling othered in female-dominated educational settings such as early years and primary education (e.g. Robertson and Brott, 2013; Skelton, 2009) – disability or minority background status (Carrington and Skelton, 2003). Role models and mentoring continue to play a role once established in the profession, especially as increasingly senior roles are taken on, reaping benefits for both mentor and mentee (e.g. Hansford and Ehrich, 2006; Lofthouse, 2018).

Reflection point 2:4

- *Is there anyone who acts as a role model for you (whether they know this or not)?*
- *Do they come from within or beyond your work experience?*

Opportunities for more inclusive PD opportunities need to and are being offered, including pan-national collaborative initiatives such as illustrated in Vignette 7.

Vignette 7: Collaborative higher education provision for inspiring and transforming practice – the ECDVU (Alan Pence)

The Early Childhood Development Virtual University (ECDVU) is a capacity development initiative focused on countries in Africa, but with a storyline that connects with an earlier story that commenced in 1989 and focused on Indigenous communities in Canada.

'In the beginning ...' was a phone call from a large Tribal Council in north-central Canada seeking to explore a possible partnership with Alan Pence's university department that would involve the development of a contextually and culturally sensitive ECD education/training programme for community-based deliveries within the Council's territory. The students were Indigenous community members interested in being employed as staff for to-be-developed early childhood services. What became the First Nations Partnerships Program has its own, fifteen-plus years' story, largely captured in *Supporting Indigenous Children's Development* (Ball and Pence, 2006). As a result of the recommendations, the project was extended in the mid-1990s.

The interests of the donors (UNICEF and later the World Bank) were in promoting capacity through leadership, rather than directly finding frontline services.

Leaders were in a position to advance policies, programmes, training, and networks essential for the overall development of early childhood services that were the focus for ECDVU. Most of the individuals in these key, national-level positions did not have an ECD background, providing the ECDVU an opportunity to introduce a 'common ECD language'. This allows for working together across silos, across backgrounds, and across African countries (Pence and Benner, 2015). Participants, working largely asynchronously online but coming together every six months for two weeks face-to-face, form communities of learners and leaders that even now, 20 years after the launch of the ECDVU in 2001, continue to inform, shape, and motivate ECD developments through their 138 graduates (out of 145 participants), across 17 African countries.

Community spaces and relationships within these, as illustrated in Vignette 7, need to be sufficiently open to allow different perspectives and approaches to be considered and debated, as well as offering 'safe' opportunities to question policy directives (Hendry, 2020).

PD requires agency

Professionals need to be able to feel that they can follow their own trajectories of identity development, that they have an agency in finding ways to meet their own needs in the workplace and apply new knowledge to their everyday work. These concepts are reflected on further in Chapter 10. Organisations can offer an expansive, rather than a restrictive learning environment (Evans et al., 2006). In these workplace settings, there would be:

- opportunities for close collaborative working;
- out-of-institution educational opportunities, including to reflect and think differently;
- an explicit focus on educator learning, as a dimension of normal working practices;
- supported opportunities for PD that go beyond those linked to policy initiatives;
- opportunities to engage with other working groups, inside and outside the institution;
- opportunities to extend professional identity through boundary-crossing into other departments/teams, across-institution activities and beyond institutions;
- support for variations in ways of working and learning, for different educators and departments/teams.

(adapted from figure 3.1 in Evans et al., 2006: 3)

However, PD is not only something that is made available but requires educator proactivity.

There are increasing opportunities for self-generated PD not bound by the workplace, with particular relevance for educators who do not have peers close to hand, such as teachers of specialist subjects or working in small educational teams/settings. Engaging in open courses, as mentioned in Chapter 1, is one option. Social media offers more sustained social interactivity (e.g. Emke, 2019; Kontopoulou, 2019) and hence spaces for enacting PD. Vignette 8 provides an example of this.

Vignette 8: In-service PD for independent language professionals through social media (Martina Emke)

This vignette draws on a doctoral thesis which investigated freelance language teachers' Twitter-based professional development (Emke, 2019). Freelance language teachers are employed in all educational sectors, yet their number is difficult to ascertain, due to definitional and statistical problems. For this diverse group of educators, PD is crucial for keeping up with the changing demands of volatile educational labour markets and for securing work contracts.

However, in seeking opportunities for meaningful PD, freelance language teachers face severe challenges regarding availability, accessibility, and appropriateness. Institutional PD offers are often not available for freelance staff, or they take place face-to-face, which increases the cost for freelance language teachers in terms of time and money. Granted, this may not be such a big issue in the current COVID-19 pandemic, but it will become an issue again for freelance language teachers once face-to-face PD offers will be returning. Finally, PD offers may simply not cover the topics that freelance language teachers need for their work, leading to freelance language teachers turning to informal learning to satisfy their PD demands. Educational chats on the social media platform Twitter provide opportunities for freelance language teachers to pursue their PD interests in self-directed and collaborative ways.

For a mixed-methods study (Emke, 2019), six freelance language teachers were asked to indicate the Twitter educational chat they deemed most important for their PD. Data were collected from questionnaires, research participants' tweets, three educational Twitter chats (#ELTchat, #TBLTchat, #LTHEchat), and from interviews with the six participants. Data analysis involved the development of a novel method (relational cross-reading of data), which drew on situational mappings and social network analysis. The study suggests that educational Twitter chats can provide interesting PD opportunities for freelance language teachers across professional careers, making new professional roles available (chat organiser, chat moderator, chat summariser), and contributing to the production of new teacher identities (e.g. teacher-entrepreneur) in some cases.

Virtual networks and their use of the internet to access digital resources allow an educator to search for information, be kept informed on topical issues, and make direct connections with peers and experts. Skills in evaluating the information available, as discussed in Chapter 1, will be important. Further opportunities for PD through freely available resources, in particular Open Education, are covered in Chapter 4.

If an educator's workplace setting does not engage in collaborative practitioner inquiry such as professional learning communities or lesson study groups (e.g. Baker, 2020; Xu, 2020), applied postgraduate study is a way forward for individuals to seek out peers to engage in practitioner research. Inquiry is increasingly built into initial teacher education (Carter, 2015) with the intention of building evidence-generation through practitioner inquiry as a form of continuing PD expected by education professionals. This aspiration is explored further in Chapter 8. Examples in this chapter highlight the need for collaborative learning opportunities at all career stages. Showing leadership, offering mentoring or support for other professionals are also opportunities that are likely to provide mutual PD benefits.

In conclusion

This chapter has shown that PD should be invitational, inclusive, and celebrate the potential all educators bring to their roles. Rather than always being an individual activity, PD is something from which others can benefit from the unique qualities, skills, ideas, and passions each educator brings. This means that PD is relevant to all stages of a career and should involve professionals across stages in their career for a mutual sharing of ideas about how the profession should move forward. In learning together through PD, professionals can shape the profession.

Personal Development Planning Table 2 Focus: Personal and Professional

Question	What can I do?	What do I need from others?
	Short-term action	Medium-term action
1. How well do my personal and professional aspirations connect?	Find time for reflection on how comfortable a fit my current role is with what I value	Plan a meeting with someone who can help guide my next steps
2. What are my PD needs at the moment?	Think of an incident you have not felt fully confident dealing with, an idea you have not been able to follow through into action or an opportunity you felt you couldn't take	Plan to talk to someone to identify barriers and what would be helpful to tackle/ address this (these)

(continued)

Personal Development Planning Table 2 Focus: Personal and Professional
(*continued*)

Question	What can I do?	What do I need from others?
	Short-term action	Medium-term action
3. How do I evaluate my workplace in terms of being an expansive learning environment? (see bullet list on page 20)	Identify opportunities where you could reach beyond your immediate workplace and peers	Identify what those responsible for supporting you might do to expand the opportunities for you

NB: *Recommended Open Access Readings are highlighted below, using asterisks as follows: *Leaders and Teacher Educators, **Practitioners, ***Early Career Professionals.*

Recommended reading

* Baker, B., Graham, S. and Williams, S. (2003) Teaching under a glass ceiling: A study of gender equity in federal education career fields, *Advancing Women in Leadership Journal*, 13 [http://advancingwomen.com/awl/spring2003/BAKER~1.HTML].

* Le Cornu, R. (2013) Building early career teacher resilience: The role of relationships, *Australian Journal of Teacher Education*, 38 (4): 1–16 [https://files.eric.ed.gov/fulltext/EJ1013933.pdf].

** Emke, M. (2019) *Freelance language teachers' PD on ... and with ... and through Twitter*, Doctoral dissertation, The Open University [http://oro.open.ac.uk/60076/1/2019_Thesis_Martina_Emke_final.pdf].

** Nuttman-Schwartz, O. (2017) Rethinking professional identity in a globalized world, *Clinical Social Work Journal*, 45: 1–9.

** Stoll, L., Harris, A. and Handscomb, G. (2012) *Great professional development which leads to great pedagogy: Nine claims from research schools and academies.* Nottingham: National College for School Leadership [https://assets.publishing.service.gov.uk/government/uploads/system/uploads/attachment_data/file/335707/Great-professional-development-which-leads-to-great-pedagogy-nine-claims-from-research.pdf].

*** Carter, A. (2015) *The Carter Review of Initial Teacher Training.* London: HMSO [https://www.gov.uk/government/publications/carter-review-of-initial-teacher-training].

*** Hendry, H. (2020) Becoming a teacher of early reading: Charting the knowledge and practices of pre-service and newly qualified teachers, *Literacy*, 54 (1): 58–69.

3 PD in a crisis

#EC #ML #SL #TE

Coping with a crisis cannot be solved by attending a one-day course. Change happens whether as professionals we are ready or not.

This chapter considers professional development (PD) responses when education is disrupted by emergencies, from the COVID-19 pandemic, education in fragile contexts, to the forced displacement of refugees. Responses to crises focus on two major global themes: remote learning and responses to wellbeing, including opportunities as well as challenges for professional learning (Petrie, 2020).

Extreme disruption to society, to health systems, to education norms may leave many vulnerable economically, professionally, as well as emotionally (Grint, 2018). The challenges from such a crisis might be local, national or international, professional or personal and require a rethink of priorities. Such challenges expose inadequate resources and entrenched 'wicked' problems (Grint 2008: 11) that are beyond 'fire-fighting', highlighting the need to understand change management and responsive leadership (Harris and Jones, 2020: 246).

On the other hand, a crisis can present opportunities for trust, resilience, rapid learning, creativity, and advocacy in professional settings or home learning. For example, in one area of Norway (Bubb and Jones, 2020), school leaders found there was more creativity and better teacher feedback in lockdown during the COVID-19 pandemic.

Remote learning – who has access?

In a crisis like the one precipitated by the COVID-19 pandemic, remote learning has been promoted as a solution to not being able to meet in person due to health and safety fears and learning in isolation. During 2020, an estimated '1.8 billion school children in 188 countries were locked out of their schools' (OECD, 2021) with serious implications. Although different countries experienced different school and university closure patterns, there were urgent schemes to set up remote learning across the world. Remote learning includes independent study packages, online synchronous video lessons, and audio broadcasts according to context. The goal was to maintain learning, teaching, and professional learning in some format, despite the pandemic.

Reflection point 3:1

- *After experiencing COVID-19, is there anything you have learned or changed in your practice which you would want to keep?*
- *What advice would you give to other professionals based on your experience?*

Remote learning where there is no teacher is not new. In some parts of the world, it is already a large-scale strategy to bring learning to otherwise isolated communities. For example, the Australian School of the Air was an innovation developed in the same era as the Flying Doctor remote health service for the Australian Northern Territories. Black and white Pathé news reel from the 1960s (British Pathé, 1962) shows a teacher on a two-way radio prompting children in the outback to talk about a worksheet in a call and response dialogue.

Broadcast, distance learning, and other large-scale approaches are considered in Chapter 5. For example, in some parts of the world during the COVID-19 pandemic, there was an adaptation of rapid revision of national broadcasting and associated online materials to offer for home learning. *École à la Maison* in Francophone countries and *BBC Bitesize* and *Oak Academy* in the UK were promoted as quality educational free resources. Although some struggled to pay extra broadband connection charges for schooling at home, leading to a need for PD on closing gaps.

Reflection point 3:2

How is your teaching or own learning different if you have moved to online or blended teaching and learning?

Engaging and appropriate materials can make a big difference to home learning or self-directed PD but their potential is not maximised without equal access and some mediation, such as teachers offering blended versions of lessons, telephone tuition, family liaison or materials on preloaded sim cards.

When the educational establishment doors are closed, there is a major challenge of who has access to remote learning and which groups of learners might be missed. Educators have important local knowledge of groups who might be at risk of marginalisation through disability, poverty or gender. This highlights the need for professional development to consider context, inclusivity, and social justice, as discussed in Chapters 6 and 7.

Access to learning by laptop or smart phone varies considerably within and between countries. PD during a crisis helps educators to network to benefit from the social aspects to learning. The following Zimbabwean example (Vignette 9) shows how rural community educators without access to the internet adapted their team PD through WhatsApp.

Vignette 9: Using text-based WhatsApp for community educator PD to support girls' learning (Liz Chamberlain, Charlotte Chishava, and Claire Hedges)

Context

Globally, girls are less likely to attend school than boys; over 132 million girls are out of school, and most of them are in the world's poorest countries (United Nations Children's Fund, 2020). Whilst there have been positive developments across Africa, over 20 per cent of secondary school-age girls in Zimbabwe are not attending school, and continue to fall behind in many areas of society where they face major challenges (Chamberlain et al., 2021) and barriers to accessing education, including gender, age, religion, economic status, ethnicity, and disability. It is estimated that half of all young people with disabilities of school-going age have no access to education (Deluca et al., 2014).

SAGE (Supporting Adolescent Girls' Education) is a UK Aid-funded programme through the Foreign, Commonwealth, and Development Office's *Girls' Education Challenge* initiative[1] led by Plan International and involving a consortium of six partners and the Ministry of Primary and Secondary Education, Zimbabwe (MoPSE). The Open University team works as part of the *Accelerated Teaching and Learning (ATL)* group to co-design and co-author a girl-centred teaching and learning programme and resources enabling over 13,000 out-of-school or never-been-to-school girls to return to learning.

Prior to the pandemic, PD for the SAGE educators in Zimbabwe had been face-to-face. This quickly shifted to an online model using WhatsApp, due to its accessibility and affordability (Woodward et al., 2020). Over eight months, nine sessions of training took place for participants, made up of community educators, learning assistants, and school buddies.

A key component of the training was a co-authored document created by the SAGE ATL team covering topics such as *Preparing to teach the next module* and *Strengthening learning conversations with girls*, with usual content including: a case study, key principles, and/or top tips. The draft document was shared with the SAGE District Coordinators for discussion at an internal team meeting where changes/refinements were made before a final version was agreed and circulated to participants. Participants were expected to have read the shared document ahead of the training, ready to answer/respond to prompt questions set by the facilitators. Training was often in the form of four or five key components, each of which asks a set of key questions before facilitators summarise the discussion.

Reflections

The training model was quick and accessible, leading to contributions from many. The use of case studies, questions, and summaries enabled succinct messages to be shared quickly, and kept people connected. Participants did highlight that, on occasion, because the WhatsApp interaction was so fast, it was easy to feel lost because of balancing reading the prompt question, reading others' contributions, and then responding. This mainly affected those who type slowly. However, all participants felt that they had learned new things which were helping them improve their practice.

---

1   The views in this vignette represent those of the authors and are not necessarily those of the Foreign, Commonwealth, and Development Office.

Remote learning – innovation quality and access issues

The rapid drive to adapt to remote learning during the COVID-19 pandemic brought many challenges including training, quality, and access. For many, it was a professional learning opportunity like no other and, as exemplified in Vignette 9, a chance to exemplify distributed leadership and collaboration (Gurr, 2020). For others, it was a challenging and isolating period without opportunities for PD. In a public health crisis like that caused by the spread of COVID-19 or the earlier Ebola or SARS outbreaks, it is usually the most vulnerable communities (of learners and professionals) who are impacted most. Issues of equity in relation to PD are covered more substantially in Chapter 7.

As the pandemic highlighted learning gaps, inequalities, and safeguarding issues for learners, leaders were involved in rapid new strategies for catch up issues (Sutton Trust, 2021). This involved teachers being proactive and needing to collect evidence of learner needs in new circumstances. Teachers as activists and educators involved in collecting evidence is discussed in Chapter 8.

Many leaders started to audit learners' needs in order to adjust strategies to gaps in knowledge, understanding, and skills as a result of the disrupted education. Research on the leadership and professional needs arising from COVID-19-related experiences is still emerging (Baxter, 2021). A pilot project on Leading School Learning through this pandemic found that a new pedagogy was needed and that wellbeing was important (Jewitt, 2021). Key themes emerging from the qualitative pilot study, Leading School Learning were that:

> "Online learning has enabled schools to address their blind spot/intolerance for pupils who do not find school works for them in the one size fits all model and some schools have been exploring the use of artificial intelligence for better differentiation."
>
> Jewitt (2021)

One solution to these issues has been to open up the teacher community to learn from and with one another across borders. Brighouse and Moon (2020) suggest the lessons of the COVID-19 pandemic presented an opportunity for national or even international Open Schools. This could help to diversify new curricula, as:

"... schools might start to feel different. The preoccupation with crowd control, behaviour, even exclusion, could become part of history in a move towards individual, personalised timetables."

Brighouse and Moon (2020)

This suggests an important role for PD networks and innovations at scale, as discussed in Chapter 5.

As the experiences and examples in this book show, a leadership strategy for remote learning needs resources, PD, and collaboration to think beyond traditional walls of one organisation.

Reflection point 3:3

- *How would you plan to audit your students' access to online learning and the consequences if they do not?*
- *How are members of your team learning to teach online and what is different?*

Other projects to develop resources available for remote learning include the digitisation of museum collections and books, remote access to science experiments or simulations. Where these are provided as freely accessible, they can enrich what teachers can bring to the learning environment of their learners. Vignette 10 from Afghanistan, a fragile state, is an innovative partnership considering local needs, particularly access to materials in minority languages, which are often overlooked (Oates and Hashimi, 2016).

Vignette 10: Online library for quality PD in Afghanistan (Lauryn Oates and Deborah Cooper)

In 2008, our organisation began delivering in-service teacher training in Afghanistan. As we set off to prepare the curriculum and look for materials the teachers could use for their own PD and in their classrooms, we found very little at all.

On the other hand, by that time, the open education resource (OER) movement was taking off, and the Internet was overflowing with good quality and completely free material for teachers, often developed by other teachers. Better yet, as OERs, teachers were free to adapt and use the materials in any way they liked for the most part. Yet the overwhelmingly majority of this material was in English, putting it out of reach for the teachers we were working with in Afghanistan.

So, we started to translate it. Most of the OERs were short documents – lesson plans, games, experiments, brief texts introducing a topic – and we were able to recruit multilingual volunteers to do the translations, most of whom came from the Afghan diaspora. Our volunteers could do this work remotely from their homes and they found the work meaningful, giving them a connection to their homeland and the power to make a contribution to education there.

Today, there are over 6,000 resources in what became the Darakht-e Danesh Library (DDL), the 'knowledge tree' library, available in nine languages: the two official languages of Dari (Farsi) and Pashto, plus English, and six minority languages spoken in Afghanistan such as Uzbeki and Pashai. In fact, the Library was the first in the world to ever use the language of Munji on the Internet!

At the time of writing, over 260,000 people had 'visited' the Library in the past 30 days, and they represent all of Afghanistan's 34 provinces, even the most rural and remote parts of the country. From their cell phones mainly, but also laptops, tablets, and from computer labs at teacher colleges where we installed 'DDL Lite', the offline version of the library using a local area network (LAN), thousands of people – now well beyond teachers – use our materials to build their knowledge on their own time, in their own way. In addition to written materials, there is now a wealth of multimedia resources including video lessons and Afghanistan's first ever audiobooks, plus a growing collection of children's storybooks, and accessibility features so people with disabilities can use the Library too.

The COVID-19 pandemic prompted us to do more: we developed a courseware platform in Afghan languages, DDL Courses, where people can enrol in massive open online courses (MOOCs).

Reflection point 3:4

Find a MOOC (looking at FutureLearn, Coursera or OpenLearn) which might be of interest to you and colleagues, and plan how to work together on common professional development goals.

Meeting local and unplanned needs

For front-line education leaders, the COVID-19 circumstances of firefighting with no preparation were unprecedented:

"School leaders are walking a tightrope without a safety net. There are no precedents and no guides to leading schools in a pandemic..."

Harris and Jones (2020: 244)

The work had to go beyond the usual duties. Some schools and universities found themselves distributing meals during the COVID-19 pandemic, others found themselves in rubber gloves spraying the desks. For example, a survey of headteachers in the most deprived areas of England (Moss et al., 2020) found that for 68 per cent, checking that families had food, welfare, and mental health support during COVID-19 lockdown was a priority.

A literature review of global responses to unplanned school closures during other natural disasters around the world such as earthquakes in New Zealand and tsunamis in Japan (O'Connor and Takahashi, 2014) showed that local leaders play a central role and are better placed to respond to unplanned needs with their local knowledge than central authorities (Harmey and Moss, 2020). In all cases, local leaders played a vital role in understanding the immediate needs of vulnerable groups and coming up with appropriate strategies such as taking account of social and emotional needs in the curriculum and providing staff training for mental health needs. This implies agency and trust as well as training.

The mounting list of challenges for front-line workers, including educators, during the COVID-19 pandemic must have seemed never-ending: closures, reopening, absences, ensuring safety measures, setting up testing, cancelling exams, switching to online teaching and blended learning, onerous extra preparation time, sourcing equipment for staff and students, safeguarding issues around children and cameras, the loss of leisure or play time, the loss of practical work, the wellbeing and mental health of isolated learners, short notice for enacting new guidelines, juggling home schooling, and financial pressures.

This list of demands meant that many front-line lecturers and teachers were overwhelmed and at risk of burnout. Rubber gloves were not enough. Safety was physical and emotional wellbeing. For many staff and students, a mix of fear, anxiety, anger, guilt, and loss impacted on their work. This presented not just a health crisis but a psychological crisis – and new needs for PD.

Wellbeing – taking care of one another and ourselves

Wellbeing was always a key part of educators' pastoral duties but after the pandemic came higher up the list. Data on wellbeing and the connection with retention has been established (OECD, 2021). The UK Chartered College of Teachers recognised the impact of teachers in restoring normality and stability after a time of uncertainty. In this context, looking after ourselves especially with kindness when working without trauma-related training is vital:

> "… in addition to processing their own stress, they are also supporting students through theirs. Ensuring that teachers are supported to manage stress and avoid exhaustion is imperative for both teacher and pupil wellbeing."
> Müller and Goldenberg (2020: 29)

Providing psychological support became a leadership and organisational issue. Leaders had to strategically carry out risk assessments, account for the hygiene, safeguarding, and wellbeing strategies in place and monitor their effectiveness, being held accountable for student and staff absence. The challenge for leaders was to embed the values of compassion through their plans and resourcing. As wellbeing has become a strategic priority, the question is: how prepared have educational leaders and front-line educators been for this expansion of their responsibilities? Ideally, PD offers support to maintain their own wellbeing in order to carry out their responsibilities for others.

Reflection point 3:5

* *Which professional associations or networks can you recommend to colleagues to support staff wellbeing?*
* *What are the implications of not responding to staff wellbeing?*

Nurses dealing daily with a high level of death and bereaved relatives, as experienced during the COVID-19 pandemic, are also at long-term risk of burnout and even post-traumatic stress disorder. Evidence-based practice in the US recommended that nurse leaders can make a positive impact by supporting and communicating with nurses by offering empathy and compassion about the intensity of their workload and its impact on their wellbeing (Shanafelt et al., 2020). The rationale for this approach is that nurses need to safely care for patients by caring for themselves with strategic support. The expressed need of nurses as professionals working under stress was to:

> "hear me, protect me, prepare me, support me, and care for me."
>
> Shanafelt et al. (2020: 2134)

This is relevant to other professionals and educators working under stress as empathy becomes an essential team skill with ability to witness but not to absorb others' distress. Practising self-compassion and self-kindness such as a restorative self-care plan and access to telephone help lines or online resources and training are some examples. In the nursing profession, these aspects of PD have been developed with professional bodies such as the Royal College of Nurses and The King's Fund, drawing on rapidly produced evidence-based advice as online resources as part of PD in these crisis circumstances. In England, there is a government charter with guidelines and resources (Department for Education, 2021) setting out commitments and principles of promoting wellbeing.

Working collaboratively on wellbeing

Education experts interested in quality have been arguing for some time for greater emphasis on the social and emotional aspects of learning as part of what counts as quality in teaching (Akiba and Letendre, 2017). Caring for young people through developing professional relationships is a key function of teachers all over the world. Historically this role was an important shift from the family care as mass schooling developed. Everywhere teachers are expected to help guide and support the emotional and social development of children as part of professionalism and their duty of care. This is very different to the focus on international competitiveness and academic progress measures of international tests.

Developing students in a holistic way beyond grades may be motivating for teachers and support retention. Similarly, ongoing support and collaboration among other professionals can improve motivation, trust, and job satisfaction (Ovenden-Hope and Passy, 2021). Collaboration and support for one another can help isolation, share workload, and pool expertise.

Therefore, collaboration in a crisis is more important than ever and this suggests leaders of PD should actively plan for collaboration in ways which take account of one another's wellbeing. This may involve training new teachers to be aware of tools for mapping self-awareness and support networks (Dale et al., 2021; Fox et al., 2021).

Opportunities for partnerships and collaborations to share common problems, such as making wellbeing a strategic priority, are part of a PD opportunity. For example, the UK higher education sector was already aware of serious issues around student mental health (Lister et al., 2021) well before the COVID-19 situation accentuated issues of isolation and uncertainty.

Student Minds (https://www.studentminds.org.uk/) recommends specific interventions, such as training for staff to spot and respond to student mental health issues in combination with a whole-university approach to health including staff wellbeing. However, one-off training is likely to be limited in its impact on practice and should be part of a wider service with clinically trained experts. Staff wellbeing and mental health is essential and is linked with student wellbeing in universities and schools (Salimzadeh et al., 2017).

Reflection point 3:6

- *What do you think are the current training needs to support the wellbeing of students in your community?*
- *What are the ways of measuring the success of PD aimed at improving wellbeing?*

Vignette 11 shows how UK universities have worked together to pool knowledge on wellbeing. The project was a collaboration to share lessons on leadership during the COVID-19 pandemic via rapidly produced reports drawing on interviews and workshops. The focus was on socially-distanced campuses and wellbeing is a theme running through the project where a shared assumption was 'the challenge is about people not about technology' (Parkin and Brown, 2020: 4).

Vignette 11: Collaborative learning project in UK higher education (Deborah Cooper)

'Never waste a crisis' is one creative way of looking at the disruptions of the COVID-19 virus as an opportunity to develop potential in people and organisations when new rapid ways of doing things become essential. This is illustrated in the university sector on a collaborative learning project during the COVID-19 pandemic. A large group of UK universities worked to share learning and ideas in progress. A series of workshops and reports were organised around themes of Leadership, Communication, Partnership, and Wellbeing, many of which overlapped.

Crisis management when there is a threat to health might lead to a directive style but beyond the extreme circumstances was not a path for long-term trust or change. Instead, the project considered the need for balance and consultation. Transformational leadership might be a combination of courage, compassion, collaboration, and creativity. Leadership experts have been writing and researching in these areas for some time. Courage includes authenticity if you do not have all the answers, risk-taking in uncertainty, showing vulnerability, and getting the moment right to give clear guidance. Compassion may involve showing humility and kindness and asking, 'how can I help you?' and acknowledging 'collective wisdom' (Parkin and Brown, 2020: 15).

Collaborative leadership includes valuing pulling together, explaining choices, and seeing students as partners in co-creation and a call for communities to work together beyond the crisis.

Throughout this book, collaborative PD shows the need to think globally.

The importance of data and global perspectives

The international examples in this chapter take us beyond our everyday worlds. When the media portrays conflict through images of people forced from their homes to survive, we can imagine the devastating impact, the risks to health and wellbeing, economic livelihoods, and disrupted education. Our common humanity makes us want to take action and to provide restorative care, but a strategic approach is needed to understand the impact of the refugee experience on learning (Cerna, 2019). How does our awareness of PD leadership equip us to support global issues including refugees and those who are forcibly displaced and experiencing trauma?

Images do not explain the background context, history or geo-politics to migration. As educators, we can choose to make it our professional business to find data about context to support training and to develop student support with welcoming policies in the face of xenophobia or tokenism. This role of educator to counter negative discourse is introduced in the next vignette, and culturally appropriate PD and equity and social justice are taken up again in Chapters 6 and 7.

Data by the United Nations High Commission for Refugees indicates refugee attendance at primary school at 77 per cent, dropping to 31 per cent at secondary level and just 3 per cent in higher education. The report (UNHCR, 2020) argues for a partnership approach, training and resources to take action to improve. For example, university scholarships and removing bureaucratic obstacles to inclusion for all, such as providing access to school for undocumented children (UNHCR, 2020: 45).

Delving into data about Education in Emergencies shows that most refugee populations are in the Global South not in the Global North. Most countries have few refugees but a handful such as Lebanon, Jordan, Turkey, and Uganda have the highest percentages of refugees from neighbouring countries. Refugees may transit in several countries before resettling (Christopherson, 2021).

Reflection point 3:7

- *What opportunities, if any, do you have for international perspectives as part of professional learning, such as exchanges or reading research or blogs?*
- *What opportunities did you have for learning from international perspectives during your initial training?*
- *How would you begin to plan for the opening up of a discussion of sensitive issues?*

The OECD has pointed out the limitations of viewing refugees as a homogeneous group instead of finding out about language, educational background, and community links. The OECD (2016) recommends training teachers, early assessment of wellbeing needs, and improving monitoring and data collection, for example, on years spent out of education, languages and achievements, and support received. If data is missing, it is hard to design the best support.

In planning professional learning for inclusion, we need to make the case in favour of a global perspective and not shy away from sensitive topics such as whose culture or language is missing from the curriculum. We can share reliable data and research as part of setting up PD where these issues are placed firmly on the table and arguments made for what matters to those found in these situations. Exploring global perspectives can be part of the ongoing PD of teachers and initial training either through networks or through courses (formal or non-formal).

In destination countries of resettlement, educators can play a role as change agents in welcoming, actively including, and improving the life chances of refugee students and in countering hostility, bullying or racism, and supporting the collection of audits and data. Vignette 12 from an Australian researcher explores building knowledge of global issues into the PD of those working with refugee resettlement countries to counter negative and deficit views of refugee groups and children. It highlights the importance of Education in Emergencies not just for education but for peace, security and human rights, and for quality standards.

Vignette 12: Revisioning roles for educators – reversing the negative discourse on 'refugees' (Alison Fox)

The rise in provision for people experiencing forced migration and/or living in fragile contexts is known as 'Education in Emergencies' (EiE). The need for PD for the educators involved in EiE raises questions.

One challenge is to think beyond donor country notions of education and look at the non-formal settings and approaches which offer more culturally appropriate ways to organise the curricula, pedagogies, and assessment of education appropriate for those in such fragile situations. This means educators overturning any notion of 'saviours' for facilitation roles, as part of equity and social justice.

Another challenge is to ensure quality standards. The International Network on Education in Emergencies (INEE) was set up to construct a 'global architecture' for international engagement in education (Cardozo and Novelli, 2018: 236). The INEE sets standards for EiE responses. Minimum Standard 1 includes expectations of community participation from inception through to evaluation. This could move representation away from tokenism towards empowerment and equity, which 'would be decolonial by default' (Oddy, 2021) if educators were trained to work in these ways with networks of stakeholders.

Such equitable design of educational programmes is not only needed in the fragile contexts themselves (whether zones of conflict or transient or more permanent camps), but also in countries offering resettlement to ensure their educational offer contributes to social justice.

Education can play a key role in making the host country a restorative space where the forcibly displaced feel accepted and no limitations are placed on their aspirations. It is important that teachers are equipped not only with sufficient knowledge and skills to address the needs of newly arrived students but also that they are supported in holding positive beliefs about these needs and their role as educators (Barnes, 2021).

This is an issue in Australia, one of the world's key refugee settlement countries, as immigrants have been increasingly dispersed regionally. There is a difference between urban centres like Sydney where multicultural education is likely to have been included in PD (Forrest et al., 2016), and regions where educators might have had previous limited exposure to cultural and linguistic diversity (Mellom et al., 2018). Such educators need to be prepared to overturn the negative discourse about refuges, and be aware of its geopolitical roots, to release the power of education for social integration and mobility.

In conclusion

A crisis, whatever its causes, has profound implications for both leadership and the PD of leaders and educators and those made vulnerable by the new situation. Coming through an emergency and adjusting priorities and practice raises questions of what needs to change and who has been made vulnerable by the new situation.

Remote learning is not a panacea (Menashy and Zakharia, 2020) even if it is sometimes sold as such. Since disrupted learning is not new to the pandemic (Burns and Orne, 2020), it is up to us to take the opportunity to reimagine education and use the potential of appropriate technology to reach marginalised groups. This means taking account of local context, solutions and partnerships, and to keep raising gender and disability voices in designing programmes and policies. It means working collaboratively across borders. The lessons of educators' work in crisis are to agree with lessons of interest for the enquiring practitioner. Lessons of supporting one another as professionals will not be lost.

Around the world educators and leaders of PD have demonstrated adaptability, innovation, and creativity in crisis situations. Technological approaches to maximise learning at a distance and open access are important. Renewed attention to wellbeing PD requires resources and tools to build in social and emotional learning for continuity. Educators can learn from this crisis as well as acknowledging the complex challenges to maintain quality, equity, and wellbeing.

Personal Development Planning Table 3 Focus: Professional

Question	What can I do?	What do I need from others?
	Short-term action	Medium-term action
1. Do I know which groups of students and individuals might be especially vulnerable in a crisis?	Speak to colleagues and students and review data or set out what data would help us to identify those at risk	Plan data collection, new resources and training for inclusion that will support students most disadvantaged by educational disruption
2. What aspects of my work environment support or hinder wellbeing for staff or students?	Write a diary or list or discuss with a mentor	Work with a group towards wellbeing policies and resources
3. How can the social aspects of learning be planned into remote learning?	Discuss interactive activity ideas for remote learning with colleagues	Include student feedback in learning design processes

NB: Recommended Open Access Readings are highlighted below, using asterisks as follows: *Leaders and Teacher Educators, **Practitioners, ***Early Career Professionals.

Recommended reading

* Parkin, D. and Brown G. (2020) *Creating socially distanced campuses and the HE Project*. Final Capstone Report [https://www.usaf.ac.za/wp-content/uploads/2020/07/Advance-HE_Social-Distance-Project_Final-Report_July-2020.pdf].

* Sutton Trust (2021) *Learning in lockdown*. Research Brief, January [www.suttontrust.com/wp-content/uploads/2021/01/Learning-in-Lockdown.pdf].

** British Pathé (1962) '*School Of The Air*': *Lessons broadcast to Outback* [video] [https://www.youtube.com/watch?v=WgZO7Ht_0M0].

** Burns, M. and Orne, P. (2020) *Will the COVID-19 pandemic speed a global embrace of online learning?* London: UKFIET [https://www.ukfiet.org/2021/will-the-covid-19-pandemic-speed-a-global-embrace-of-online-learning/].

4 PD at a distance

#EC #ML #SL #TE

This book was written by academics at the Open University in the UK at a time when it celebrated its fiftieth anniversary. To make education available to all regardless of background, to be open, was still a revolutionary idea at its inception. There are Open Universities throughout the world, as well open content in different formats bringing professional development (PD) to groups of learners who would not otherwise have access and leading to a reimagining of teaching as a distance educator. As covered in Chapter 3, the COVID-19 pandemic threw distance education into the path of educators and consumers of PD globally, as they and their institutions sought to continue providing education even when societies went into lockdown. As we move into post-pandemic times, time will tell how much PD will move to online delivery and how much will become blended provision of online and local face-to-face support. This chapter looks at the international growth of Open Education (OE) through Open Universities, open education resources (OERs), and massive open online courses (MOOCs). It considers the potential for open access content to be innovative, inclusive, and responsive to the PD needs of those teaching or studying at a distance and/ or in open educational settings.

What is distance education provision?

In distance and open education, learners can study where they live in ways which are flexible to their circumstances and prior attainment. They are not required to come to a physical location and the entry requirements may be open. Such courses, from webinars to remote labs, open up access to education (Saykili, 2018), particularly for those living in areas remote from campus-based settings, with declared disabilities, caring responsibilities, employment and/or in secure environments, or who have had interrupted study or personal experiences leading them to underachieve (e.g. Hoare, 2012; Pike, 2009; Sengupta et al., 2019). They have a role in upskilling, supporting career change, and other support for in-career development. Distance education therefore has the potential to democratise education (Gunawardena and McIsaac, 2004).

Distance education has evolved alongside technology from print and radio as first and second generations to a third generation of two-way communication (Saykili, 2018). These changing media have changed the pedagogy of courses: the social construction of knowledge with interaction now underpins learning design and delivery, replacing a more didactic view of teaching and learning lectures (Anderson and Simpson, 2012). These exemplify asynchronous learning design (when learners can interact with one another, the teacher, and/or materials at different times to one another). The OE movement forms the fourth generation, aiming to maximise the equality of access for increasing social justice. These evolutions reflect a shift to a more social and learner perspective of learning (Bozkurt et al., 2015), when synchronous (in real-time) opportunities for learner interaction and co-creation are also being sought.

The fourth generation has not replaced the third but exists alongside it, offering a wider range of types of PD learning opportunities (see Table 4.1).

Table 4.1 The development of distance education

Generation	Media	Directionality (Holmberg, 2005; Padilla Rodriguez, 2014)	Learner experience
First: Correspondence	Print	One-way (learner with content) and/or two-way (learner with tutor, tutor with learner)	Course materials posted to learner Learner response posted to course tutor Tutor sends feedback to learner
Second: Broadcast	Radio or TV	One-way or two-way	Course materials broadcast to learner On some courses: Learner response posted to course tutor Tutor sends feedback to learner
Third: Online	Virtual learning environment (VLE)	Multi-way	Learners interact with materials hosted on VLE, with tutors, potentially also with peers and possibly also with invited experts
Fourth: Open Education	Virtual learning environment or static multi-media resources	Could be one-way, two-way or multi-way	May involve but does not necessarily involve interaction with tutors Often involves interaction with peers

Reflection point 4:1

Think of yourself as a learner about to engage in PD at a distance. What do you feel about engaging:

a) with the content independently?
b) with a tutor?
c) with peers?
d) with any of the above, using multimedia?

Learning at a distance for PD

Study might be formal or informal; accredited or not (Table 4.2). In terms of PD opportunities, learning at a distance offers a flexible and accessible way to increase skills, knowledge, and understanding, at the same time as continuing to work. These courses might lead to university-level credits or recognition of study through a certificate of participation or digital badge.

Table 4.2 Forms of study at a distance

	Curriculum	Outcome	Value	Open-ness
Formal	Structured	Credits of national or international recognition	Accreditation helps demonstrate content learnt and capacity to take on new roles	Often have entry requirements and fee
Non-formal	Learner choice over some of study content and how to study	Certification of achievement or participation, statements of participation, digital badges	Can be used in professional contexts but do not have approved international status	Courses often free but outcomes often charged. Only pre-requirement usually an internet connection
Informal	Learner has free choice of what to engage with and how	No outcome other than learner self-evaluation	Learners can find advice to solve practice problems or gain ideas for practice	If in the public domain, freely accessible

Reflection point 4:2

- *Think about any experiences you have of studying at a distance.*
- *Identify whether your study was formal, non-formal or informal.*
- *For any examples, why did you engage with that particular kind of study?*

Design and delivery of PD at a distance

There are key considerations when providing distance learning provision. These affect design, presentation, and quality assurance decisions. Due to the opportunities for different models of communication available between the learner and provider (see Table 4.1), 'teaching' as a distance educator can involve the following roles:

- Subject expert
- Tutor or mentor
- Course designer

In addition to academic roles, Papathoma (2019), studying MOOCs offered by the FutureLearn platform in the UK, identified technical staff as key to online provision. These staff help ensure that the platform and tools help rather than hinder learning and support learner access to and knowledge about tool use. The activities each role might be involved in are summarised in Table 4.3.

Table 4.3 Activities performed by three roles in MOOC delivery

Activities	Academics in subject expert and course design roles	Tutors in mentoring role	Collaborators such as educational technologists
Securing funding	⚐		⚐
Allocating work	⚐		
The design process	⚐	⚐	⚐
Ensuring rights clearance	⚐	⚐	
Presenting videos	⚐	⚐	⚐
Editing videos	⚐	⚐	⚐
Creating the course on the platform	⚐		⚐
Facilitating discussions	⚐	⚐	⚐
Extending the educator role outside the platform	⚐	⚐	⚐
Repurposing the course/resources	⚐		⚐

Adapted from table 9 in Papathoma (2019: 181).

A first phase is *course design* to accommodate learner needs when studying at a distance. This involves platforms, online tools, as well as material and activity development, bringing together different skillsets. Design can provide opportunities for asynchronous learning to facilitate learner independence, offer flexibility of study and self-pacing. However, it needs to recognise the dangers of learner isolation and, associated with this, potential declining self-motivation. Maximising a sense of teacher presence, offering opportunities for timely feedback, and building in peer interaction can develop a sense of community amongst learners (OpenLearn, 2020).

A second phase is *course presentation* in which a key role is in supporting learners in their engagement – with academic and pedagogic support, as a tutor, and pastorally, as a coach/mentor. These roles can be taken on by the same educators or separated and develop the concept of higher education teaching 'as a distance educator'. Staff offering distance learning might sit within a subject discipline either employed solely for direct learner support or as part of teams responsible for wider course design and provision. This could involve creating printed materials posted to students, hosting materials on virtual learning environments, tutors working with learners online, supporting assessment submissions, marking, and reporting to learners via post or e-assessments.

To ensure *quality* there is a need for interaction, including sharing student feedback, between teams of distance learning educators, and between educators and the institution. For example, teachers sharing experiences and students co-creating courses can improve the quality of courses and develop understanding of technologies (Su et al., 2005). Such PD can take place at a distance or through social media and may be with educators inside and beyond the institution (Emke, 2019; Padilla Rodriguez, 2014).

The OER course 'Take your teaching online' designed to support educators during the COVID-19 pandemic (Figure 4.1) promotes how courses can harness peer collaboration to 'create, build and share' (OpenLearn, 2020). The reference to 'we' is intentional.

Figure 4.1 Pedagogical outcomes of distance learning

Source: Denise Krebs

How can open provision contribute to PD?

The OE movement has taken its inspiration from open source software communities as the internet evolved. Academics across the globe are united by the belief that:

> *"knowledge should be free and open to use and re-use; ... collaboration should be easier, not harder; ... people should receive credit and kudos for contributing to education and research; and ... concepts and ideas are linked in unusual and surprising ways and not the simple linear forms that today's textbooks present."*
>
> Baraniuk (2007: 229)

Teaching and learning programmes such as OERs and MOOCs represent a shift to involve individuals and collectives in co-creating materials. Beyond textbooks they can include; images, audios, videos, simulations, wikis, blogs, and/or games.

Reflection point 4:3

Wikipedia is an example of an OER. Reflect on OERs you are aware of.

- *How have you come across these?*
- *What were you looking for?*
- *How did you determine whether they were useful to you?*

However, there are challenges to this vision and creativity of OERs in terms of cost, choice, and quality. The plethora of offers may make it difficult to find and select from the point of view of learners and quality can be variable linked to a lack of peer-review in this innovative, inclusive, and responsive provision. There are costs for institutions to host and sustain these repositories and hence differentials in where they are offered, due to different economic support and funding priorities (Baraniuk, 2007). These costs also apply to any learner support to be offered, summarised below in relation to the Open University in the UK.

> *"A network of local tutors provides additional support including marking assignments, giving feedback, and offering help to students. Over 200,000 students at The Open University learn by this method, but it is costly to recruit, train and employ the tutorial staff, so the approach is only viable on paid-for courses."*
>
> Ferguson and Sharples (2014: 100)

Other challenges include creating easily editable materials that can be reused, how to involve learners or institutions in adapting, and identifying which creative commons licensing should be linked to open resources. Balancing the desire to make the resources as open as possible are fears of commercial exploitation if resources are made available for this usage (Baraniuk, 2007).

Open Universities are institutions which have embraced these principles of distance and open education. Their growth comes with a history, which helps explain their contribution to the provision of PD and quality education in general.

What PD opportunities do Open Universities offer?

A history of Open Universities reflects the socio-political context; as social circumstances change, their attractiveness and usefulness can be challenged (Tait, 2008). For example, the University of South Africa (UNISA), established in the 1920s, was the first institution to offer accreditation by examination at a distance and, later, in the 1960s, by including teaching only at a distance. It survived pressures during the Apartheid period to offer racially separate education and, by 1995, students were roughly equally distributed between 'Black African' and 'White' (Tait, 2008). However, the high drop-out and failure rates suggested insufficient support for all students, leaving those from the most privileged sectors of society to succeed. These challenges also appeared in the former USSR. In the 1950s, Nikita Khrushchev sought to increase the pool for political recruitment by offering low-cost higher education to those in work through part-time study by correspondence. Whilst this increased access, the quality was considered to be low by those who could afford to choose alternative provision, with a two-tier higher education system developing.

Harold Wilson's vision of higher education was to remove the standard entry requirements to reach more of the population, leading to his establishment of the Open University in the UK in 1971 (Tait, 2008). It is open to all four nations of the UK and those based internationally, with its courses drawing on the University's international research and development work. This was followed in 1972 by the Universidad Nacional a Distancia in Spain. That it was National was, and still is, controversial, given that regions of Spain seek to become autonomous and celebrate their particular languages and cultures. In response, in 1994 the Open University of Catalonia was established to promote and offer Catalan-speaking higher education provision at a distance. Again, political and social factors affect not only the provision but also the curriculum of these institutions, all seeking to offer open education at a distance and at scale (see Chapter 5).

Open Universities now exist worldwide. Their current position as higher education providers can be summarised through a Strength-Weakness-Opportunity-Threat analysis (Paul and Tait, 2019) – see Figure 4.2.

The strengths and opportunities in Figure 4.2 cover the potential for Open Universities to reach large proportions of the population and invite them to engage in higher education courses. These could boost their employability, if seeking employment or career advancement, or, for those already in employment, offer continuing professional development. The flexibility of provision helps those in work to study part-time and decide when, where, and how to study, to fit this around their employment and additional responsibilities. This flexibility is a significant enabler for those with physical disabilities and mental health conditions, for whom traditional campus-based provision is a barrier to sustaining study, course completion, and gaining further qualifications. There are also learners who participate in OE who are not driven by employability concerns, studying mainly for personal interest and fulfilment. This is the case as much for Languages and the Arts as it is for the Social Sciences and STEM (Science, Technology, Engineering, and Maths) subjects.

Figure 4.2 A SWOT analysis of Open Universities

STRENGTHS	OPPORTUNITIES
• **Commitment to openness** • **Capacity for large-scale provision** • **Support and flexibility for part-time study** • **Commitment to technology-enhanced learning**	• **World-wide access to the internet** • **UN Sustainable Development Goals support expansion of higher education** • **Use experience to develop quality assurance at scale** • **Build on trends to international collaboration and the OA movement** • **International trend to acknowledge lifelong learning and professional upgrading as continuous process**
WEAKNESSES	THREATS
• Completion and graduation rates • Reputation and brand risks • Staff resistance to change • Models usually on very large student-staff ratios	• Mainstream university sector increasingly involved in online and blended learning • Government disenchantment with OU model • Enduring value of elite educational provision • MOOCs and other innovations from mainstream universities

Adapted from table 1 in Paul and Tait (2019: iii).

Reflection point 4:4

- *Think about when you have sought courses or resources to help your skill development.*
- *Were these purely to support you in your work role or can you identify examples where you just wanted to get better at doing something or were interested in understanding something better?*

PD at a distance has grown from correspondence courses in the late nineteenth century to radio and television broadcasts in the twentieth century and distance education in 1996, but does not need to involve single institutions. System-wide provision in Brazil (Da Silva et al., 2019) was set up in

2005, focusing on teacher education in a consortium of public national, state, and regional educational institutions, who also offer face-to-face provision. Here, recruitment is not open, as learners need to have finished high school and pass an entrance exam.

Investing in PD for distance and open learning educators

As countries and regions locked down because of the spread of the COVID-19 pandemic, the move to teaching at a distance affected all phases of education, from kindergarten through to higher education. As seen in Chapter 3, when teaching needed to move online, it was clear there was a need for training and investment, given the distinctive nature of teaching at a distance (e.g. Donitsa-Schmidt and Ramot, 2020).

To sustain quality production and delivery of PD at a distance requires investment in staff PD, recognising the skillsets needed to complete the kinds of activities outlined in Table 4.3. Given that teamwork is required across the roles, PD offered together is also recommended to understand how the roles complement one another. If educators and educational technologists are themselves at a distance, the PD will need to be designed with the same considerations as for the learners they will be supporting (de Laat, 2012; Gregory and Salmon, 2013).

Five key aspects of PD for both pre- and in-service teachers emerged from educational research in response to the pandemic (Hartshorne et al., 2020):

1 The importance of building communities.
2 The use of online professional development and coaching.
3 The need to adapt to simulated and online teaching experiences for pre-service teachers.
4 The broadening use of and creativity in using digital tools.
5 Recognising and overcoming equity issues of access to tools and hence to PD.

For higher education academics, needs were identified in skill development relating to digital literacy, supporting interaction with learners, encouraging learner motivation and participation, using time effectively, as well as support for course material, presentation, assessment, use of tools, and programme development (Elçi, 2021). A review of literature on PD for educators transitioning to online and blended learning recommended: a supportive programme with clear goals as part of strategic support for transitioning to online and blended learning, with appropriate evaluation measures (Philipsen et al., 2019). This might include the following components (see table 4.4).

Table 4.4 Evidence for PD needs and implications for providing PD to pre- and in-service educators moving to online teaching during the COVID-19 pandemic

Dimensions	PD needs (Elçi, 2021; Hartshorne et al., 2020)	Implications for provision of PD (Philipsen et al., 2019)
Purpose	To adapt current practices and learn new skills	Set clear goals relevant to both online and blended learning
Support	To feel part of a peer community	Create a supportive programme and learning environment
	To be coached	Sit within a strategic programme of ongoing support
Curriculum	To learn about simulated and online teaching opportunities	Draw on and adapt the wide range of existing knowledge
	To know how to create assets using appropriate tools	
	To identify and know how to overcome equity issues	
Pedagogy	To develop confident and creative use of digital tools	Support teacher change in pedagogy
	To know how to facilitate participation and interaction between learners	
	To understand how to encourage learner motivation	
Assessment	To know how to develop programmes of study in which assessments are linked to units of study	
Impact		Identify knowledge, skills, and attitudes about and for online and blended learning as measures to evaluate the PD programme against

A reflexive strand could be added in which the learners, in this case educators, chart the connections being made between their emerging understandings and skills and existing practice. This is where personal development planning could highly benefit and support their PD, helping empower the educators to align the changes needed in their practice with their values. It can also help self-evaluate the changes to their knowledge, skills, and attitudes so that they can go with confidence into new blended and/or distance learning teaching opportunities.

Reflection point 4:5

- *What are your skill levels in relation to the points listed above?*
- *To whom or where can you turn to for support in the areas you feel least confident?*

Initial PD for teachers at a distance

In Wales, prior to the pandemic was a period of educational reform, which included the identified need for a national ITE programme, which could be offered at a distance. Following a review (Furlong, 2015), a new accreditation process for ITE was introduced, which was key to achieving the national mission 'to raise standards, reduce the attainment gap and deliver an education system that is a source of national pride and confidence' (Welsh Government, 2017: 3). As outlined in Vignette 13, a programme was designed, which needed to accommodate the implementation of a new curriculum and assessment strategy as part of this national vision for improving the quality of teaching. ITE was becoming transformative and 'a major step forward' in positioning schools and communities at the centre of the process of reform through training its teachers (Waters, 2020: 37). The programme sought to reflect practices that have been reported to improve teacher training, such as aligning to professional teaching standards, integrating theory and practice by supporting work in settings, and research-informed clinical practice (Burn and Mutton, 2015; Darling-Hammond et al., 2017; Hagger and McIntyre, 2006; Tucker, 2019).

Vignette 13: The delivery of a flexible PGCE programme for Wales (Sarah Stewart)

The Open University Post Graduate Certificate in Education (PGCE) programme in Wales, launched in 2020, offers either a salaried or part-time route into teaching – the first routes of their kind in Wales. At the time of its creation, the salaried route was the only employment-based accredited offer in Wales and the part-time programme the only such offer available in Wales.

The vision underpinning these routes into teaching was to offer a flexible, distance, and blended learning approach to supporting ITE. Available to students across Wales, the programme is also the only fully national ITE provision. By doing so, it seeks to widen access to those from a broad demographic background and make the qualification accessible in more rural areas of Wales. Secondary provision is also designed to support specific areas of hard to recruit shortage subject areas. All routes and pathways are available for study through the medium of Welsh, making it the only bilingual teacher education programme in the UK.

The programme is founded on the principle of collaboration and joint accountability with partner schools across Wales. The Partnership is formed of 24 strategic lead partner schools and over 200 associate and employer schools as the sites for student learning, overseen by a strategic decision-making committee. It is based on the view that each member of the partnership brings different forms of professional knowledge and expertise. Together, joint teacher-educators, school mentors, and university tutors support student teachers to integrate theory and practice. Also intrinsic to the programme design is a recognition that all teachers in Wales teach in a bilingual country, so student teachers are actively supported to develop both their own language proficiency and their pedagogic approaches to supporting children and young people's language skills. Central to all of these approaches is the golden thread of research and scholarship, with lesson study and small-scale master's level research sewn into the fabric of the programme. This is designed to enable student teachers to both engage critically with research to support their understanding of practice and simultaneously improve their practice through becoming teacher-researchers themselves.

The programme positions student teachers as at the beginning of a career-long journey of professional learning, in which ITE is just the initial steps on the path. As the reform programme continues in Wales, a seamlessness of ITE into induction is likely to feature more prominently.

Programmes like the one covered in Vignette 13 and others which offer online, at a distance, ITE support to training teachers, such as pre-service English Language teacher education in Argentina, might have been thought to have been protected by the demands of the COVID-19 pandemic. However, in such settings challenges for trainee wellbeing, anxiety, access to resources, the lack of flexibility in any move to synchronous online tuition, the demands of home-schooling and economic stability have been cited (Banegas, 2020), needing responses from the ITE providers to offer support to allow trainees to continue and complete their programmes.

The pandemic has also been a time of opportunity as well as coping for trainees joining the profession. There is evidence that new and early career teachers have been a resource for their more established colleagues, partly as a result of their more recent training, which has itself gone online, and partly due to their personal use of online tools, which include the ability to draw on networks beyond their workplace. Early career teachers have also been motivated to engage in personally sourced online professional development to help them solve some of their frustrations with moving online (such as engaging learners in dialogue and motivating learners) by undertaking PD, itself online. Such teachers talked about the key enablers as; people, tools, and a lowering of expectations in helping them be seen as a resource for their peers, without the usual pressures of exams or expected ways of working (Shanks and Carver, 2021).

As well as on-the-job upskilling, a rebalancing of the entire workforce reflected the rebalancing of online versus face-to-face working as the pandemic progressed. In Israel, the Ministry of Education saw this as an opportunity and responded by creating an ITE programme for those with graduate qualifications but who had lost their jobs as a result of the pandemic, helping them to retrain as teachers with strong digital skills (Donitsa-Schmidt and Ramot, 2020).

Building on the scene-setting from Chapters 2 and 3, the growth of education being offered at a distance not only includes courses of different lengths and with different target markets in mind (D'Antoni, 2009; Wiley et al., 2014) but also embraces the OE movement. Internationally, educators are broadening the range of resources other educators and learners can readily draw on – captured under the broader heading of OERs.

As illustrated already in this chapter, distance education need not be carried out through correspondence or online, relying only on virtual learning environments, but can also include locally organised face-to-face learner support, as a blended approach. In Vignette 14, a spotlight is placed on an established teacher education initiative across sub-Saharan Africa, focusing on how a blended approach reached and supported in-service teachers.

Vignette 14: Supporting professional development for teacher educators at a distance (Kris Stutchbury)

The Open University runs a number of international development projects. The longest running of these is Teacher Education in sub-Saharan Africa (TESSA) (Wolfenden, 2008). TESSA provides a resource bank for teachers to support the primary and secondary science curriculums in Africa. The resources are available as open education resources (OERs) and support teachers in planning engaging lessons which actively involve learners (www. tessafrica.net).

Teacher education in Africa is highly theoretical. It is assessed through exams with very little emphasis on practical teaching. Active teaching approaches are talked about, but not modelled – Professor Bob Moon tells the tale of how he once sat through a two-hour lecture on group work in an African university, with no opportunity to actually work in a group.

In order to mediate the TESSA resources for teacher educators and support them in modelling the pedagogy they espouse, we developed and ran a successful MOOC – Making Teacher Education Relevant for 21st Century Africa (https://www.open.edu/openlearncreate/course/view.php?id=2745). At the time of writing, nearly 9,000 people have registered for this course and there is research evidence that this has impacted on their professional practice. The whole course is still available on OpenLearnCreate. It is not running as a facilitated MOOC but it is available for anyone to use to support PD in their institution.

The same approach was used in a project with partners in South Africa (https://www.open.edu/openlearncreate/course/view.php?id=3287). Again, for many early years practitioners, this course was their first ever experience of online learning.

We have learnt that, despite practical issues such as erratic electricity supplies and poor connectivity, if the learning design and support are right, people are motivated to work together to solve local problems.

In both courses, teams of local facilitators completed the course themselves and armed with a 'Facilitation Guide' supported colleagues in their own institutions and organisations in studying the courses.

WhatsApp, Facebook, and text messages have been very helpful, not only in connecting the teachers and teacher educators with one another to share practices, but also to stay in communication with the local facilitators and the UK-based TESSA team, to ask questions and make suggestions (Stutchbury et al., 2019). By ensuring the content remains available beyond the end of the facilitated MOOC, the courses support a more sustained PD process. MOOC participants were situated across seven sub-Saharan contexts, which means that WhatsApp groups and Facebook are sustaining an international professional learning community.

Key to this initiative is the importance of giving control to local coordinators in its delivery and involving them in the co-production of the programme's curriculum and content development, to allow adaptation and illustration relevant to their own particular context. The use of social media for local, national, and international interconnectivity and networking maintained a collaborative model of PD at a distance. The TESSA model is similar to a newer initiative in Zambia, in which Raspberry Pi hubs have been established to enable teachers to use their personal devices to access digital resources, co-construct knowledge, and explore possibilities in their own schools to inform and develop their teaching practices (Gaved et al., 2020).

Non-formal PD and its accreditation

The accreditation and recognition of learners' achievements have also diversified alongside provision of courses and OERs. As well as traditional university undergraduate and postgraduate credits, non-accredited certification and digital badges are also available (e.g. Law, 2015). A certificate of participation is the common recognition of course completion of MOOCs, as with many online, blended or even face-to-face short courses.

Sometimes, these certificates indicate achievements, but more often a declared agreed minimum level of participation in the course activities. In the MOOCs discussed in Vignette 14, the relatively high completion rate (50 per cent) and high levels of participant satisfaction were linked to the provision of a free certificate of participation. Increasingly in MOOCs, even when the course itself is free, a certificate of completion (achievement or participation) would need to be purchased. Additional sponsorship of the TESSA MOOCs was sought to cover the costs of their certificates to offer a tangible recognition of the time committed to PD to use in the teachers' educational setting which matched the reports of pride from course completers (Stutchbury et al., 2019).

A further source of recognition has been the growth of digital badges as alternatives to certificates of participation. The chapter concludes with a case study about how digital badging is used at the Open University to recognise non-formal learning through its suite of non-accredited courses.

Case study 1: Digital badging and professional development – using digital badges (Patrina Law)

The OpenLearn website (openlearn.com) was launched in 2006 to be a platform for free learning resources in support of the Open University's (UK) (OU) commitment to its social mission. It now hosts thousands of articles, videos, and nearly 1,000 short courses. Pre-pandemic it was reaching around 10 million learners a year with numbers significantly rising, from March 2020 to March 2021, to around 17 million.

Content on the site is a mix of taught course excerpts, adapted for an online audience, and commissioned courses, videos, and articles. Besides a strong social mission to open up free learning to everyone, the platform's aims are:

- to be topical and engaging;
- to reflect the output of university research;
- to serve student needs for induction and study support;
- to deliver content that supports employability.

All material on the platform requires a self-directed approach to study and learners can use the resources at their own pace; no course has a start or finish time. Almost all of the learning materials on the University's IP, are published with a Creative Commons licence to allow reuse and (for courses) are downloadable in a variety of offline formats, e.g. Word and PDF.

A recent study showed that 38 per cent of learners use OpenLearn to upskill for career development and 20 per cent are teachers/trainers (noted as being at any educational level).

Recognition for non-formal learning

Whilst all courses on the platform deliver a free certificate to those who complete an online course, digital badges are awarded for completion of a 24-hour long course with online assessments which much be passed and which cannot be gained by repeatedly inputting different responses. These badged open courses (BOCs) have fulfilled a need for the recognition of non-formal learning achievements and remain some of the most popular content on the platform (Law, 2015). By March 2021, a full year since the first UK lockdown for COVID-19, over 133,000 digital badges had been issued for completion of OpenLearn BOCs, 76,000 of which were in the first 12 months of the pandemic alone.

Of the 70 BOCs on the platform, around 20 have been commissioned to support employability, including some of the so-called 'soft skills' needed by employers (Taylor, 2017) such as leadership, resilience, and communication skills.

Figure 4.3 Examples of professional development badged open courses

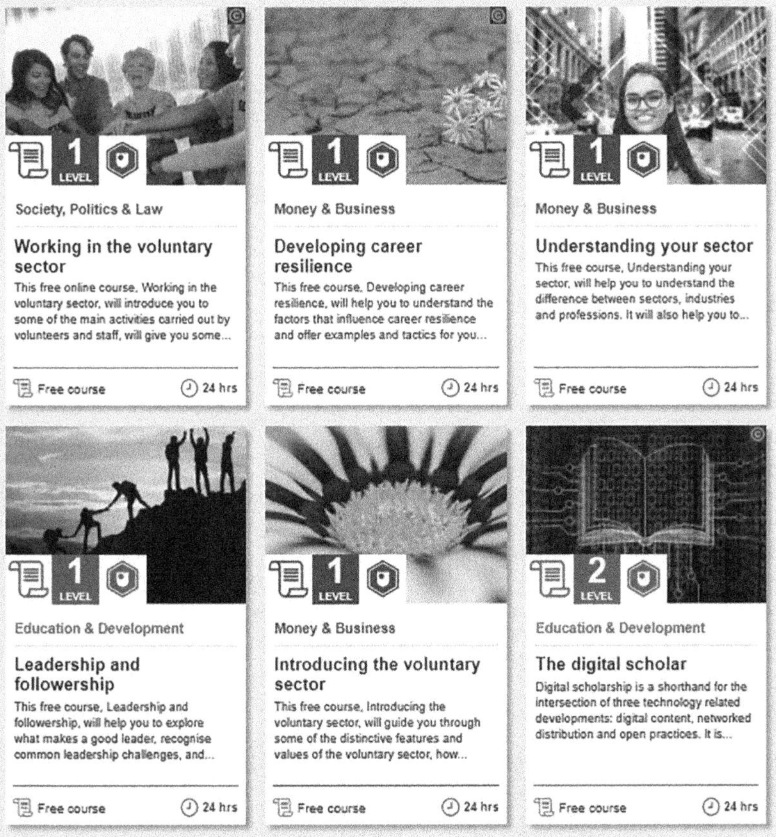

Source: Screenshot taken from OpenLearn.

Open digital badges contain metadata particular to the badge, the issuer, and the recipient, and can be used to match badge earners with employment opportunities. They are considered to be a key component of the digital credentials landscape, recognising skills and educational achievements that are not degree shaped.

In 2021, a review of the end of course surveys for 22 of the BOCs on Open-Learn was undertaken to learn more about learner demographics, motivations to study, and how learners might practically apply their achievements (Law, 2021). The study examined 42,195 survey responses.

Learners can share and display digital badges in a variety of ways, including their OpenLearn Profile, exporting to e-portfolios or downloading and sharing via social media (Figure 4.4). The study showed that 86 per cent of learners intended to share their badge in places other than their OpenLearn Profile, with LinkedIn, Facebook, and their employer being the top three places.

Figure 4.4 Uses of a digital badge

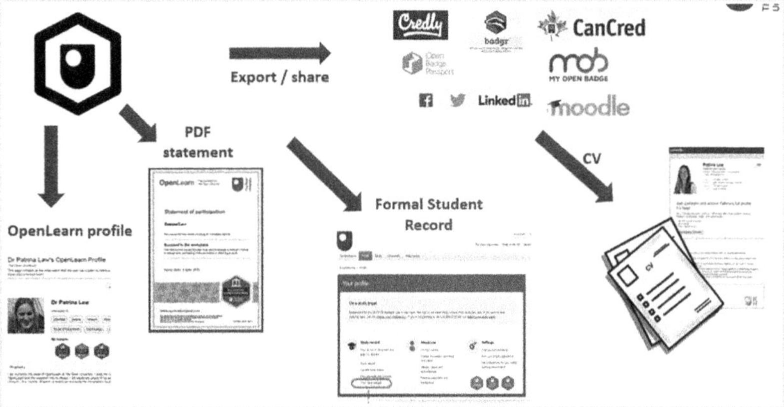

Source: Patrina Law.

When asked if learners thought whether the digital badge was more important than a printable/downloadable PDF Statement of participation, 65 per cent said that they were equally important, 21 per cent that the Statement of participation was more important, and 9 per cent that the badge was more important. Figure 4.5 shows that badges offer a sense of achievement in a free learning context, a tool for motivation, and to gain university recognition.

Figure 4.5 Responses to the question 'What does earning a badge mean to you?' (learners could select more than one option)

Few studies exist that examine the perception of digital badges by employers, although OpenLearn survey data show that they have a value to learners, with 77 per cent declaring that they would be sharing their badge with an employer or prospective employer.

Reflection point 4:6

- *What incentives are you aware of for engaging in PD online?*
- *Does it matter to you whether your study is accredited, certificated or badged?*

Digital badges have become a popular means of recognising achievement for non-formal learners, particularly in support of career development. For educators, they provide a means to motivate and reward learners for co-curricular or non-formal study. The huge rise in uptake for non-formal learning and digital skills recognition, reported by the team responsible for the OpenLearn covered in Case Study 1 in the first year of the COVID-19 pandemic (2020–21), has provided a fresh view of commissioning to support non-formal learners' professional development goals. Universities are now exploring how informal learning might be recognised through digital badging, for example through evidence of reflection on skill development, linked to employability (Carey and Stefaniak, 2018). This needs to draw on understanding the perceptions and value of these badges to learners and employers (Dyjur and Lindstrom, 2017).

In conclusion

To cover the characteristics of PD at a distance, you have been taken on a tour through the principles and practicalities of open and distance education. This has allowed a focus on the needs of those who can be reached by PD without the need to physically travel somewhere to access training, illustrated by the experiences of educators during the COVID-19 pandemic. Limited access to resources, whilst the most obvious factor in making the most of these opportunities, is not the only one. The role of social interaction and motivations for learning are also important. PD at a distance can also involve locally sourced support such as through local facilitators and tutors. This is a way to blend online and face-to-face provision and provides the important opportunities to empower learners to situate their learning for their particular context.

Personal Development Planning Table 4 Focus: Personal Skills

Question	What can I do?	What do I need from others?
	Short-term action	Medium-term action
1. Do I know what PD resources I have access to online/at a distance?	Search for OERs which might be relevant to you, for example from OpenLearn, FutureLearn	Ask colleagues or peers what online PD resources they have used and have found helpful

(continued)

Personal Development Planning Table 4 Focus: Personal Skills (continued)

Question	What can I do?	What do I need from others?
	Short-term action	Medium-term action
2. When and why would I study at a distance?	Undertake a SWOT analysis to help identify why you would or would not be interested in undertaking PD at a distance	Ask colleagues or peers why they have or have not used online PD
3. Can you contribute to the PD of others at a distance?	Reflect on any expertise you have which you might be able to share with others and how this might be shared	Explore with colleagues whether collectively you can share some of your expertise more widely than your immediate work situation

NB: Recommended Open Access Readings are highlighted below, using asterisks as follows: *Leaders and Teacher Educators, **Practitioners, ***Early Career Professionals.

Recommended reading

* Philipsen, B., Tondeur, J., Roblin, N.P., Vanslambrouck, S. and Zhu, C. (2019) Improving teacher professional development for online and blended learning: A systematic meta-aggregative review, *Educational Technology Research and Development*, 67 (5): 1145–1174.
** Hartshorne, R., Baumgartner, E., Kaplan-Rawoski, R., Mouza, C. and Ferdig, R.E. (2020) Special issue editorial: Preservice and inservice professional development during the COVID-19 pandemic, *Journal of Technology and Teacher Education*, 28 (2): 137–147.
*** Shanks, R. and Carver, M. (2021) New teachers' responses to Covid-19: Getting by or getting ahead? [blog post], *BERA blog*, 27 April [https://www.bera.ac.uk/blog/new-teachers-responses-to-covid-19-getting-by-or-getting-ahead].

5 PD at-scale

#SL #TE

In this chapter, the examples discussed range from small to large-scale and from top-down to bottom-up professional development (PD), with examples of educational reform and policies.

In practice, these categories don't divide so neatly: PD may start as top-down originating from change required by a national policy but then grow horizontally or organically across places and people. It is worth noting that scaling up PD might have unintended consequences, both positive and negative. In some cases, it might be a worthy pilot, but not readily scalable. These are all considerations for leaders of PD, as well as policy-makers.

Why scaling matters

The spread of large-scale education innovations, especially distance learning for mass education, including the growth of massive open online courses (MOOCs) for PD (as covered in Chapter 4), illustrate the potential of 'at-scale' changes and innovations to address major global problems in education.

Although there is growing evidence on what works at-scale, less is known about why or how to scale for impact and sustainability (Price-Kelly, 2020). The stories and evidence of scaling are relevant to system leaders and policy-makers as well as practitioners. Through their actions, all stakeholders may have influence as change-makers, although the voices of local actors may not always be heard.

For leaders of PD, this means taking a broad perspective of what reforms are happening at system level whilst at the same time using deep knowledge of the local context to lead in ways which actively engage teachers. For policy-makers, this implies dialogue and listening to the voices of practitioner champions:

> "... education reforms to improve quality are likely to fail unless teachers are actively engaged in the reforms and buy into the planned changes. Interventions or reforms that work do so because ... key stakeholders change their reasoning ..."
>
> Akyeampong (2019: 16)

The vision and practice of scaling matters as a link to themes throughout this book: of agency, local adaptation, and technology. For this reason, examples in this chapter refer to scaling at different (micro, meso, macro) levels.

Big problems, big solutions

Education systems and infrastructure are often designed and rolled out at large scale. The impact can be national or international. For example, South Korea is often cited as a model of a country with rapid economic development and investment in human capital through its long-term education policy. The policy is key to South Korea's development from a low-income nation to a regional success story, with a highly valued education system (Hultberg et al., 2017). Finland is often cited as a country with an excellent record of educational efficiency and equity, underpinned by strong teacher professionalisation and research (Sahlberg, 2021). The time and resources for PD are planned.

Education at-scale often attempts to tackle major quality problems which are seen as valuable to society: improving literacy, numeracy technology skills, supplying and training a workforce, improving quality of teaching and provision, addressing equity in gender or inclusion, preparing for the future.

National policy-makers may consider economies of scale, evidence, and/or the wider socio-economic context. Think, for example, of the historical reasons for examples of mass compulsory schooling as reflections of the economic, political or religious priorities of that context and era. Sometimes the rationale has been focused on improvement, sometimes on equity. Other reasons for education at-scale might be economic, political or educational drivers, including:

- seeking greater capacity of labour;
- developing human capital;
- promoting child socialisation;
- supporting or suppressing a culture or language;
- equity and universal human rights;
- responding to technological change.

Some of these drivers might be behind the introduction of compulsory schooling or other at-scale reforms such as: lowering or raising the school entry and leaving age; introducing compulsory examinations.

Think about countries from Wales to Tanzania where the language of instruction has been changed. Consider legislation on the de-segregation of schools in the USA, Canada, South Africa or Northern Ireland. Reflect on changes in attitudes towards single-sex schooling or the inclusion or segregation of children with special educational needs. Recently, educational leaders have pointed out how promoting girls' education globally may be more powerful in combating climate change than expanding wind turbines (Kwauk, 2021). Such large-scale changes have the potential to be transformational and not just incremental.

Reflection point 5:1

- *What large-scale educational change has taken place in your educational context, probably directed from national government?*
- *What were the underlying drivers for it?*
- *How was PD included to support this change?*

All of the above examples have implications for PD, which should be part of the roll-out plan for any large-scale reform. Top-down, large-scale educational reform is likely to have impacted all of us as educators, whether we agree with the changes and PD roll out or not.

PD can be planned into educational reform, such as with the launch of the National Strategy for Educational Research and Enquiry (Welsh Government, 2021). Four Collaborative Research Networks have been established to support teachers in their grassroots implementation of the strategy, focusing on: (a) Curriculum and pedagogy, (b) Leadership and professional learning, (c) Welsh language and bilingualism, and (d) Equity and inclusion. The aim is for institutional and classroom practice change to be evidence-informed. The benefits and challenges of PD through inquiry are explored further in Chapter 8.

Creative uses of technology at-scale

The demand for more teachers and quality teachers is one of the Sustainable Development Goals in pursuit of education as a right for all. Shortages in the teacher workforce is a global issue as student numbers increase, projected to double in some low-income countries (Akiba and LeTendre, 2017).

Demand for teachers in the Global South will increase according to UNESCO's International Task Force for Teachers 2030 working on an Education Workforce Initiative project aimed at policy-makers. Teacher shortages and subject shortages require new approaches, especially for marginalised groups.

As discussed in Chapter 3, educational technology with appropriate design, support, and infrastructure offers huge potential for teaching and learning at-scale; for PD and for wider access by hard-to-reach groups. Allocation of teachers, distribution of resources, and closing equity gaps for marginalised groups are interconnected key challenges in every country and within countries. Technology can be part of a support structure for capacity-building and developing quality teaching in challenging circumstances.

A creative approach to such regional inequity is needed. In the Global South, the most marginalised learners in remote rural areas may live too far away from a secondary school or from regular electricity or telephone internet infrastructure. Teachers trained in urban areas may not want to live in such challenging circumstances or may be too far from training centres to benefit from face-to-face training and quality professional development.

To address the teacher shortage in rural areas of Ghana and the issue of girls' drop-out between primary and secondary phases, 'Making Ghanaian Girls Great!' (MGCubed) provides live distance learning via web cams and projectors using satellites and solar power. Such technology enables marginalised children to take part in 'MGCubed' primary lessons led by a master trainer working in Accra and local facilitators supporting student-centred Maths and English lessons across the country. This programme provides positive role models for girls, whilst also supporting the accreditation of local teachers (Varkey Foundation, 2018). This model has the potential to be scaled to address teacher shortages, girls' attendance, and PD.

Another example of at-scale technology for equity and redistribution is the potential to use satellite geospatial data and mapping software to help select the best places and distances to locate schools for equitable access (Education Commission, 2021). This might also help policy-makers decide how to share teachers across more than one school where specialists are lacking and is part of scaling across boundaries.

Throughout this book, there is evidence of how innovations for improvement may be taken up in more than one context. Borrowing ideas and adapting them may happen on a local or global scale, between or within countries. Leaders of PD may reflect on: why and how ideas are taken up? How to make sure they are appropriate? Do reforms promote or hinder inclusion and equity in practice?

One criticism of global borrowing (Harris and Jones, 2017) is that, as this is a centrally regulated activity, it may place pressure on teachers without taking account of teachers' or parents' needs or the language, culture or local context – assuming one culture instead of many.

Building agency and adaptation into large-scale CPD

Policy-makers may be driven by economic development and pressure for competitiveness or equity in borrowing global models. However, Harris and Jones (2017) highlight poverty, power, and inequity as 'inconvenient truths' of scaling. The predominant focus on international league tables, such as the Programme for International Student Assessment (PISA),[1] drives national competitiveness. This relies on outcomes measures which do not account for the different circumstances and opportunities for learners. Scaling which did account for differences is illustrated in the following case study of large-scale PD for rural teachers in seven of the poorest states in India where many teachers are too far from regular quality PD opportunities. The focus was on developing active and motivated teachers with readings, reflections, and classroom activities as part of building practitioner communities of teachers, district officials, and teacher training institutions to learn from each other and move beyond prescribed text-books (Wolfenden and Adinolfi, 2019).

As in many cases of reform, the starting point was a new national policy framework on professional development. As part of the roll out, technology was a key part of the scaling infrastructure and involved different stakehold-ers, taking account of rural schools and language contexts, as important dimensions to culturally relevant PD (as covered in Chapter 6). The open edu-cation resources (OERs), as examined in Chapter 4, were available in multiple formats, including offline and via SD^2 phone memory cards. Creative Commons licensing of materials enabled them to be adapted.

Case study 2: TESS-India – a case study of large-scale teacher PD (Freda Wolfenden)

In India, the 2009 National Curriculum Framework for Teacher Education (NCFTE) signalled a paradigm shift in conceptualisations of pre- and in-service teacher education and articulated a clear vision for teacher PD (TPD) – ongo-ing with opportunities for teachers to observe learners, engage in self-learning and critical reflection, and become confident in trying out new ideas (NCTE, 2009). The recent National Education Policy (MHRD, 2020) reiterated the commitment to regular TPD for all teachers.

Finding ways to achieve these ambitions with almost 10 million teachers and highly diverse contexts is challenging. Much TPD provision in India is acknowl-edged to only rarely lead to significant improvements in classroom teaching, particularly in rural areas and under-served communities.

But the increasing availability of ICTs in different forms, particularly mobile phones, offers support to move towards more equitable, effective, and per-sonalised TPD at-scale. The TESS-India programme offers one example (Wolfenden, 2015). TESS-India (www.tess-india.edu.in 2013–2019) was a multiple stakeholder partnership led by the Open University, UK working with the Indian Ministry of Human Resource Development (MHRD) and Depart-ments of Education in seven states in India.

At the heart of TESS-India is a large resource bank of open education resources (OERs) collaboratively created by educators from across India. The OERs reify the participatory pedagogy advocated in Indian national policy (NCERT, 2005; NCTE, 2009) as structured activities for teachers to carry out in their own classrooms. These are complemented by authentic case studies (text and video). The basic premise of the OERs is that learning is a social practice and the learner (whether child, teacher or teacher educator) is agentive, knowl-edgeable, and intrinsically motivated. Through participating in the activities of the OERs, teachers are guided to generate local solutions to improve their pupils' participation in learning.

In the TESS-India approach, teachers' practice is recognised to be deeply influenced by the contexts in which they work, the resources they are able to draw on, and the institutional demands on them. Hence the original TESS-India OERs were subsequently localised (translated and adapted) by educators in different Indian states to reflect geographies, curriculum, resources available, and local cultural and institutional practices. Teachers and teacher educators can further adapt the OERs to their local contexts, and doing so has been shown to create communities and local ownership of the OERs (Wolfenden and Adinolfi, 2019).

These derivative, localised OERs are freely available in multiple forms – print, offline (CD or SD cards or institutional intranet), and online. They can be integrated into formal teacher education programmes such as BEd courses (Wolfenden et al., 2017a). But equally importantly the OERs can be used independently by individual teachers or teachers collaborating in professional learning communities: the format of the OERs enables teachers to be agentive in developing their own learning journeys. Many teachers access the materials via their phones, often through social media platforms where they also share stories of use. The TESS-India video OERs have been particularly highly valued, with over 3 million YouTube downloads to date.

This case study demonstrates both scale and local ownership. The adaptations for each state included not just translation into local languages but also different nuances of photos, stories, and references. Paying attention to learners was one feature of the roll out, as illustrated in this reflection from members of the research team:

> *"Whenever I felt there was something missing from the OER, I used to take help from a child from the class itself, I recorded [with the tablet] the activities of children (UP3)."*
>
> Wolfenden and Adinolfi (2019: 337)

Reflection point 5:2

* *What do you see as the potential for educational technology to provide access to MOOCs and other OERs as PD?*
* *How can stakeholders, such as teacher educators, support such PD at-scale?*

Creative approaches to diversifying the workforce for equity

One potentially scalable and creative option to teacher shortages, especially in rural areas, is to train local people or develop existing stakeholders. This might be informal community education, paraprofessionals, teaching assistants or volunteers in supporting formal education.

In countries with a low percentage of female teachers, teacher shortages are linked to systemic issues such as girls' attendance and drop-off at puberty between primary and secondary schools. One access scheme in Sierra Leone has trained rural females in hard-to-reach areas as classroom assistants to provide support in classrooms and at the same time prepare for teacher training college. This involves a support structure for the women to return to study and shows a high retention rate at teacher training college, which had previously been male dominated (Chamberlain and Safford, 2019).

The need for new team approaches to teacher workforce issues arises partly as the introduction of universal primary education revealed teacher shortages in low- and middle-income countries and, among unqualified teachers, low levels of access to CPD. Untrained and unqualified teachers may not have the same opportunities for PD. There is a need for scale with equity.

For example, although early childhood education provision is low throughout Africa (Kabay et al., 2017), in Ghana the government introduced an additional two years of pre-primary early years education. This required PD for new pre-primary educators. A creative approach involved a play-based learning programme that engages both teachers and parents (J-PAL, 2017–2018). In one scheme, illiterate mothers were trained in: playing games, the importance of handwashing, supporting home play, and preschool learning (Institute for Fiscal Studies, 2018). Where such schemes can become linked to national policies and infrastructure, sustainability is more likely. Access to support for early childhood development and early years education is related to increasing social mobility and reducing intergenerational poverty and in many communities has been the focus of investment (Institute for Fiscal Studies, 2019).

Scaling through collaboration

Even if you happen to be a light-house keeper, in your day-to-day work you are likely to have experienced learning, influence, and inspiration from working and discussing challenges alongside others. You may have been challenged by working in different teams, through networks or with external partners to make a change or perhaps to resist a change. As covered in Chapters 1, 2, and 8, collaborative learning may be formal or informal and the leadership of inter-school PD involves different skills such as brokering and initiating new networks.

PD and collaboration links to scaling from the bottom up because it involves teachers as stakeholders and leaders. Although many lecturers and teachers have tended to work in isolation, as foregrounded in Chapter 2, PD might involve: being mentored, taking part in shadowing, observing, jointly designing a curriculum or contributing to a needs analysis to decide priorities. You might be involved in an inquiry, a learning set or research project to improve practice. You might be a key contributor to blogs or social media feeds to share what you passionately believe to be professionally important.

In this way, some small-scale innovations may grow from the bottom up. On an individual level, learning from others may be part of your values and, hence, your professional identity. On an organisational and system level, leaders may strategically plan time for collaboration. If practitioners are to share and learn from each other, they need time and trust for adaptation and ownership as we have seen. This needs to be considered at an early stage of scaling.

Boylan (2016) considers system-wide change and 'teacher system leaders', for collaborative organisation of scalable PD, taking key ideas from adaptive leadership and systems thinking. For example, a national UK Maths network involved groups of teachers leading improvements by identifying local needs and then leading PD and inquiry networks not just in their own schools but beyond the school boundary in a local area. Rather than bottom-up, this is more bottom-across. It was reported to give more ownership, agency, and passion, and was seen as less prescriptive than national top-down numeracy strategies. Importantly, it may also lead to seeing wider horizons, a shift in thinking about a contribution to practitioner knowledge as system-wide change as in this Maths example:

> "... we see their motivation extending beyond their school or immediate networks of schools to a sense of being part of a larger or wider movement with an expansion of focus from a school-to-school system."
>
> Boylan (2016: 12)

Successful inquiry networks across schools have been well evidenced (e.g. McLaughlin et al., 2007), growing from an international interest in networked learning communities (e.g. Chen, 2003), into large-scale developments in other regions such as Singapore (Academy of Singapore Teachers, n.d.). In the UK, there has been a sustained national interest in establishing bottom-across inter-school support from the seminal work of David Hargreaves (Hargreaves, 2003), the Networked Learning Communities programme, involving 137 networks (1,500 schools) between 2002 and 2006 (e.g. Jackson and Temperley, 2007; Katz and Earl, 2010), through to the current UK government funded Teaching (Department for Education, 2020) and Research School networks (Education Endowment Foundation, n.d.). School-to-school PD is written into the 'big 6' requirements to become a Teaching School (Bart's Training and Support Alliance, 2021). Teaching Schools in England will be replaced by hubs to focus on across-school PD and initial teacher development (Department for Education, 2020). The leadership of such inter-school PD involves identifiable skills such as brokering and initiating new networks.

An internationally widely-used example of systematic peer collaboration in education, also covered in Chapter 8, originates from Japan: Lesson study or *jugyokenkyu*, where learning from colleagues involves an organised and regular way to watch one another's teaching and share knowledge. Whilst in many of the ways it has been adapted for other national contexts, opportunities to observe the final research lessons in Japan (and sometimes in China) are offered at a regional level and may take place in stadia (Xu and Pedder, 2014). When adopting at-scale PD, cultural relevance and context remains important.

Reflection point 5:3

- *Do you belong to networks outside your organisation and, if so, how does this contribute to your PD and that of your colleagues?*
- *What opportunities do you have in your context to share knowledge about practice? How does this contribute to your PD and that of your colleagues?*
- *What do you consider the barriers are to offering these opportunities for PD to colleagues?*

Working for improvement can also be reflected in the ethos and in the strategic plans to promote a culture of leadership for professional development. As part of this, leaders need to plan into their strategies an understanding of and approaches to mitigate the likelihood of staff resistance to change (e.g. Fullan, 2007).

Changing practice: who decides what is useful?

Changing practice is complex in education. One approach to scaling is tinkering or testing, adapt, and then share. Involving teachers as stakeholders may make the difference between success or failure. Such an approach is at the heart of scaling science and networked improved communities (Price-Kelly, 2020). Japanese lesson study may be considered a series of small changes that are tested and grow as a shared product (Morris and Hiebert, 2011). Not all successful practices can or should be scaled. A good idea is not necessarily scalable and an at-scale idea may not have impact across the larger contexts to which it is taken (Price-Kelly, 2020)

Research from the US illustrates the complexity of how scaling occurs:

> "… governmental decision-making about scaling is neither linear nor purely rational. Instead, it's a three-dimensional zigzag in which technical and financial features of an innovation interact with personal relationships, political incentives, and competing innovations."
>
> Olsen et al. (2021)

Leaders of PD may find themselves as intermediaries called on to interpret large-scale macro policy change to be applicable to micro-levels, recognising and building on the varying degrees of agency of those being expected to implement the changes. For example, how best to teach reading is a particularly contested area which may be received as a top-down prescriptive erosion of autonomy. This might be using synthetic phonics or teacher promotion of stories and literature (Cremin et al., 2008). The National Literacy Strategy in England, 1997–2011 based on phonics and word recognition contrasts with the whole book and whole language approach of New Zealand (Soler and Openshaw, 2007). A critique of the former National Literacy Strategy became part of the debate on 'whose knowledge counts'? (Moss, 2013), referring to how scaling large initiatives for the public good involved cascading only one particular method. Moss argues against commercial interests and a simple view of knowledge transfer and calls for an open dialogue and involvement of teachers and students in evaluating what is transferred into new practices:

> *"... which forms of knowledge are most apt for whom, under what circumstances and who is in a position to decide. ... to produce, reflect upon, sanction, endorse, adapt, challenge or dismiss knowledge in different forms. These are deeply social... subject to change."*
>
> Moss (2013: 247)

An interesting example which has changed practice in many contexts internationally and which has the potential to give students more agency is discussed in Vignette 15. All over the world teachers are involved in assessment, often driven by external exams or summative assessment. Teachers also assess on the spot in response to learners and this is known as formative assessment. Learners need to know what to do to improve and a problem is how to take the information from formative assessment to improve student learning and for students to become more involved in their own learning. Research on approaches to using formative assessment for learning can be influential (Marshall and Drummond, 2006) and rolled out to teachers at-scale as described in Vignette 15. The movement of the Assessment for Learning practices from national to international contexts illustrates how a 'good idea for practice', which makes sense to policy-makers and practitioners alike, can travel and become embedded in practices at-scale.

Vignette 15: The spread of assessment for learning practices (Alison Fox)

A meta-review of studies of assessment practices revealed the potential efficacy of formative assessment in supporting student learning (Black and Wiliam, 1998a, 1998b). Today, the practice of formative assessment in supporting learning experiences has become firmly established and promoted (OECD/CERI, 2008; UNESCO, 2015; World Bank, 2011). Based on both constructivist (Black, 2015) and socio-cultural theories (Elwood and Murphy, 2015), formative assessment lays the groundwork for changes in the structure and content of evaluation-oriented thinking, calling for teachers and students to work interactively in relation to classroom assessment procedures (Shepard, 2000).

Black and Wiliam led two subsequent projects to understand factors affecting the effective use of formative assessment in UK schools. The first was a two-year study involving six schools and 40 teachers, known as the King's Medway Oxfordshire Formative Assessment Project (or KMO-FAP). This has been reported in research articles (Black and Wiliam, 2003; Harrison, 2005; Lee and Wiliam, 2005; Wiliam et al., 2004) and a book for practitioners (Black et al., 2003). In parallel, the Classroom Assessment Project to Improve Teaching and Learning ran over four years in the United States and reported at about the same time (Coffey et al., 2005). The second project involving members from the KMOFAP team was a broader development and research project running for four years across 40 schools. This UK Research Council-funded project, entitled 'Learning How to Learn: In classrooms, in schools and in networks', reported in a special issue of *Research Papers in Education* (e.g. Black et al., 2006) and through two books (James et al., 2006, 2007), one aimed at practitioners (James et al., 2006). These studies have created insights into the way formative assessment can become embedded into UK teachers' practice, including practical advice. However, they warn that teachers need to fully take on the implications of its underpinning principles, noting a tendency towards procedural and limited application (Marshall and Drummond, 2006).

The findings of such UK-based research around formative assessment have been used to introduce it into Kazakh schools, for example through the 'In-service training programme for the pedagogic staff of the Republic of Kazakhstan' project of the Center of Excellence AEO Nazarbayev Intellectual Schools (running since 2012). Up until this point, Kazakhstan's assessment practices in secondary schools were based on the principles of Soviet education with current and final assessment located within a four-point summative assessment system. Consequently, innovation through bringing in formative assessment can be considered challenging, if thought about negatively, or helpful in redefining the possibilities of what constitutes quality processes in evaluation in positive light. The perspective of the teachers in Kazakhstan will depend on their level of awareness of the values, vision, and understanding of formative assessment as well as their attitudes to change. Like other countries seeking to adopt formative assessment in schools, such as Canada (DeLuca et al., 2015) and Singapore (Ratnam-Lim and Tan, 2015), teachers are likely to face difficulties in interpreting and formulating formative assessment and the relationships between this and the regularly collected summative assessment data. The materials of the OECD/CERI International Conference 'Learning in the 21st Century: Research, Innovation and Policy' (2008) recorded similar barriers from wider international practice in terms of: (a) the tension between formative assessment and summative testing cultures, and (b) an unsystematic vision for assessment and evaluation at the different levels of implementation.

It has been advocated that those seeking to improve the quality of formative assessment, need to consider the current teaching contexts and realities of teacher positions (Black and Wiliam, 1998b; Lyon, 2013; Weurlander et al., 2012). As teacher educators, we therefore need an understanding of teacher perspectives in our contexts. Giving the teachers a 'voice' can help us locate our advice more appropriately in the cultural context for their practice.

There were strong external factors influencing how it is being adopted and adapted (bottom-up, bottom-across, top-down). Teacher beliefs will affect how well locally appropriate formative assessment practices are embedded into practice, with unintended consequences and variation according to teachers' interpretation and design (Marshall and Drummond, 2006).

Educators can create lesson plan frames, learning intention frames for communicating with learners, and/or worksheets to capture learner self-assessment, but these can be used without a deep engagement with what Marshall and Drummond termed the 'spirit' of assessment for learning. To embed this 'spirit' requires more creative and responsive practices that might need constant revision. This is where constant inquiry into the applications of the new intervention or reform are needed to hold up against evidence from the context of how well the practices are achieving what was intended – local evaluation of at-scale reform.

In conclusion

Scaling to widen impact requires appropriate PD and teacher involvement. Where it is possible to plan adaptation for local context, whether that is language, culture or inclusion, may give agency. Technology and technical solutions are not enough for success and quality without leadership and time to adapt. For many professionals in education, our values and identity lead us to share and collaborate. Leaders of PD can build on this agency at all levels for small changes in system change.

Personal Development Planning Table 5 Focus: Academic (Policy)

Question	What can I do?	What do I need from others?
	Short-term action	Medium-term action
What could working with organisations beyond your boundary bring to PD around an issue of common interest?	Mind-map key areas of PD that you are interested to work on and potential links to nearby organisations that you work with already	Arrange to discuss possible PD connections with leaders from one or more of the organisations that you have identified

(continued)

Personal Development Planning Table 5 Focus: Academic (Policy) (*continued*)

Question	What can I do?	What do I need from others?
	Short-term action	Medium-term action
How can leaders plan to support local adaptation of top-down schemes?	Work through materials/expectations from a current top-down scheme. Identify any challenges in implementing this in your context	Together with colleagues, generate possible ways to overcome these challenges. Draw together contextual examples that are more relevant to your organisation before rolling out the PD
If you could influence national policy in your specialism, what would you want to change?	Research current national policy in your educational sphere/specialism. List the key areas for PD	Discuss with colleagues which of these policies seem most relevant to your context. Identify those that seem less well aligned

NB: *Recommended Open Access Readings and Resources are included below for Leaders and Teacher Educators.*

Recommended viewing/reading

View any of the videos from the TESS-India site [www.tess-india.edu.in] and think about what similar resources or practice you would recommend or like to create.

If you have not come across it already, read the following pamphlet made widely available in the UK in 2003: Hargreaves, D.H. (2003) *Education Epidemic: Transforming Secondary Schools through Innovation Networks*. London: Demos [https://www.demos.co.uk/files/educationepidemic.pdf]. Note your reactions to how this vision relates to the current reality of across-educational setting PD where you are.

Notes

1 PISA is the OECD's Programme for International Student Assessment. PISA measures 15-year-olds' ability to use their reading, mathematics, and science knowledge and skills to meet real-life challenges [https://www.oecd.org/PISA/].
2 SD stands for Secure Digital and refers to non-volatile memory cards which can be used to share data.

6 Culturally relevant PD

#SL #TE

Culture and context

In this chapter, we focus on the idea that professional development (PD) must respond to the culture and context of each education setting and community. Every education setting is influenced by the context in which it is situated, the histories and identities of its workforce and those of the communities it serves. Each education setting is therefore situated in a complex local, regional, and national culture. In addition, education settings develop their own professional cultures over time; these are the normative practices of educators, including actions and interactions that can support or constrain progress towards institutional goals (Hallinger, 2016).

PD in education has historically been situated in a discourse of leadership derived from research in the Global North, which may not support cultural relevance in other locations around the globe. PD from this perspective has been dominated by a focus on organisational roles and a hierarchical approach (Hallinger, 2016; Hallinger and Kulophas, 2019). In a review of research into leadership and teacher professional learning between 1960 and 2018, the most cited sources were predominantly from North American studies and therefore potentially hold limited application for leading professional development in diverse contexts around the globe (Hallinger and Kulophas, 2019). This picture is changing with new studies emerging in Europe and the Global South. However, whilst new PD research may link to a wider range of countries, effective PD must still be appropriate to the multiple, individual, and collective cultures and contexts relevant to any educational setting.

We suggest that PD can be culturally appropriate in two main ways:

1 by adapting to the educators' needs and contexts; and
2 by equipping the educators to examine the cultural relevance of their practice.

Ensuring that PD is culturally appropriate is challenging when many studies, programmes, curricula reforms, etc. are developed with a 'one-size-fits-all' perspective. For example, Hallinger (2016) argues that studies of educational leadership tend to present an overview of strategies considered to be effective without answering the question, 'How should I apply these findings to leading learning in my educational setting?' He goes on to point out that school leaders will always be influenced by their contexts at an institutional, local, and national level, so indicating that any recommendations for PD must be scrutinised through this lens. As we have seen in Chapter 3 (PD in a crisis), contexts can change rapidly and be challenging but it is not just crisis situations which require culturally relevant PD. All settings will need PD that can adapt to cultural contextual influences such as the social economic status of their learners, the setting's history of inspection, local conflict, or specific urban or rural constraints on resourcing and environment.

One aspect of leading culturally relevant PD may involve encouraging approaches that are school-/setting-focused and learner-centred. In a recent study of secondary schooling in Thailand (Kulophas and Hallinger, 2020), the importance of moving away from a centralised approach to PD was endorsed. Instead, school-based professional learning communities, focused on learner-centred PD, were seen to be instrumental in fostering a culture of 'academic optimism' (Kulophas and Hallinger, 2020: 606) – that is, where school staff believe that learners can and will thrive academically, and trust parents and children will collaborate with them to achieve this (Hoy et al., 2006). In this case, locally driven PD was culturally relevant, as it allowed teachers to cooperate and motivated them to believe that they could make a difference to children's learning. This contrasted with the previous 'cascade' model of PD that relied on de-contextualised training of individuals. Kulophas and Hallinger (2020: 619) assert that creating 'a school culture of trust, collaboration and high expectations' through these learning communities was a more effective way of supporting the PD of teachers. They also suggest that 'in collectivist Asian societies, principal leadership acts as a kind of connective tissue linking the efforts of different stakeholders' (2020: 620).

The secondary school principals in this study established a new culture for PD, that reflected the local context by supporting teachers to collaborate on action research, school-based PD and learning about their students' home-background and challenges (Kulophas and Hallinger, 2020). In this shift of focus for PD, it became not just PD developed for the context, but PD shaped by the context. Professional learning communities and other forms of teacher assemblage are defined and discussed in more detail in Chapter 8 (PD through inquiry).

Reflection point 6:1

- *How do you identify the cultural contexts of your setting?*
- *Which of these might influence the PD needs of the staff?*

Humanist approaches to PD

It seems obvious to say that the impact of PD on educators may rely on the way that it is communicated and organised. More specifically, the approach to PD should be adapted to respond to the cultural context of the educational setting and the staff that participate (Dzamesi and van Heerden, 2020). Different styles of leadership for PD may be more, or less, supportive in different contexts. As Kulophas and Hallinger (2020) suggest, the role of senior leaders in collectivist cultures may be to draw together different stakeholders and provide an environment conducive to collaboration. The underpinning approach to leading PD in different locations may also be influenced by a traditional local philosophy or worldview. For example, whilst no location can be said to have a single culture (Elonga Mboyo, 2017), traditional African philosophies such as Ubuntu may need to be reflected in PD approaches in Africa (Ncube, 2010).

Ubuntu, or humanism, underpins most traditional African cultures. It relies on an understanding of interconnectedness and interdependence leading to respect, strong relationships, and learning from one another's differences (Ncube, 2010). Although there is some debate as to whether Ubuntu is unique to African contexts (Elonga Mboyo, 2017), leadership of professional development from this perspective should offer direction and a vision for the future that benefits the whole educational community. It should also involve democratic, communal enterprise and inclusive decision-making that reaches a consensus view. Teamwork is a key element of an Ubuntu philosophy.

The design of PD activities may be more effective if it aligns with Ubuntu in contexts where Ubuntu already influences the educators' culture. For example, in teacher education for adult literacy in South Africa, Ubuntu informed the way that the tutors worked with their students. The leader incorporated supportive teamwork through group tasks that required the students to help one another. Student teachers had to collaborate to identify possible solutions to set problems and agree on actions. The PD content also included discussion about social issues affecting the community and their tutor supported students to work with one another on local enterprise outside of the course which led to small business collaboration (Quan-Baffour and Romm, 2014). This connection between Ubuntu and physical and financial support within the community is also part of Bulala, a Kenyan practice of 'togetherness' where communities group together to carry out farm work, pool resources, and share food (Lutomia et al., 2018). PD approaches imported from other countries may not automatically reflect the connection between educator learning and community support seen in these traditional philosophies.

> **Reflection point 6:2**
> - *What kind of 'shared philosophy or worldview' seems to be underpinning the way PD is led in your context?*
> - *Is this locally relevant or imported from a different context?'*

Co-constructed PD

Perhaps the best way to ensure that PD reflects traditional or indigenous philosophies is to design PD in partnership with the community population.

As mentioned in Chapter 2, Vignette 7, the First Nations Partnership Programs (FNPP) in Canada developed PD in this way. One example of this involved The University of Victoria working with the Meadow Lake Tribal Council to create culturally appropriate childcare training that was community-based and reflected their values, language, and spirituality. Two important factors contributed to make this PD sustainable and successful, the 'Generative Curriculum Model' and 'Borderland' location and funding. The Generative Curriculum Model involved co-construction of the curriculum for the programme with community members. Notably, this was not a 'one-off' event. Instead, before each programme began, there was a new cycle of review and co-construction with the community to ensure that it reflected current issues and needs (Pence et al., 2010). Pence and colleagues (2010) also suggest that housing the headquarters of the programme away from the main university campus and being funded by sources external to the university allowed them to operate in a 'Borderland' which gave more freedom for the PD to be fully community focused and led, whilst remaining within university regulations.

Challenging historical practices

PD for culturally appropriate practice in education settings may involve supporting educators to question existing beliefs. In some cases, educators may need to 'undo' accepted ways of working to connect with the culture and context of their learners. The following vignette focuses on PD for early years educators in Ghana.

Vignette 16: PD for play-based learning in Ghana (Esinam Avornyo)

'Traditionally, the Ghanaian culture values child social integration through a combination of consciously motivated teaching with a non-didactic method' (Harkness et al., 2009: 144), relying mainly on the child's own observation and learning through participation (Nsamenang, 2009). However, formal education has been rooted in rigorous teacher-directed instructions, emphasising the rote memorisation of factual information (Agbenyega, 2018). This contrast in cultural childcare and formal education practices possibly reflect different conceptions of child developmental domains that can or should be developed in fundamentally different ways. Efforts are now being made to integrate non-didactic ways of learning into the formal education context.

In 2018, the Ghana Ministry of Education set forth a new curricular framework for education, which specifies a learner-centred approach to learning, highlighting play-based learning especially at the early childhood level. Moreover, Right to Play has launched an in-service training agenda that supports professional development at different levels – teachers, teacher educators, and officials of the Ministry of Education – in order to make a more significant and sustainable shift in didactic teaching practices.

While the move towards equipping professionals to use play-based activities in Ghana is a critical piece in the teaching and learning discourse, it is important that models of play-based activities do not over-emphasise Western play activities but support educators with the knowledge and skills to integrate local and culturally relevant Ghanaian games and play. For example, Ghanaian folktales, 'Kwaku Ananse' (Kwaku, the spider), are rich traditional oral storytelling that can be used to support children's learning. The stories of 'Ananse' follow the adventure of how he uses his cunning and intelligence to get whatever he wants. These stories can be used as a way of exploring ideas and supporting children's learning, particularly through communication and language development, where children have the opportunities to experience rich language through discussions, speaking, and listening, as well as through expressive arts and design, where children play with a range of materials. Another example is 'ampe', a group game that involves clapping, jumping, and feet coordination, which is mostly played by girls. These play sessions have the potential to teach young children counting and older children concepts of the probability theorems (Akayuure and Nabie, 2021). Not only can 'ampe' be used to develop mathematical concepts, it provides opportunities for developing teamwork. Also, traditionally viewed as a girls' game, 'ampe' has the potential to foster gender inclusivity, encouraging the involvement of both boys and girls. To sustain the use of these play activities, it is important that professional development is designed to help educators establish links to the relevant curriculum objectives.

These Ghanaian play activities can be best supported and promoted when professional development draws attention to how 'learning' is conceptualised within the Ghanaian context. The evidence suggests that learning is conceptualised narrowly as 'knowledge acquisition' (Avornyo, 2018). If educators are to create supportive learning environments where all children can access learning, they will need significant opportunities to examine their own beliefs about learning and this should be a crucial part of professional development.

The challenges highlighted in Vignette 16 were also experienced in a small action research study of Ghanaian kindergarten teachers. PD that involved them in indigenous play-based learning and modelled how this could be used to implement the new curriculum had some impact on their practice. However, as the project did not really question or challenge their beliefs about a teacher-led approach they, to some extent, reverted to old practices following the training (Dzamesi and van Heerden, 2020). This problem is not unique to Ghana, as persistent 'colonial' approaches to education are embedded within the system of many nations.

A colonial approach to education can create a barrier to the inclusion of certain population groups within education settings whether in the Global

South or Global North. This can also include linguistic imperialism (Phillipson, 1997), where certain languages or dialects are privileged by the education system. For example, in the case of the nomadic, pastoralist Turkana people in north-western Kenya, the embedded historical approach to education in Kenya marginalises these children by using materials that do not reflect their everyday lives. In addition, classroom practice rarely draws on indigenous home languages and so limits the educators' opportunities to support children's literacy development (Ng'asike, 2019).

In the UK and USA, the Black Lives Matter movement has highlighted how education policies and practices may also marginalise the experiences and history of black students in a way that contributes to inequitable educational outcomes (Dixson, 2018). There is some agreement that, in contrast, when the culture, curriculum, and pedagogy of an education setting build on learners' home culture and language, students will achieve (Biraimah, 2016; Ng'asike, 2019). For this reason, culturally relevant PD may involve a focus on decolonising the curriculum or introducing practices that enable educators to better connect with the contexts of their learners. PD for equity, diversity, inclusion, and social justice are considered further in Chapter 7 (PD for equity).

Local facilitation and materials

It could be assumed that local facilitation of PD will ensure a connection to the local context. However, examples from previous research indicate that facilitating PD locally may not ensure that it is culturally relevant. Even after local PD, educators may not be able to embed their learning in practice. In a geographically remote area of Indonesia, a community-based model of teacher education was established with local training and facilitators to promote a new active-learning approach but training sessions, without ongoing class supervision and support, resulted in limited impact on practice (Harjanto et al., 2018). In addition, limitations to the available resources in these remote contexts were also cited as possible barriers to embedding the pedagogy championed in training. Therefore, effective locally facilitated PD will need to help practitioners to reflect on the cultural relevance of their curriculum and pedagogy and to consider the materials to which they have access. Ng'asike (2014: 48) gives the example of an early childhood practitioner who shared a story with her pupils about climbing a mango tree, even though these did not grow in the region, simply because this was one of the few books available. She later revealed that she had knowledge of local stories she could share but had not experienced professional development that would encourage the use of these. Following on from this, a PD project was initiated that focused on creating story books with family members as a basis for future teaching. This ensured that that teachers developed practice using resources relevant to children's lives (Ng'asike, 2019).

The importance of helping educators to access and create culturally and contextually relevant resources through PD is not unique to 'lower income countries' in the Global South. In England, the Royal Society for the Arts, Manufacture and Commerce (RSA) ran an 'area-based curriculum' project in three schools in Manchester and five in Peterborough with the aim of enhancing the educational experience of young people. The project involved working with parents, pupils, and other local stakeholders to create a curriculum that reflected and drew on the local area, people, and resources in a way that met National Curriculum objectives (RSA, 2010). Some area-based interventions have been a way of tackling a regional or local problem of disadvantage and for this reason may begin with a deficit view of the communities that the interventions serve (Facer and Thomas, 2012). Instead, this project set out to draw communities in by celebrating local culture and history and using this as a rich starting point for learning. Teachers reported that pupils were more engaged and therefore learned more with this approach. This way of working relies on positioning teachers at the centre of curriculum design (L. Thomas, 2012). It not only will include parents and communities but give them a democratic voice in the learning opportunities provided for their children.

In any location, PD can improve outcomes for students if it connects with their home experiences. Rural and urban schools will need to diversify their PD to reflect their circumstances and draw on local resources. Schools might connect teachers with local businesses and sites of interest to plan learning for pupils and design a local curriculum as set out in the 'area-based curriculum' approach (Facer and Thomas, 2012), Alternatively, PD might enable teachers to draw on pupils' funds of knowledge such as herding, caring for livestock, the seasons, and natural environment. Such an example has been given of potential teaching opportunities in rural Turkana to support the aims for the Science curriculum in Kenya (Ng'asike, 2014). In Rwandan setting-based PD, early years classroom teachers learned the importance of connecting to children's homes and the natural environment by using local materials for play activities, as reported by teachers:

> "A theme of study makes a connection to the village, to Rwandan culture, and to the children. Then you find different materials from around us which help children to understand more ... like found materials outside: stones, bottle caps, grasses, banana leaves."
>
> Gerde et al. (2020: 2442)

PD for culturally relevant early years practices was led by local 'seasoned' educators rather than internationally trained instructors. These PD leaders developed the sessions and mentored the participants. The PD followed four stages.

1 It began with educators observing practice with follow-up discussion about how to adapt pedagogy.
2 Then educators participated in four practical skill-based workshops to practise their new approaches with individual observations and feedback.

3 This was followed by a mentoring discussion and chance to reflect on teaching, sometimes using a video of their practice.

4 In this mentoring conversation, the educator planned for changes to embed this practice (Gerde et al., 2020).

This way of working empowered the ECD educators. They reported that they viewed themselves as professionals who studied the impact of their practices on learning and developed these to meet the needs and interests of the children (Gerde et al., 2020). This example, in common with the First Nations Partnership Programme, shows that the content of PD and resources used within it can be co-constructed with community members to ensure relevance.

Reflection Point 6:3

How does PD in your setting help educators to connect to the home lives and experiences of the students they work with?

Responsive, participatory approaches

Materials and programmes for PD may be most culturally relevant if they are built on what educators say about their needs and circumstances. Vignette 17 presents findings from a study developed to understand the impact of a set of open education resources (OERs) for tutor professional development in Uganda.

Vignette 17: Teacher educator stories of professional development in Uganda (Alison Buckler)

"I have come to realise as a tutor that learning does not stop. At any time you can learn new knowledge and skills. I did just this, and this is my story …"

This and the following quotes come from a story written by Samuel, a teacher educator (tutor) who participated in a storytelling research study in Uganda (Buckler et al., 2021). The study aimed to understand the impact of a set of open education resources (OERs) for tutor professional development. It also wanted to engage more creatively and optimistically with teacher educators' worlds in Sub-Saharan African contexts: in the literature they are presented as under-qualified, discontented, and lacking in innovation, motivation, and agency.

Thirty-nine tutors were supported to write a short story about a personal experience as a tutor that would help people to understand what it was like to work in the profession.

> "I will admit that I had inadequate experience in teacher education ... But I thought that I would try and learn on the job and got on with it."

PD was the predominant focus across the stories. Tutors presented themselves as committed, dynamic, and open to change and most stories were about proactive attempts to learn new pedagogies and skills to deal with the challenges of their role. Sometimes this was sparked by formal training courses, but these were rarely available, and it was more common that professional development trajectories were self-directed. Fascinatingly, the OER – a free tool designed to support tutors' professional needs – was not mentioned once.

Collectively, the stories suggest interrelated reasons for this. First, internet access was much more limited than the researchers had anticipated. While tutors had smartphones, only two referenced the internet as a place for professional learning. Second, tutors framed 'formal' professional development as an opportunity to attend a course. They were selected to attend by senior staff, so engagement also had an esteem factor. Other kinds of professional development were seen as everyday, ad-hoc responses to immediate challenges. A structured but optional OER sat uneasily between the two: it did not align with tutors' collective understanding of opportunities for developing professionally. Third, the issues that the OER aimed to address (challenges with teaching and learning in schools) were not primary concerns for the tutors. They were consumed with the immediate difficulties of working in the college – especially a lack of resources for teaching and student wellbeing. Their professional development goals were focused around these local issues, leaving little time or energy to engage with more widespread education challenges.

> "I therefore say that learning does not end. Expertise is not a single pursuit – we think we must become an expert in one thing, to stick to the thing we were trained in. I don't believe this is true. I encourage colleagues to take on new learning opportunities whenever they can. You should be open to many paths in life. You never know where they will lead you."

The stories of ITE tutors in Uganda highlights how the culture of the education institution can inhibit or support PD. In Vignette 17, tutors had limited access to organised PD or the internet as a means for further study and connection with the OERs designed to support them. Perhaps more importantly, the OERs had low status amongst the tutors for PD and so were disregarded. This shows that education settings need to promote the range of PD available and emphasise its value to encourage educators to participate. When promoting or designing PD, leaders should also take time to find out about educators' expectations, needs, and access. Furthermore, the participatory method of gathering educator experiences of PD through story-telling shows the potential of listening to educators before deciding the focus of future PD.

The need to listen to educators and gain their views about culturally appropriate PD also surfaced in a study of trainers and trainee teachers in Cyprus (Symeou and Karagiorgi, 2018). In-depth interviews and focus groups post PD on working with Roma children and families showed that teachers had felt isolated and helpless without PD around this issue. Although they had attempted individually to learn about what to do for this marginalised group, there had been limited professional development available. However, when they did access PD about Roma children, they were still frustrated as they felt it did not offer practical solutions to their day-to-day issues or clear guidelines for practice. This finding raises another challenge for culturally relevant PD in that educators may take an 'instrumental approach' in which they want to be given a plan to follow that will 'solve' this cultural difference in their classrooms. Of course, PD that addresses cultural diversity cannot offer a blueprint for educators to follow, as every child and family is different. However, attention can be paid to ensure that PD does at least offer some practical strategies and starting points or applied examples so that teachers are able to relate their learning to their everyday responsibilities. Similarly, the teachers in the study had, in some cases, years of experience of working with Roma children and families and had their own ideas about what worked. Another important aspect of PD that is appropriate to the culture of the educators is that it considers their lived experiences and draws on these as a foundation.

> "Training that fails to consider the professional contexts in which educators operate or set connections between training activities and school agendas appears meaningless. Professional development needs to be tailored to educators' prior background and establish channels for exchange of the wealth of participants' experiences."
>
> Symeou and Karagiorgi (2018: 318)

The examples of challenges experienced by educators who have found limitations to their PD suggest that a participatory pedagogy for professional development may support culturally relevant educational practices. Participatory PD can include a 'hands-on' active approach to learning but also ensure that what educators know and have experienced matters. Educators in participatory PD are agents in the process and construct knowledge through interaction (Wolfenden et al., 2017b).

Bridging the gap between theory and practice

Culturally appropriate PD may involve working with educators to review the curriculum or plan new strategies that help them to apply theory in context.

The following vignette refers to a process engaged in within the context of a group of teacher education providers in Pakistan who delivered a shared Bachelor of Education (BEd) programme. This was initiated when faculty members realised, as a result of an analysis of their policy context (Behlol et al., 2014), their desire to reform the curriculum, pedagogy, and assessment of their initial teacher education programme. The existing programme had been constructed through a Global North aid project which provided a curriculum and IT computer suite in each of the four teacher training providers. Vignette 18, in common with other examples in this chapter, highlights issues of importing curricula in the global marketplace for teacher development previously illustrated in Vignette 2, Chapter 1.

Vignette 18: ECD multisectoral training in low resource contexts – Pakistan (Alison Fox)

A joint Pakistan and UK team was formed using British Council Pakistan funding (2014–2017) to collaborate on the 'Promoting Inquiry Informed Practice: Bridging the gap between theory and practice for participants of pre-service teacher education program'. The team began with a curriculum evaluation following an approach recommended by Porter (2004), which examines four dimensions: the intended, assessed, enacted, and learned curriculum. This was assessed against the local National Professional Standards for Teachers in Pakistan (UNESCO, 2009). The first and second dimensions were approached through paper-based activity, analysing handbook materials, teaching resources, and assessment documentation, which served as an orientation phase for the UK partners and a chance to engage in critical reflection with those in Pakistan. The third and fourth dimensions required fieldwork. Joint observations and a range of interviews with teacher educators across the teacher education providers, cooperative teachers in three school settings, and with prospective teachers were complemented by a questionnaire to all prospective teachers on the BEd programme (Behlol et al., 2017b).

The data from this analysis of the curriculum informed three days of workshops with representatives from all stakeholders, working together in the same working space. The sessions were built around nine self-evaluation guides termed 'Building Bridges Guides: An Initial Teacher Education self-evaluation toolkit', which addressed questions such as: How can we evaluate our curriculum? How do we know what the student teacher experience is? How can we support student teachers in the practicum? How might we develop school and university partnerships? How can we assess initial teacher development?, and an associated international conference.

As part of the initial activities in this workshop, the participants scoped their ideal characteristics for a teacher in Pakistan which was used as a reference point, as represented in Figure 6.1.

Figure 6.1 A representation of the ideal teacher in Pakistan

Image included with thanks to the participants of the 'Promoting Inquiry-Informed Practice: Bridging the Gap between Theory & Practice for Participants of Pre-Service Teacher Education Program' workshops, 16–18 May 2017.

Following this, the National Professional Standards for Teachers in Pakistan (UNESCO, 2009) were reviewed as a basis for the teacher education curriculum. Each standard has three parts: (a) knowledge and understanding, (b) dispositions, behaviours, attitude, and values, and (c) performances (skills). Of these dimensions to a teacher's development it was concluded that knowledge and understanding were privileged in the BEd programme and new methods of assessment were needed to value dispositions and skills, many of which are represented in the workshop participants' views of the ideal teacher. This has led to research and development activity led by the Pakistan team to further teacher development practices, looking at relationships which support teacher development (Behlol et al., 2019; Fatima and Behlol, 2018), the importance of garnering student voice (Behlol et al., 2017a), and how to support higher-order skill development in prospective teachers (Behlol and Cajkler, 2018; Fox, 2021; Masood and Behlol, 2017). This team have challenged whether what they term the 'brain drain' of their early career teacher educators to studying in Global North settings will prove a curse or a boon for teacher education in Pakistan (Behlol and Dad, 2020).

Vignette 18 points to the importance of PD that develops dispositions and skills as well as knowledge. This is a common issue also evident in Vignette 17 and other global contexts. In East Africa, teacher education programmes are often separated from the context of schools and local communities (Akyeampong et al., 2013; Wolfenden et al., 2017b). Pre-service teacher education frequently focuses on subject knowledge rather than pedagogy and student teachers may experience a lack of agency. 'It's like everything at college – it's not real, it's a game we play to pass our exams and then we learn how to be a real teacher when we graduate' (Buckler, 2020: 856). It seems clear that to bridge any divide between theory and practice, culturally appropriate PD should draw on student and educator ideas. This PD should also be built on relationships that support ongoing development of practice (Gerde et al., 2020; Wolfenden et al., 2017b). An approach to PD for university educators for health professions in Brazil included a peer mentoring system of mid-career faculty members who met for reflection, advice, and support. Significantly, it involved educators in carrying out authentic project work focused on curriculum innovation with students (Amaral et al., 2012). Such approaches can also include gathering perspectives from the community that the educators work with to inform their PD (Soni et al., 2020).

Vignette 19 highlights a way of working with early years educators in England to identify health education priorities specific to their setting and develop strategies to address these in context.

Vignette 19: A model for promoting children's health (Jackie Musgrave)

As I was embarking on research with a colleague into young children's health in 2018, I realised that there was a great deal that educators can and could do in promoting the health of children from birth to five in their nursery, pre-school or home. But what interventions for health promotion were likely to work? Health promotion is not something that can be done to people, instead it must be in collaboration and consultation with the practitioners in their setting. This is where the idea for *Child Health Promotion: A Toolkit for Early Childhood Education and Care Practitioners* started. As well as providing knowledge and information about child health, the toolkit includes a model for practitioners to use to assess the health needs of the children in their setting – this is the *5-Step Approach*. The steps support practitioners to identify the health priorities, to identify, implement, and evaluate the effectiveness of the intervention (Figure 6.2).

This model has been piloted in one pre-school nursery in an area of high deprivation in England (Musgrave and Payler, 2021). My co-researcher was the Family Support Worker in the nursery, and she led the practitioners to identify that there was a need to promote healthier eating for the children. This decision was taken because the contents of lunches sent from home frequently included processed and high sugar content food.

Figure 6.2 The 5-step approach to child health promotion

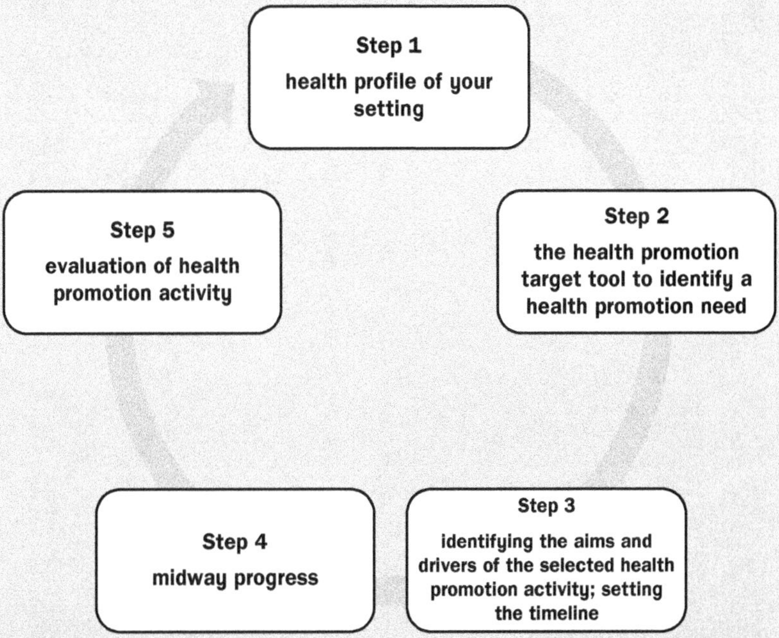

```
                        ┌─────────────────────┐
                        │       Step 1        │
                        │  health profile of  │
                        │    your setting     │
                        └─────────────────────┘

┌─────────────────┐                          ┌──────────────────────┐
│     Step 5      │                          │        Step 2        │
│ evaluation of   │                          │  the health promotion│
│ health          │                          │  target tool to      │
│ promotion       │                          │  identify a health   │
│ activity        │                          │  promotion need      │
└─────────────────┘                          └──────────────────────┘

           ┌─────────────────┐   ┌──────────────────────┐
           │     Step 4      │   │        Step 3        │
           │ midway progress │   │  identifying the aims│
           │                 │   │  and drivers of the  │
           │                 │   │  selected health     │
           │                 │   │  promotion activity; │
           │                 │   │  setting the timeline│
           └─────────────────┘   └──────────────────────┘
```

Reproduced from Musgrave and Payler (2021: 773).

As the practitioners used the 5-Step Approach, it became apparent that key to the success of the proposed model was the ability of the practitioners to work as a community with children and the parents at the centre of the health promotion initiative. It is imperative to be sensitive to the cultural and socio-economic factors that can influence parents' health beliefs and practices and result in less than healthy choices being made.

One example of how my co-researcher approached working with parents was to create a bank of visual resources which were placed strategically around the nursery. At parents' evening, a display showed the sugar content of the foods that were frequently included in the children's lunch boxes. As I had been invited to attend parents' evening in case any of the parents had questions about our research, I saw for myself the impact the display had on parents, many expressing their surprise.

Figure 6.3 Sugar content display

By engaging with trialling the use of the toolkit, the practitioners were able to reflect on their knowledge of health promotion and working together they were able to unpack some of the complexities of promoting children's health and initiating change. That they were able to initiate such change was because they adopted a whole-nursery approach, embedding healthy activities in everyday routines. They demonstrated their commitment to health promotion in their nursery by taking responsibility for contributing to identifying the health needs of the children and working closely with parents in collaborative ways, using sensitivity, respect, and understanding.

Vignette 19 exemplifies many of the key principles in this chapter. It highlights the value of an enquiring collaborative approach that simultaneously develops educator practice and addresses the specific needs of the community and pupils. This long-term approach to PD, with built-in opportunities to review and develop, offered a way to respond to and reflect the unique culture of the setting.

In conclusion

This chapter has provided examples of culturally relevant PD at all stages of an educator's career. It has highlighted that PD can be developed in partnership with educators and the community – whoever that community might include, whether student teachers, early childhood practitioners, parents, businesses or tribal leaders. It may involve examining and challenging long-held practices. In doing so, it has the potential to change educators' practice and understanding in a way that is more meaningful and sustainable than PD designed from the 'top down'. This approach includes taking time to ensure that the focus of PD, materials and examples used, are in tune with the local context, and the needs and experiences of the learners. It involves listening to educators to build on their prior experiences and respond to their concerns. Leading culturally relevant PD may also require a leadership style that reflects traditional philosophies. This may influence the way that roles are assigned, the tasks and activities that are included, as well as strategies for communication and decision-making within PD.

Personal Development Planning Table 6 Focus: Professional

Question	What can I do?	What do I need from others?
	Short-term action	Medium-term action
1. What aspects of culture and context of my setting do I need to consider in PD?	Make a mindmap or list of contextual influences on your setting (local, regional, national, staff, community)	Talk to other members of staff to find out what current contextual issues might need support through PD
2. How could PD be co-constructed with educators and the community?	Note down key stakeholders in the community who might make a valuable contribution to staff PD	Gather ideas from parents or other community members around the planned focus of PD
3. How can PD draw on educators' existing knowledge and experience?	Think about ways that you could gauge educator starting points	Plan a 'Pre-PD' exercise to gather educators' prior experience, concerns. and questions before planning PD to incorporate these

NB: Recommended Open Access Readings are highlighted below, using asterisks as follows: *Leaders and Teacher Educators, **Practitioners, ***Early Career Professionals.

Recommended reading

* Pence, A., Anglin, J. and Hunt-Jinnouchi, F. (2010) Institutional engagement with Indigenous communities: The First Nations Partnership Program and the use of a borderland space, *Ngoonjook: A Journal of Australian and Indigenous Issues*, 34 (1): 57–71.

* Quan-Baffour, K.P. and Romm, N.R.A. (2014) Ubuntu-inspired training of adult literacy teachers as a route to generating 'community' enterprises, *Journal of Literacy Research*, 46 (4): 455–474.

** Musgrave, J. and Payler, J. (2021) Proposing a model for promoting children's health in early childhood education and care settings, *Children and Society*, 35 (5): 766–783 [https://onlinelibrary.wiley.com/doi/full/10.1111/chso.12449].

*** Thomas, L. (2012) *Thinking about an area based curriculum: A guide for practitioners*. London: RSA [https://www.thersa.org/globalassets/pdfs/rsa_thinking-about-an-area-based-curriculum-a-guide-for-practitioners.pdf].

7 PD for equity

#EC #ML #SL #TE

Every educator is likely to be concerned about the unequal educational outcomes that persist for learners from marginalised groups, in comparison with their more advantaged peers (Schleicher, 2019). How educators can address educational inequality and challenging circumstances through professional development (PD) for equity is linked to theories and practices of inclusion and social justice. Disadvantaged learners are likely to have intersecting identities that influence their experience: factors of race, ethnicity, class, gender, sexuality, religion, citizenship, ability, socio-economic status. These may be linked to limited opportunities to participate, to differential power relations and structural inequalities for the learners individually, their families, and their wider social group (Tefera et al., 2018). Educators need to understand the diversity of their students and support them through responsive pedagogy. Beyond pedagogy, PD for equity requires a critical approach in which assumptions, practices, and systems are challenged and ultimately changed.

In this chapter, we explore how educational disadvantage might be addressed through PD, and suggest how educators may be supported to develop inclusive, socially-just pedagogy in different contexts. PD for equity is a complex field and, rather than attempting to cover all aspects of educational inequality in depth, we draw out key issues including poverty, cultural diversity, disability, and special educational needs. The language used to refer to learners and their characteristics in this chapter follows that used in the original research studies we draw upon.

Reflection point 7:1

- *Who are the learners that are marginalised in your context?*
- *How do you know? If you do not know, where would you look for data?*

Three elements identified in recent research inform PD for equity with staff in any setting:

1 Knowledge about diversity, diverse learners, and life experiences.
2 Teaching *to* diversity by adapting practice to respond to the needs of individuals.

3 Teaching *for* diversity by enabling future educators to work to transform the education system, not reproduce existing inequalities, and recognise and challenge limiting practices and structures (Rowan et al., 2021)

Knowledge about diversity, diverse learners and life experiences begins by enabling educators to reflect on their own assumptions and establish the values that drive their pedagogy. Teachers commence initial teacher education (ITE) with beliefs about teaching, learning, and learners that are difficult to shift (Bondy et al., 2007; Mutton et al., 2010). So, work in this area begins with identities. Teachers need to be supported to examine their own prior experiences and preconceptions to develop understanding of the contexts in which they will be working, as well as responsive learner-focused pedagogy (Goodwin and Darity, 2019).

This may begin with an examination of their own social, ethnic, and cultural identity and how this could influence their view of teaching, for example via a survey to gauge perspectives on diversity (Clarke and Drudy, 2006; Ellis et al., 2016). A survey of postgraduate trainee teachers in Northern Ireland revealed tension between the trainees' generally positive disposition to diversity and more negative assumptions about the impact of immigration on job prospects and the social welfare system (Clarke and Drudy, 2006). Survey responses could provide a starting point for a sensitively handled discussion about how we establish the veracity of such views, where they come from, and how they might relate to our own identity and actions as educators. Boylan and Woolsey suggest these emerging views are treated with compassion and respect, therefore modelling the appreciation of difference that we want the teachers to develop:

> "Compassion because the identity work needed to negotiate changing identity is uncomfortable and challenging, and respect because identity is rooted in personal histories."
>
> Boylan and Woolsey (2015: 63)

Reflection point 7:2

- *How do you find out about the assumptions and perspectives on equality, diversity, and inclusion of the staff you work with?*
- *What could you do to learn more? How would you make the case?*

Teaching *to* diversity may involve data collection and analysis to identify students who are not reaching their potential and may be most at risk of falling behind. Then educators can review their practice in supporting different groups and individuals (Collins et al., 2015; Demie, 2005). They may draw on assessment data and informal observations and conversations with learners. This should also support educators to recognise the achievements of pupils with special educational needs and disabilities (SEND) beyond those assessed through standard testing (Belli, 2018).

Teaching to diversity can be supported by opportunities for 'inter-professional' PD. In Canada and the United States, university social work courses gave students work experience of collaborative practice to address social justice issues. Students were paired with others from different disciplines (e.g. social work and medicine) to shadow the members of a clinic for patients with HIV and Aids; students from occupational therapy, physiotherapy, social work, and nursing worked as a team with members of staff from the prison (County Jail) to provide a health and wellness programme. Students become better prepared to address inequalities through their team-working experiences and reflections on competencies for effective inter-professional working (Rubin et al., 2018).

Reflection point 7:3

Who could you work with to provide opportunities for inter- and/or intra-professional learning with an equity and/or social justice focus?

Teaching *for* diversity builds on educators' understanding of the intersectional inequalities experienced by learners so that they advocate for children against discriminatory or harmful school practices as part of modelling equity (Goodwin and Darity, 2019). One example is PD that provides reflective activities and discussion around critical whiteness. In an American study, 57 trainee teachers on a teacher education programme in the Midwest were exposed to information about the racism of white historical figures and racism and homophobia in the civil rights movement and asked to compare with the content of children's books on these subjects. However, even with this PD, educators may not recognise their own responsibility to find out more about the histories and lived experiences of marginalised groups (Aronson et al., 2020). Others may attribute learners' challenges to deficit factors stemming from the individuals and their families rather than pedagogy or structural inequalities (Sleeter, 2017). For these reasons, teaching for diversity requires sustained and critical approaches to pedagogy and PD.

Culturally responsive and culturally relevant pedagogy

Rather than viewing any students or communities from a deficit position, culturally responsive pedagogy examines how policy, curriculum, pedagogy, and assessment may be influenced by cultural assumptions and then working to change the barriers (Gay, 2013; Vass, 2017). Culturally relevant pedagogy takes this further by developing students' critical understanding of race, racism, and white supremacy in society (Matias, 2016). Equity for learners of colour and from linguistically and ethnically diverse backgrounds presents a particular challenge in countries where white teachers dominate the teaching profession, such as in the USA and the UK and the teacher population does not represent the diversity of the learner population (Aronson et al., 2020; Ellis et al., 2016). There is criticism that initial teacher education and school experiences can perpetuate the inequalities and racism endemic in society with teachers who are not well-prepared to teach students from diverse backgrounds (Pearce, 2014; Sleeter, 2017). Some teachers may not be aware of the inequalities in the education system (Aronson et al., 2020), whilst others may be aware of issues of racism and inequality but unsure of how to change their teaching to address racism and effect social equity (Bhopal and Rhamie, 2014). Others may believe themselves to be prepared to teach diverse learners without having any real-life experience to draw on:

> "… at a US urban-focused teacher preparation program, my white teacher candidates professed a readiness to teach urban students of color though most had had no previous interactions with people of color; this is akin to saying one is ready to work with children despite never having interacted with them."
>
> Matias (2016: 198)

Critical whiteness

Involvement in critical reading activities and subsequent discussions may raise teachers' awareness of what Aronson and colleagues (2020) described as 'whitewashing'. Providing opportunities for teachers to read about and discuss critical whiteness with peers could also encourage them to reflect on any discomfort experienced at these revelations. However, these challenging issues may require support for PD leaders and teacher educators themselves. Aronson and associates assert that:

> "Teacher educators (who are predominantly white) themselves have a responsibility to unlearn, relearn, and do the self-work that is needed to tell the truths about history, however ugly it may be."
>
> Aronson et al. (2020: 317)

Research suggests that mainly white teacher trainees in both the UK and the USA were more willing to hear about critical whiteness from a white academic. Black lecturers were unfairly viewed as biased and teaching from experience and emotion, rather than academic expertise (Matias, 2016; Smith and Lander, 2012). Sadly, university educators may not fully recognise the challenge faced by their colleagues of colour when they attempt to talk to trainees about race, racism, and whiteness (Matias, 2016; Smith and Lander, 2012). School leaders may also overlook the responsibility, often unequally placed, on educators of colour to address issues of equity for pupils (Kohli et al., 2021; Lisle Johnson and Kohli, 2020). White PD leaders and teacher educators will need to take on the responsibility of such teaching, perhaps working in pairs or teams to support any colleagues of colour and ensure that all teachers engage with the theories and ideas surrounding critical whiteness.

Service learning: An integrated approach

Service learning refers to training experiences of working with marginalised groups planned to equip educators to 'serve' the best interests of these individuals and communities. This can be via work-based learning in an area of low socio-economic status, with a very multi-cultural or multi-lingual community, or with learners with disabilities. Service learning is important because some educators may have very limited understanding of the experiences of learners with different needs, different ethnic, cultural, social, and economic backgrounds or the impact of these factors on their experiences. For example, Ellis et al. (2016) highlighted a study of 166 training teachers as they commenced their initial teacher training at Oxford University, UK, 76 per cent of whom did not believe there was a link between poverty and educational attainment and offered a deficit model of low parental aspirations and pupil attitudes as the reason for why children with low socio-economic status do not achieve as highly in education.

Service learning needs carefully planned support. Trainees sent to a 'challenging' school in an area of socio-economic disadvantage in Ireland (Brown, 2017) and from mono-cultural educational backgrounds, teaching in schools with a diverse pupil population (Hendry, 2008) experienced a 'culture shock' in the school where they were placed. However, with preparation and support, they became familiar with school-based strategies to support the learners and developed greater empathy.

One successful strategy for service-learning involved training teachers in planning, teaching, and reflecting on one-to-one support for children who were struggling academically. Ellis et al. (2016) reported on an initiative in an economically deprived area of Scotland, where trainee teachers worked in teams of four to support a specific child with their reading. They each supported the child for half an hour, one day a week, and shared ideas by phone. Working as a team allowed trainees to make collaborative decisions, discuss teaching strategies, and base their responsive pedagogy on shared knowledge of the pupil. Personalised planning activities have also been used to good effect as a regular part of placements for teaching trainees working with pupils with special educational needs and disabilities in New Zealand and Australia (Arthur-Kelly et al., 2013).

Some ITE providers have found that a more long-term integrated approach to pre-service teacher preparation involving multiple experiences of working with diverse groups of learners and combining theory and practice has been effective. Walton and Rusznyak (2020) highlight the importance of a structured interplay between coursework and school experiences to develop trainee teachers' pedagogy for pupils with SEND. This could include activities such as guiding trainees through a reflective process of lesson planning in which individual needs and teaching strategies are carefully aligned. In Australia, the National Exceptional Teaching for Disadvantaged Schools programme recruited high-performing trainee teachers during their undergraduate degree to focus on preparing to teach in disadvantaged schools (Burnett and Lampert, 2019). The programme followed the existing ITE curriculum but introduced trainees to educational theory on poverty and educational disadvantage as well as critical race theory, before placing them in high-poverty settings. Placement school leaders worked collaboratively with university staff to plan elements of the course, modelling an emphasis on reflection and communication within a community of peers and mentors.

Integrating a service-learning approach into ITE could involve a planned practice experience in every year group of an undergraduate programme (Petersen and Henning, 2018). However, even well-planned service-learning experiences, supported with reading and reflective tasks, may inadvertently re-enforce any negative assumptions on the part of the ITE trainees. Kirkland (2014) found that some trainees viewed their urban teaching practicum with fear and looked for evidence of students' and community connections to crime and violence. This emphasises the importance of discussing trainee bias in preparation for service learning and giving them responsibility for specific social justice projects so they could decide if they had a future in this role. Another possible challenge with service-learning is ensuring that these planned experiences are flexible enough to offer the time needed to establish reciprocal learning with the children and young people involved (Sitter and Nusbaum, 2018). ITE providers need to consider the identities of the training educators taking part and how this might shape their experience. For example, service-learning literature in the USA focuses on non-disabled trainees supporting children and young people in schools, rather than the experiences of trainee educators with disabilities. This is an area that could be explored further (Sitter and Nusbaum, 2018). The experiences and perspectives of LGBTQ trainee educators are similarly rarely considered, as service-learning is designed and implemented with a focus on the young people they will be working with rather than support for their own equity as learners (Donahue, 2018).

It seems that to prepare teachers to **teach *for* diversity** service-learning should not rely on direct experience alone: 'students need opportunities to experience carefully designed acts of care and social justice' (Petersen and Henning, 2018: 440) with 'input from literature, research provocations, and collaborative challenge' (Ellis et al., 2016: 495). These should be multiple and built up over time through practical experience and opportunities for theoretical challenge and critical reflection within a community of practice that includes the in-service teachers and children/young people. However, care should be taken to co-construct service-learning so that it challenges any underlying assumptions of student educators and is created by, for, and about the community (Donahue, 2018; Kirkland, 2014).

Mentoring for equity

School-based mentoring has the potential to support trainee teachers with **teaching *to* diversity**. Even trainees who begin their placements with a well-developed pedagogy for equity may find that they struggle to reconcile this with resistance from school leaders and the real-life demands of 'teaching to the test' in some locations (Sleeter and Owuor, 2011). In Australia, a small study found that some ITE mentors perpetuated a culture of low expectations and a deficit view of learners and their families. Students experienced barriers to making any curriculum or pedagogic changes and they were very conscious that it was unwise to 'rock the boat' in a context where they would be assessed by their mentors. They particularly cited the pressures of curriculum, standards, and accountability as a barrier to teachers engaging with culturally responsive schooling (Vass, 2017).

Mentors have a crucial role to play in developing trainee teachers' and early career teachers' understanding of equity, but to enable trainees to enact culturally responsive pedagogy during practicum, some school-based mentors may need extra training. In the lifelong learning sector in the UK, in common with ITE, government standards for mentoring have led to a focus on subject knowledge (Duckworth and Maxwell, 2015). However, mentors could provide:

> "spaces for critical reflection, support trainees to experience different cultures, develop inclusive critical pedagogies, and generally act as advocates and foster passion for social justice."
>
> Duckworth and Maxwell (2015: 4)

As Lofthouse (2018: 258) points out, mentoring can prompt critical inquiry so that trainee teachers develop 'the disposition to act truly and justly according to one's values and moral stance'. To achieve this, mentors first need their own PD, perhaps including opportunities to video and reflect upon their mentoring interactions with student teachers. Furthermore, leadership is needed to ensure mentors develop their understanding of and for whole-school change.

Reflection point 7:4

What training is available in your workplace to support mentoring for equity?

PD for leaders of equity

Creating a long-term community of practice can support PD as well as building trust between different communities such as schools and higher education institutions (Burnett and Lampert, 2019; Sleeter, 2017). This targeted collaboration can also build an employment pathway for trainees who are well-prepared to work for equity in education (Burnett and Lampert, 2019). Torrance et al. (2021) report that social justice is still rarely part of conventional leadership development. Instead, school leadership programmes are often influenced by a focus on raising attainment without surfacing issues related to equity and fairness. Another limitation is that leadership PD for social justice may focus on the needs of some marginalised groups and exclude others, paying less attention to gender, sexuality or special educational needs (Pazey and Cole, 2013; Torrance et al., 2021).

Critical pedagogy as part of in-service or postgraduate programmes for leaders and teacher educators, can offer the stimulus for critical examination of their own practices and assumptions. Vescio and associates found that for some teacher educators, participating in a critical pedagogy seminar series and completing a reflective essay were transformational:

> "They talked about changes in their perspectives toward personal and professional aspects of their lives and how they had attempted to, or planned to, include some of these changing views in their work."
>
> Vescio et al. (2009: 13)

The success of this approach rested on the relational intra-personal dialogue in sessions. The teacher educators reported that the tutor created a feeling of equality between themselves as learners and the tutor, which meant they were able to explore perspectives. The group also established shared understanding that it was normal to feel unsettled by the discussions and readings. They reported that the extra time given to think during the reflective activities was needed because of the demanding intellectual and emotional load. Sessions began with manageable connections – in this case, starting with a familiar text. Time was taken to clarify shared terminology and the assignment focused on documenting their experiences of putting theory into practice (Vescio et al., 2009). Autoethnographic case studies of social justice dilemmas faced by academics can offer a critical starting point for reflection and discussion (Dover et al., 2018). Creating a faculty learning community of like-minded educators also offers protection from burnout for those attempting to champion equity and challenge existing perspectives (Dover et al., 2018, 2019). After a year of regular CPD meetings between faculty members with this shared focus, they had forged strategic alliances and connections, which increased their confidence and productivity (Dover et al., 2019).

School leadership for equity is the responsibility of all 'layers' of leadership (Forde and Torrance, 2017). Middle leaders need to work through what this means for practices in their subject areas. Through critical reflection, discussion, and collaborative planning with a focus on equity, leaders at all levels can acknowledge the dilemmas they face and explore ways to address them (Forde and Torrance, 2017).

Reflection point 7:5

- *How are educators of colour, or from other marginalised groups in your setting, supported by PD networks with other similar educators?*
- *How could this be developed?*

Re-framing social justice across the life-course of educators

Opportunities to 're-frame' social justice challenges encourage educators to reflect on the way inequalities intersect and how their practices are influenced by class, culture, and politics (Poekert et al., 2020). Practical engagement with re-framing can involve collaborative reflection on 'professional dilemmas of practice' (Nicholson and Kroll, 2015). A regular space is set aside for a member of staff to share a concern or challenge with their colleagues in a designated meeting time. First the member of staff presents their concern and their feelings about it as colleagues listen. Then staff members are guided to use coaching techniques to facilitate a collaborative problem-solving space such as:

- listening and allowing the practitioner to talk about their feelings and experiences;
- suggesting how the problem could be broken down into manageable elements;
- identifying improvements and strengths;
- offering a new perspective/re-framing;
- raising a question or challenging assumptions;
- suggesting an alternative way forward;
- offering possible resources to support.

This technique was implemented with early childhood professionals including a leading SEND teacher and a mentor for practitioners across a school district. Setting these discussions in the context of trusting relationships allowed them to explore the roots of the issues, reconnect with internal values, suggest how they could use different connections for help, and enabled them to re-focus on the needs of the children (Nicholson and Kroll, 2015).

Other suggested approaches for PD include creating a safe network in which to share practice. This has been particularly important for black educators in the USA who reported gaining the ideas and confidence to introduce youth-led participatory action research and culturally supportive curriculum activities in their classrooms. The Network of Black Educators allowed them to share their own experiences of marginalisation and emotional load and provided opportunities to develop classroom activities together, such as using a community family game as a starting point for artwork and discussions of cultural gender expectations (Kohli et al., 2021).

PD for equity applies to leadership of higher education, for example approaches to de-colonisation. A critical starting point could be for faculty members and senior leaders to reflect on the way that different articulations of colonialism may be shaping pedagogies in their institution and how these might be changed. For example, de Oliveira Andreotti et al. argue that, if higher education providers recognise the dominance in education that privileges white males, 'radical reform' would offer 'recognition, representation, redistribution, voice and reconciliation' (2015: 26). Practices would involve re-education of the existing dominant workforces, empowering marginalised groups, and redistributing material resources.

PD for equity and student voice

PD can support equity if it is based on understanding the complexities of learners' identities and experiences, including their relationships with educational institutions and systems (Poekert et al., 2020). For example, attention should be paid to the intersectional nature of identity in order to recognise the individual experiences of people with disabilities (Sitter and Nusbaum, 2018). However, children and young people's views and experiences of inequality may be marginalised by longstanding practices that do not include student voice. As reported in a study of students' views on gender inequality, students may feel powerless and disengaged (Keisu and Ahlström, 2020). Student voice can inform PD with pre-service or in-service educators through participatory action research with children and young people. In this way, students can shape changes to educational practices:

> *"Too often, youth – especially those historically marginalised due to race/ ethnicity, gender, and socioeconomic status – are the subject of policies rather than actors in shaping policy."*
>
> Mansfield (2014: 398)

Sitter and Nusbaum (2018) argue that participatory research with students with SEND should be based on genuine collaboration about how to change practice; any research and collaboration should be flexible enough to accommodate the timing needed by the participants. It could involve 'counterstorytelling' or other arts-based forms of inquiry, such as poetry writing to really encourage participants to tell their stories in a way that enables educators to see things from their perspective. Educators can also use student-led videos and follow-up discussions to capture student perspectives on learning that inform PD (Florian and Beaton, 2018).

School leaders must also take responsibility for social justice by improving their own understanding of special education, including evidence-based practices for both general and special education, rather than expecting this to be taken care of by leading teachers and coordinators for SEND (Pazey and Cole, 2013).

Case Study 3 explains how portage workers were supported to shift their perspective by learning from each child in context.

Case Study 3: In-the-Picture: Using PD to see from a child's perspective (Jonathan Rix)

In-the-Picture is an innovative approach which helps those supporting very young children with learning difficulties explore everyday experiences and activities from the child's perspective (Rix et al., 2020). It involves first-person narrative observation of the child in the learning context and photographs of the child's focus of interest. These are a precursor to reviewing the photographic record with the child and undertaking reflective discussions with the practitioners and family involved. In-the-Picture began life as a research method in a project undertaken by Jonathan Rix and Alice Paige-Smith/ Matthews between 2008 and 2009. Alice and Jonathan had been interviewing parents involved in early intervention programmes since 2004. Policy since the 1990s has increasingly placed emphasis on such programmes for children with learning difficulties. Professionals and policy-makers expect parents to carry out developmental 'activities' on a daily basis with their children, and through early intervention to counteract children's identified problems and 'deficits'. The parents that Alice and Jonathan interviewed had reported that these early intervention activities were a regular source of tension with their child, and that they only engaged with activities they enjoyed and found easy to do. Jonathan and Alice wished to explore this further, but recognised they had to develop a research approach which facilitated listening to young children with learning difficulties in a family context.

Over the next few years, In-the-Picture was used mainly by Alice and Jonathan, together with John Parry, to study interactions and learning between young children, practitioners, and the children's parents in home and early childhood settings. To their delight, practitioners involved in these projects expressed an interest in using the tool themselves. In response, John and Jonathan started to offer training to staff in early years settings and home visitors. Unsurprisingly, John and Jonathan then wanted to find out how useful people found In-the-Picture in practice; so they undertook training and interviews with ten portage services in England.

The portage home visitors perceived themselves as being listeners in their jobs, but they talked about In-the-Picture shifting their ways of thinking so they could more readily engage with the child's voice and facilitate family-centred and child-centred practice. This encouraged them to draw upon their professional knowledge, too, which they felt had been subsumed by an assessment and target agenda. There was a degree of surprise about both the capacity of In-the-Picture to achieve these things and the strength of the resultant insights. Consequently, the practitioners believed that In-the-Picture would be of value to the practice of many others. This was not because of a specific aspect of the process or its robustness and rigour, rather it was because of its simplicity, flexibility, and capacity to create space and engender reflection within a very brief time-frame. For time-pressed practitioners, it therefore seemed to serve as a useful tool, one which could be tried occasionally or which could be built into regular practices; one that might not provide answers but was likely to suggest useful questions about the child and their participation within their developing world.

As a result of these discussions, John and Jonathan developed a course for the National Portage Association, which aimed to help practitioners use the approach as part of their everyday working practices.

Reflection point 7:6

- *How could you and your colleagues find out more about students'/pupils' experiences as a basis for PD?*
- *What datasets and other evidence can you draw on, or would you need to commission new research?*

Languages and translanguaging

The language of instruction matters in all education sectors as a social justice issue, where one language is privileged over others or indigenous, home or local language goes unacknowledged:

> "... students with language practices that differ from that of the national elite have undergone some form of 'othering,' a product of colonization and political formations that then enregister these students as inferior."
>
> Garcia (2020: 12)

'Translanguaging' involves supporting multilingualism in educational settings to address language discrimination and enable learners to feel that their home culture and language is valued. Duarte and Günther-van der Meij (2020) suggest that translanguaging practices in school help learners to recognise that different language practices are of equal value.

PD for translanguaging in the North Netherlands used a 'design-based intervention' in which pre-service teachers, teacher trainers, and researchers developed and 'experimented' with new multilingual activities, then discussed the impact, before moving on to adapt or add another new approach. Over 18 months they held six PD workshops in which they could debate and plan approaches; they also examined video footage of classroom interactions and received feedback from other members of the project. Results showed that, through experimenting in a safe environment, teachers gradually embraced their pupils' multilingualism (Duarte and Günther-van der Meij, 2020). A key influence on their changing understanding came from the opportunity to observe and reflect on their multilingual interactions with children. A similar impact was felt in a German study of translanguaging in day care settings, where ethnographic observational data was shared with staff, so they had the opportunity to examine their daily practices and reflect on their own competencies through a close to practice focus on interactions (Pangiotopoulou and Hammel, 2020). PD in the global development sector could also benefit from engaging with translanguaging as a way of including all learners (Sriprakash et al., 2020).

Cultural literacy

PD for educators needs to offer them opportunities to examine their own practice as well as to experiment with suggested strategies. One part of this may be to support educators to develop the language and confidence needed to involve their students in discussions that facilitate reflection and cross-cultural learning. Case study 4 exemplifies how teachers and university colleagues developed a cultural literacy learning programme for teachers and students.

Case study 4: Promoting cultural literacy as a dialogic practice (Fiona Maine)

DIALLS (www.dialls2020.eu) was a three-year project funded by the European Commission running from 2018 to 2021, involving ten partner universities and over 350 teachers in seven different countries. The central aims of the project were to support the development of cultural literacy in schools, through teaching children and young people the dialogue and argumentation skills to become tolerant, empathetic, and inclusive. As a core concept, cultural literacy was defined as a dialogic social practice (Maine et al., 2019) and seen as crucial for twenty-first-century intercultural living and the navigation of multiple perspectives. Researchers in the project investigated central values that underpinned European social policies and developed a cultural analysis framework which featured several cultural themes clustered around social responsibility, living together, and belonging. From this, a core set of cultural texts (wordless picture books and films) were gathered where themes of, for example, democracy, human rights, and solidarity were key to the stories they told.

This was not a project that researchers forced on teachers, rather a collaboration where different educational stakeholders came together and designed an initiative that would be meaningful and long lasting. In the first phase of the project, a small group of teachers from across four countries worked together with researchers to develop a Cultural Literacy Learning Programme (CLLP), exploring how the wordless films and picture books could be used as stimuli for culturally themed discussions. Running parallel to this thematic content, lessons were planned to include the teaching of dialogue skills, focusing on inclusive communities, developing one's own ideas and relating them to others, and dealing with multiple perspectives.

In the second phase, the professional development part of the project kept the DIALLS principles central and drew on our collective knowledge about effective professional learning. As the learning contexts in each country were very different, teams planned their professional development differently, but core values were consistent. We created a programme of spaced learning with principles of 'reflection and collaborative learning in communities of practice' (Hofmann et al., 2021). The ethos of this PD was then necessarily dialogic, as teachers worked together to reflect on their changing practice and discuss the challenges that they faced.

The final third phase of the project looked to the future. How could we engage teachers in professional learning that would 'stand-alone' beyond the three years of DIALLS? Recruiting a further set of teachers to the project we trialled online materials which included professional development interactive films and the CLLP (complete with films and lesson prompts). We extended the resources to include Scales of Progression for dialogue and cultural learning. All are available as free resources on the project website (www.dialls2020.eu). A dialogic ethos (Alexander, 2020) where multiple perspectives are heard and valued proved to be a prerequisite for both professional and classroom learning in DIALLS and we hope that many more teachers will enjoy the resources we created for years to come.

In conclusion

PD for equity in education requires that educators critically examine and change practices and connect with assumptions, privilege or marginalisation. Successful PD for equity can stimulate reflection on previously unexamined assumptions and lead to collaborative solutions to address educational inequalities. The principles underpinning successful PD for equity involve learning from and with the learners and communities themselves. This is most effectively achieved through longer-term approaches that combine reflection, inquiry, dialogue, and co-constructed practice. In every case, care must be taken to consider the identities of the educators and the learners concerned and raise challenge in a safe and supportive environment. The responsibility to change our practice must be shared across all levels of leadership and educators from privileged groups must support their colleagues. An important starting point is systematically embedding PD for equity in initial teacher education, designed with schools and marginalised communities and supported by well-trained tutors and mentors. PD for equity is not easy. There will be differences of perspective, institutional and personal resistance, and barriers. Even those educators committed to social justice will experience dilemmas and setbacks because of socially and systemically embedded prejudices. For these reasons, collaborative approaches, which include diverse peers and communities, can prove both supportive and inspirational.

Personal Development Planning Table 7 Focus: Academic and Professional

Question	What can I do?		What do I need from others?
	Short-term action	Medium-term action	
1. What areas of equity and social justice do I/we need more knowledge about?	Make a mindmap or list of areas you need to research, e.g. critical whiteness, translanguaging, critical race theory	Search for readings about key areas that could act as a stimulus	
2. What approaches to PD for equity and social justice might work well in your setting?	Identify possible approaches, e.g. critical reading seminars, participatory action research with learners, integrated approaches, interprofessional learning	Discuss ideas with other colleagues about their preferred approaches	
3. Can you find opportunities to put your ideas into practice?	Identify colleagues who are interested in taking such initiatives further	Plan ways to work with learners, the community, and other professionals to co-create PD	

NB: Recommended Open Access Readings are highlighted below, using asterisks as follows: *Leaders and Teacher Educators, **Practitioners, ***Early Career Professionals.

Recommended reading

* Panagiotopoulou, J.A., Rosen, L., and Strzykala, J. (eds.) (2020) *Inclusion, Education and Translanguaging: How to Promote Social Justice in (Teacher) Education.* Wiesbaden: Springer [https://library.oapen.org/viewer/web/viewer.html?file=/bitstream/handle/20.500.12657/41724/2020_Book_InclusionEducationAndTranslang.pdf?sequence=1&isAllowed=y].
** DIALLS Cultural Literacy resources [https://dialls2020.eu/].
*** *In the Picture: Developing perspectives upon a very young disabled child's experience.* Online Course [https://www.open.edu/openlearncreate/course/view.php?id=3590].

8   PD through inquiry

#EC #ML #SL #TE

As part of becoming a change agent in a setting (Pantić and Florian, 2015; Van der Heijden et al., 2015), educators have a responsibility to base their PD on evidence. This chapter examines how such evidence can be gathered and used to inform PD. As early as the 1970s, Stenhouse advocated that all educational practitioners should engage in systematic, self-critical inquiry on which to base practice change and adopt the identity of practitioner researcher (Rudduck, 1988).

Practitioners as activists

Sources of educational knowledge are wide-ranging.

Reflection point 8:1

How do you know what you know as a professional?

Four forms of knowledge can inform educator PD (Cochran-Smith and Lytle, 1999; Day and Sachs, 2004):

- **Knowledge *for* practice:** educational research generated by academic researchers and published through papers, reports, advice, and guidance.
- **Knowledge *of* practice:** generated by practitioners critically examining the basis for teaching and learning in their own settings.
- **Knowledge *in* practice:** generated by practitioners through systematic inquiry in their own 'classroom' environments, including gathering student perspectives.
- **Knowledge *of* self:** generated by teachers engaged in regular reflection about their values, motivations, feelings, and relationships.

Through such knowledge generation, teachers can become 'activist professionals' (Sachs, 2000), well placed to make important judgements to move on the education profession. Contemporary examples of those who base their teaching and leadership on using knowledge in different ways include:

- Alison Peacock (UK): Alison's advocation of teachers as activists from the positionality of a headteacher built through her research examining 'learning without limits' (Swann et al., 2012), extended beyond her own school and saw her become Chief Executive Officer of the Chartered College of Teaching.[1]
- Phil McCrae (Canada), as director of the Alberta Initiative for School Improvement at the University of Alberta, promotes teachers as researchers across Alberta.[2]
- Sharon Wei-Lynne (Singapore): Sharon's classroom teaching views students as sources of evidence and places them as 'teachers for the day'.[3]
- Ranjitsinh Disale (India): Ranjitsinh analyses his students' reflections to tailor his QR-coded teaching resources for them.[4]
- Ken Silburn (Australia): Ken uses student project work to collectively learn more about the role of science in sustainable living.[5]

These examples illustrate how practitioners identify and value different forms of knowledge. One challenge for professionals is not always being aware of the knowledge available to them. It often remains tacit, unless they engage in reflection, which can be an active process, as advocated by Donald Schön (1983), or by generating new knowledge through inquiry.

Reflection point 8:2

What inspires you to change your practice?

Many initial teacher education programmes support educational professionals in becoming both a *reflective practitioner* (Schön, 1987) and a *practitioner researcher* (Hodson et al., 2012). These aspirations for educator identity can be linked to calls for teaching to become a Master's-level profession (Gray, 2013; L.S. Thomas, 2012), as in Finland and some US states (Maaranen, 2009). Master's-level study requires educators to become; aware of, select, critically interpret, and plan to act upon the findings of these publications (L.S. Thomas, 2012). Through Master's study, educators get chances to engage with academics in universities and access research publications. These actions will be vital if academic outputs of 'educational research' are to extend beyond being published 'for' practice to inform practice. As not all teachers have direct access to higher education settings, this form of knowledge-sharing and application remains a challenge.

Reflection point 8:3

- *Identify places you could go to for published evidence relevant to your setting and role.*
- *How are you supported to find literature and evidence?*

Inquiry as a social activity

As outlined in Chapters 1 and 2, there is an important social dimension to teacher knowledge-building (e.g. Groundwater-Smith and Dodds, 2004) from communities of practice to action learning. Collaborative teacher inquiry is considered productive, empowering, and central to education developing as a profession from within. However, there is little agreement on how leaders might best establish this. Some international examples you might have come across are: professional learning communities, communities of inquiry, joint practice development, lesson study groups, change teams, action learning sets or simply 'sets'. See Table 8.1 for an overview of the origins, characteristics, and some key authors who advocate each of these approaches.

Each of the conceptualisations in Table 8.1 offer different visions for establishing PD through inquiry. However, even within each vision, there are multiple ways to put these into practice (see, for example, Baker, 2020 for professional learning communities; Xu, 2020 for lesson study and Stoll et al., 2012 for joint practice development).

Table 8.1 The language and characteristics of collaborative modes of practitioner inquiry

Collaborative teacher research	Origins in ...	Key characteristics	Key authors explaining and advocating in education
Professional learning communities[a]	Organisations as learning organisations (Senge, 1995)	Focus on improving student outcomes through improving teaching practice; knowledge among professionals' everyday practice; learning with peers	USA: DuFour and Eaker (1998), DuFour and DuFour (2012), Lieberman and Miller (2008) UK: Bolam et al. (2005), Stoll et al. (2006) South Africa: Botha (2012)
Communities of inquiry[b]	Originally digitally-mediated learning (Pardales and Girod, 2006; Garrison, 2009; Garrison et al., 2010)	Conducting inquiry together, based on mutual collaboration through: social presence; teaching presence; cognitive presence Focused on improving the educational experience	Willemse et al. (2016)
Joint practice development (JPD)	Factors influencing the transfer of good practice (Fielding et al., 2005): knowledge exchange between individuals, teams, schools, local authorities, and other institutions	Building relationships and trust; recognising power imbalances	UK: Fielding et al. (2005), Sebba et al. (2012) USA: Brusca-Vega et al. (2014)

(Continued)

Table 8.1 (Continued)

Collaborative teacher research	Origins in ...	Key characteristics	Key authors explaining and advocating in education
Lesson study[c]	International publication (Stigler and Hiebert, 1999) that attributed the high performance of Japanese pupils in the Trends in International Mathematics and Science Study (TIMSS) to Japanese teachers' engagement in systemic LS practices	Groups of teachers in iterative cycles of lesson planning, teaching/ observation, evaluation and revision for quality	Dudley (2012), Saito (2012), Xu (2020)
Change teams	UK, National Remodelling Team in the early 2000s	'all staff levels consider the political, emotional and practical factors of prospective change' (Hammersley-Fletcher and Lowe, 2006: 2)	Hammersley-Fletcher and Lowe (2006)
Action learning sets	The 1990s in organisational management literature before being advocated in education 20 years later (Aubusson et al., 2009)	Collaboratively reviewing experience between a person, a problem, a group (or action learning set), and an action on the problem; identification of emotional, political, and power/Western bias dimensions to engagement in these groups	Aubusson et al. (2009), McGill and Brockband (2004), Burger and Trehan (2018)
(Learning) sets	Recognising contemporary ways of people coming together, beyond organisations, through digital means (Dron and Anderson, 2014)	Common interests, topic and theme unite group, for example when engaging with social media, enabling 'just in time' learning	Kontopoulou (2019)

[a] Exemplified in Vignette 14, Chapter 4 and Vignette 27, Chapter 10.

[b] Underpinned research outlined in Vignette 21.

[c] For example, approach taken in Case Study 5 and covered further in Chapter 9 (Evaluation of PD).

Reflection point 8:4

- *Are any of the forms of inquiry familiar to you? If so, in what context?*
- *If you have been directly involved, what were your experiences of how these initiatives were led?*

Leading collaborative inquiry

Many leaders considering how to establish collaborative inquiry look for voluntary involvement, drawing on teachers' motivations and energies. Identifying research champions can help roll out inquiry more widely. This approach comes with the danger that not all colleagues will be convinced and the inquiry activity might remain siloed. An alternative approach is to offer collaborative inquiry as a strategy, embedded into the practices of the organisation, as in the following case study. This has the advantage that inquiry goals can aim to achieve impact across an organisation and be monitored through the usual appraisal/performance management processes. However, leaders also need to consider this extra accountability, especially if linked to pay, raises the stakes for practitioners and might also lead them to be more resistant to its imposition. Case study 5 offers a senior leadership account of one school's journey through different approaches to leading practitioner inquiry.

Case study 5: Through the eyes of an enquiring school (Claire Tyson and Paul Hanson)

Every school has a unique ecosystem with its own geography, climate, culture, and populations. Just like a biological ecosystem, the pressure to evolve and improve can be driven by both internal and external selection pressures. At Homewood School and Sixth Form Centre (HSSC), a school which caters for children and young people aged 11–18, a recent Ofsted[6] report focused our attention on improving our curriculum and outcomes for our more disadvantaged pupils especially.

To achieve this evolution, we are working at a whole-school, department, and individual level with our staff and students. We have implemented a new performance management system that aims to support the expertise, progression, and job satisfaction of staff. All teachers engage in an evidence-informed development project to address an area of improvement that they themselves have identified starting with an audit of Teacher Standards.

At a whole-school level, we explicitly value research knowledge as the foundation of practice and explore the evidence of 'what works?' to improve student outcomes. However, it can be difficult to translate this value and vision into improved practice. Like many schools, staff development events have not led to the intended improvement in teaching and learning.

Our new approach to performance management is to focus on small teams and individuals, with increased choice and autonomy on key areas for development. To support this increased independence, a core research resource that we have chosen to use is the Teaching Walkthrus series (Sherrington and Caviglioli, 2020, 2021). We made a conscious choice to move away from asking the main body of teachers to engage with primary research publications because of the difficulties of accessibility, workload, and variations in individual levels of motivation. The Walkthrus are a synthesis of research knowledge presented in an accessible, graphic style that has at its core a pragmatism of 'try it and see if it works'.

The adoption of WalkThrus is a key element of a tripartite approach, which includes the use of IRIS Connect (www.irisconnect.com/uk/what-we-do/) classroom recording technology and 'critical friend' lesson study. For example, after one dissemination session, a teacher offered the following feedback:

> *"Thank you for sharing your conversation with [named teacher] and your experimentation with the student seminar. Strategies where small groups engage in independent, monitored discursive activities with their peers observing and feeding back are really powerful."*

Together, these three pillars aim to support teaching staff with the improvement of their practice and enable them to fully enact the curriculum refinement undertaken since the most recent Ofsted. After a session which shared some participation strategies drawn from a study in the United States, a teacher offered the following feedback:

> *"I just wanted to share and say thank you as I haven't tried this method before. I do it all the time teaching new songs to students but never thought to do it with terminology!"*

As we emerge from the constraints of coronavirus, the needs of our students and the autonomy of our teachers will continue to be evolutionary driving forces for professional improvement. The outcomes from this new approach will necessarily be reviewed in the light of our priorities, asking: 'Is our approach to using secondary research transforming practice and outcome for students?'

The leaders in Case study 5 show how a strategic approach built into the structures and systems of the school provides teachers with opportunities to apply evidence from inquiry as relevant to their own practice. Encouraging practitioners to identify and carry out their own inquiry is insufficient. Support for knowledge, skills, and confidence is needed in design and completion.

Bridging forms of knowledge

The limitation in access to peer-reviewed published work has been noted earlier in this book, for example being addressed by the teachers' library in Afghanistan (Vignette 10, Chapter 3). A division in access can heighten the divide between what might be termed academic (knowledge generated by research) and practitioner (teachers' pedagogical) knowledge. As argued in Chapter 1, both forms of knowledge 'count'. However, they have different characteristics and can be conceptualised as at two ends of a continuum (Cain, 2015).

Academic knowledge is often narrowly focused on a particular issue, highly theorised, and written about in a way that is designed to be generalisable to a wide audience. This means a practitioner needs to interpret the relevance of the findings to their own context and PD needs. Such knowledge is also accumulated over time, with research outputs only being available a long while after the study was initiated. This might mean that there is nothing easily available for very contemporary issues, as was the situation for the first part of the COVID-19 pandemic. Educational researchers needed to design shorter studies and find quicker ways of dissemination, such as through blogging (e.g. BERA Blog COVID-19 series), to contribute their knowledge to the discussions of how education should respond.

In contrast, *professional knowledge* usually covers a range of issues, is highly connected with the context in which it is generated and the educator's personal values. It can inform practice swiftly and sometimes even unconsciously and is most readily shared between practitioners with shared experiences of similar contexts.

Whilst the former is valued for its originality and rigour, the latter is valued for its practicality and fitness for purpose.

Unlike teachers, bridging the academic and practitioner gap is built into a medical professional's expectations of PD. General practitioners (GPs or family doctors) in the UK are expected to keep abreast of key developments in their field through:

- reading internationally respected journals;
- membership of their professional association;
- reading their professional journal (*British Journal of General Practice*), which 'publishes research, news and views, debate and analysis, and clinical guidance relevant to GPs at all stages of their careers' (https://www.rcgp.org.uk/publications.aspx).

In these ways, GPs can be agentic. For example, a GP in a socially-deprived area of Wales became a model for research-informed practice (Haines, 2018).

It has been harder for education professionals to have such access, and the expectations to read research are not so explicit in the profession. However, a journal has recently been set up by the UK's Chartered College of Teaching (*Impact*: https://impact.chartered.college/issue-archive/). The move in the field of academia to more open access publication is also helping with individual researchers making their work available through web platforms such as ResearchGate, Academia.edu or via employer-focused portals such as LinkedIn.

Collaborative projects can also gather educational research together, such as the online African Education Research Database, developed by the Research for Equitable Access and Learning Centre at the University of Cambridge, in partnership with Education Sub-Saharan Africa '… to raise the visibility of African research, consolidate the evidence base for policy and practice, and inform future research priorities and partnerships' (REAL/ESSA, n.d.).

Case study 5 highlighted how school leaders can play a mediating role in identifying and synthesising publishing evidence to inform inquiry in their setting. The WalkThrus are one example of a resource helping bridge this knowledge gap through stimulating practitioner dialogue.

> *"Such dialogue would involve teachers reviewing their pedagogical knowledge in the light of research, the limitations of one being exposed by the merits of the other. It could occur mentally, as 'armchair theorising' or in actual conversation between teachers and researchers."*
>
> Cain (2015: 494)

Collaborative action research or lesson study initiatives provide examples of structures for such dialogue.

Reflection point 8:5

- *Can you identify anything from your practice setting or something you have read about in this book which you do not agree with?*
- *Or that you felt that you would need to read much more about before you would accept it as useful to you and your practice?*

A teacher reading research findings does not simply accept these as useful, relevant or even credible (Cain, 2017). Leaders should be aware that teachers might have negative responses, such as outlined in Figure 8.1.

Figure 8.1 Teachers' negative responses to reading research findings

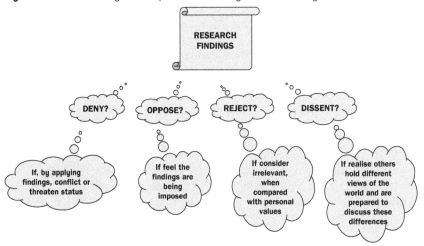

Based on ideas from Cain (2017).

The most productive form of contestation is *dissent* if the difference in opinion becomes an opportunity to talk about how views differ, providing fruitful ground for debate and revision of positions. However, this can only take place if there are safe spaces for such dialogue and these cannot be assumed to be found in educational settings. Accountability cultures, experienced by leaders and practitioners, lead to cultures of measurement. In these situations, risk-averseness develops and a search for practices which will 'work', rather than a space to explore what 'is likely to be useful' (Biesta, 2007, 2010). The danger is that what is judged as effective is limited to only what is being measured and insufficient in informing our aims for education more broadly to nurture confident, happy, and curious learners. If decisions are to be based on what professionals believe the purpose of education to be, then this vision should guide discussions about how to use knowledge for, of, and in practice in a setting. Rather than dissonance being seen as risky, it can be reframed as a collaborative, creative process.

Reflection point 8:6

- *Who can (and do) you reflect with as a learner about practice?*
- *To what extent is it possible to discuss the relationship between values and practice?*
- *Where are the spaces for you to have this kind of dialogue? If they seem absent, what would be needed to establish these?*

How we 'see' one another predicts how we act. If teachers are imagined as learners and learners as teachers (Fleet et al., 2017), this would offer a mutual and reciprocal basis for driving the focus and nature of classroom-based inquiry. Educators can position themselves as learners in a broader assemblage such as outlined in Table 8.1.

Practically, this involves educators in finding ways to gather learner views and feedback and build these into organisational structures and processes. An example of this in an open distance learning university context forms Vignette 20.

Vignette 20: Learning from students – an opportunity for tutor PD (Kathy Chandler)

Hearing about students' experiences can be a valuable way of reflecting on and developing practice. My doctoral research listened to students' experiences of online tutorials in health and social care using diaries and interviews to enable the students to share their narratives. I was interested to examine the impact that hearing about these experiences might have on tutors' practice.

I prepared a vignette of the narrative of each student's experience, which I shared with tutor colleagues via established forum communities and my research website (Chandler, 2021). Tutors responded to reading the vignettes by sharing their thoughts, mainly through the forums or occasionally by email or telephone.

This way of reflecting on practice proved effective. Reflecting on students' experiences of other tutors' tutorials, rather than their own, may have seemed less threatening than engaging with other forms of feedback and tutors had a choice about engaging, firstly with the experiences conveyed in the students' narratives, and then with the conversations with colleagues. The conversations were, for the most part, relaxed and sometimes humorous. Tutors often reflected and commented on one part of an individual narrative that resonated with them. Promoted by what students shared or by other tutors' comments, they reflected extensively on their own experiences of online tuition, both as tutors and as students themselves. Some tutors shared suggestions that were taken up by others. They tried these ideas out and reported back in the forums.

Listening to students' experiences was beneficial. Tutors were able to reflect on practice in the company of familiar colleagues and within an established community of inquiry.

Drawing on students' views as data sources is not novel as a research approach. Students can help evaluate practice (as feedback on what has already taken place). Their views can inform reform (feed forward with ideas on how to change practice). Taking into account student voice, as the focus for educational provision, might be considered an ethical responsibility, to ensure they are placed centrally in any inquiry, rather than disenfranchised or overlooked. This is the case both for practitioner researchers and external researchers coming into a setting.

Reflection point 8:7

- *How do students have a voice in your setting?*
- *What happens to their views when collected?*
- *Can you identify any actions which have resulted from student feedback?*

A rural primary school in Scotland uses consultation with learners as its starting point to identify school improvement priorities. It involves them in inquiry design, through gathering evidence to help the school evaluate initiatives. From one such learner-led idea, exploring whether bringing dogs into school could be beneficial, the school learnt about how and why the school might involve dogs, staff PD needs, and confirmed the value of the learner-led process as a sustainable strategy (Gibson et al., 2021). Learners needed to be empowered to take ownership of what should be inquired into and supported in the skills needed to participate in the enquiry.

Such principles are core to the mission of the Open University's Children's Research Centre (Kellett, 2005), which, by offering research skill training, 'support children and young people to carry out research on topics that are important to them' (CRC, 2021). The children are included in reporting the research and the Centre finds ways to include all children's views. They have shown how children with declared disabilities are able to participate, and their views should not be overlooked through preconceptions of their vulnerability or assumptions of lack of capacity (Kellett, 2011). Age also should be no barrier. Even very young children have valuable things to say, such as about their early childhood settings (e.g. 2–6-year-olds in Iceland: Einarsdóttir, 2007). In this study, as in others with children of other ages (e.g. Carnahan, 2006; Cremin et al., 2011), photovoice techniques have proved empowering. Children are given cameras and then discuss the importance of these photos.

It is possible to put children's views at the forefront of professional PD by hearing their manifestos for change. The e-Learning for Kids (2014) and DIALLS (Dialogue and Argumentation for Cultural Literacy Learning in Schools, 2020) children's manifestos speak to professionals and policy-makers about children's aspirations.

So, why engage in practitioner research?

So far, the key reasons for engaging in practitioner research have been presented as to:

• support one another as part of a learning community,
• generate locally-relevant knowledge,
• increase professional confidence and competence,
• empower educators and learners, as learners (Fleet et al., 2017).

Now turning attention to the 'how', all the approaches presented require leadership. This involves a vision and the practical work of energising and supporting those involved.

The value of partnerships

Resources for inquiry can be generated within a community/organisation, but are often strengthened by those from beyond, to test ideas and bring in new skills. Partnerships can help gauge the wider relevance of an inquiry. Although the school in Case study 5 set up structures and support within their organisation, they were not working alone and benefitted from being set within a wider Academy Trust, itself embedded in wider regional and national networks. These wider connections allow them to engage in across-organisational projects with those in other sectors, including with universities, for mutual benefit. This provides an opportunity to work across the academic–practitioner knowledge continuum discussed earlier to break down dangers of this being seen as a binary. However, power imbalances between school/college (primary, secondary or tertiary) and higher education institutions should not remain unacknowledged.

Three common forms of school–university partnership identified by McLaughlin and Black-Hawkins (2007) highlight differences in how partners are valued:

1   where a university provides a *service* – such as research training for staff in schools;
2   where the partners offer *complementary* support – by running both university and school-led projects; or
3   in a *collaborative* arrangement – involving negotiating and agreeing common research foci and methodologies.

Collaborative arrangements, whilst the most powerful, demand investment in time and resources by all partners. Trust needs to be built to explore values, understandings, and ways forward for 'reciprocal leadership' (Poultney, 2020: 36).

Reflection point 8:8

- *Identify an organisation with which your organisation might be considered in partnership.*
- *Reflect on what you think the underlying basis for this relationship might be.*
- *What can you say about the mutuality of the relationship in terms of benefits and risks?*

School–university projects can involve external partners in enquiries, drawing on their combined networks to identify sources of expertise. Vignette 21 (e.g. Cremin et al., 2018) covers how a collaboration offered a new PD opportunity.

Vignette 21: Teachers as writers – needing to engage in PD for practice (Teresa Cremin)

This partnership project between a creative writing organisation (The Arvon Foundation: https://www.arvon.org/), The Open University, and Exeter University invited teachers to participate in an intensive residential week in the countryside. The study explored the impact that professional writers' engagement with teachers had on teachers' identities as writers and their pedagogic practice in the teaching of writing, as well as any consequences for student attitudes to writing and outcomes. Following the residential, teachers worked to embrace the Arvon ethos of relaxed free writing and focused feedback in their classrooms and were supported by co-mentoring partnerships with professional writers. This, alongside group meetings, served to further their PD journeys (Cremin et al., 2020).

The study found that through engaging in workshops and tutorials, sharing their writing, and reflecting upon the experience (in audio diaries, interviews, and logs), the primary and secondary teachers grew in confidence as authors; buoyed up by finely-tuned oral feedback from tutors and affirmative responses within the group. Constructive criticism was woven throughout, yet a growing sense of authorial satisfaction was expressed, particularly in 'writing from the heart' (http://www.teachersaswriters.org/general/writing-from-the-heart/) and leaning on life to ponder, remember, and compose.

Through holding a mirror up to their own experience as writers, teachers altered their pedagogy and made new time and space for writing, for ideas generation, and sharing writing with an emphasis on students as authors and teachers writing alongside. Teachers also enabled children to draw on life experience and shifted their emphasis from planning to re- drafting and revising through peer review. The case studies showed that this increased the students' motivation, confidence, and assurance as authors, and gave them a stronger degree of ownership of their own writing. It did not impact on their writing scores across the nine months of the project and led to another project, The Craft of Writing (http://www.teachersaswriters.org/general/the-craft-of-writing/).

By bringing them out of their usual workplace, the teachers in Vignette 21 were positioned as learners – as writers – to help them, through supported self-reflection, to re-imagine their practice as teachers of writing.

Reflection point 8:9

- *What would motivate you to engage in inquiry?*
- *If you are already engaged in inquiry, what factors affect your willingness to get started?*
- *What factors would help you sustain this?*

Getting started

To initiate PD through inquiry, a focus – linked to a topic or challenge – needs to be identified. This then needs to be turned into a researchable question. Who is involved in generating the agenda for a study will determine the topic and nature of its question – whether this is learner-led, educator-led or through agenda-sharing between internal or external collaborators (Alvesson and Sandberg, 2013). A research question is a practical way of articulating a study's aims to clearly convey the objectives of the study and why it is important (White, 2013). However, such questions are not straightforward to generate. A common issue is wanting to cover many aspects to the topic and not feeling able to focus on one, feasible element. There is then the danger of feeling fixed in addressing the original question as set, even when it becomes apparent that framing it differently would be more productive.

A study with teachers in the Catholic Education Office, Sydney, Australia (Fleet et al., 2017) noted issues in getting inquiry started. Some teachers expected to engage only minimally, hoping others would take on most of the work. Others only planned to engage when directed to, feeling no sense of responsibility unless imposed on them. There were also challenges from enthusiastic but novice practitioner researchers, who required support. Encouragement, empowerment, and reassurance needed to be combined with practical support for inquiry skill development.

Next, is the need for an ethical, feasible, and robust research design that identifies which sources of data will address the question and how these can be gathered appropriately. For evidence to be generated that can be considered of quality to inform practice, three questions can be set as tests (Groundwater-Smith and Dodds, 2004: 250):

1 Is the study ethical?
   * Study design should maximise the benefits of the study and anticipate and minimise possibilities of negative consequences arising.
   * Everyone involved should be consulted and those who will provide data be informed and invited to participate voluntarily and without coercion or deceit.
2 Will the evidence be triangulated?
   * Any data-gathering method is limited by its design and conduct. Multiple methods of data collection, allowing insights to be gathered and integrated with one another, can provide a more holistic picture of the situation under study.
3 Will the findings be interpreted by more than one researcher?
   * As with the data collection methods, different researchers bring different insights into interpretation of the data. Multiple stakeholders strengthen a study's ability to generate meaningful findings.

Facilitation and sustainability

Sachs reviewed the education profession in the UK 15 years after her earlier call to practitioners to become activist professionals (Sachs, 2000). She found that a performance culture had become embedded in response to external demands on schools, which constrained knowledge generation by the profession, leading to what she termed 'controlled or compliant professionalism' (Sachs, 2016: 423). Leaders have a role to play in protecting practitioners from the factors which reduce their space to experiment, explore, and examine so they can grow as professionals. Inquiry is not going to thrive and maximise its benefits beyond individuals unless there is sufficient space and support.

There is fertile ground in the profession, however. The only College on the island of Guernsey, which until 2021 was not held accountable to inspections by Ofsted in the same way as the rest of the UK, embedded inquiry as the main form of PD. Each year teachers are expected to identify 'One Thing' to research, initiated in the first in-service PD day and reported in as many ways as appropriate to the study during the year (Education and Training Foundation, 2020). Instead of being driven by external accountabilities, teachers' enquiries drive observations when appropriate for data collection, alongside other forms of data gathering such as interviews with colleagues and pupils and in-class methods. The advanced practitioners in the College mentor the projects, supplying academic research papers where relevant.

From initiatives in individual settings, some of the early initiatives to support collaborative inquiry for development of the profession are still going strong and growing in their international reach. For example:

* The Collaborative Action Research Network, 'founded in 1976 in order to continue the development work of the Ford Teaching Project in UK primary and secondary schools. Since that time it has grown to become an international network drawing its members from educational, health, social care, commercial, and public services settings' (CARN-ALARA, 2019)
* The International Teacher Leadership Network [http://www.international-teacherleadership.org/itl.html], now established in Israel, Malaysia, and Kazakhstan, which developed from the HertsCam School–University network in England (covered further in Chapter 10), publishes outputs from teachers' projects in multiple languages (e.g. Frost, 2018).

In conclusion

To sustain practitioner inquiry, educators need to be viewed as researching professionals. Their knowledge generation is not only central to their development as professionals but also to the development of the profession. If this is accepted and valued, then structures and processes need to be in place to facilitate this, requiring facilitators to be trained and made available through support networks (Fleet et al., 2017). Practitioners need to engage with evidence produced by academic researchers alongside an ability to select and apply the findings to their own context. This requires a sophisticated research literacy. Whilst early adopters and enthusiasts can become effective research champions, cultures of inquiry are not straightforward to establish. To sustain inquiry, leaders need to:

- ensure they as senior leaders buy-in to prioritise offering practical support;
- ensure staff are given regular, dedicated time for their roles;
- expect to adapt strategies for each school's context;
- provide practical examples and materials for classroom use (EEF, 2018).

Whichever approach to collaborative inquiry (e.g. Table 8.1) leaders envision, if educators are to become change agents, their curiosity and desire to solve problems need to be encouraged. In supporting them as skilled, critical generators and consumers of knowledge there is a role for higher education institutions. School–university partnerships offer direct critical friend support for practice-focused inquiry.

Personal Development Planning Table 8 Focus: Personal and Professional

Question	What can I do?	What do I need from others?
	Short-term action	Medium-term action
1. What do you want to inquire into?	Identify a focus for which gathering evidence would help solve a problem, satisfy a curiosity or extend your knowledge	Ask whether it is possible to undertake an inquiry, ideally with others
2. How do you gather evidence to inform practice?	Identify whose perspectives (e.g. those of learners, classroom assistants, other support staff, parents/guardians) would be valuable to access	Together with colleagues, explore and evaluate different approaches to gathering evidence
3. How can you best share the findings of inquiry?	Reflect on how you find out about how others are developing their practice	Identify which structures and processes could enhance knowledge-sharing and tell someone about this
4. What external resources might support you in developing inquiry?	Spend time talking to others asking where they source ideas to support their practice	Explore whether new ways of linking out to external sources of support can be promoted, such as making links with higher education institutions or drawing on membership of professional associations

NB: Recommended Open Access Readings are highlighted below, using asterisks as follows: *Leaders and Teacher Educators, **Practitioners, ***Early Career Professionals.

Recommended reading

* Biesta, G.J. (2010) Why 'what works' still won't work: From evidence-based education to value-based education, *Studies in Philosophy and Education*, 29 (5): 491–503 [https://orbilu.uni.lu/bitstream/10993/7820/1/116%20PUB%20What%20works%20SPED%202010.pdf].

* Cremin, T., Myhill, D., Eyres, I., Nash, T., Wilson, A. and Oliver, L. (2018) *Teachers as writers*. A report for Arts Council England on the value of writers' engagement with teachers to improve outcomes for all pupils [http://oro.open.ac.uk/53501/].

** Alderson, P. (2012) Children as researchers: Participation rights and research methods, in P. Christensen and A. James (eds.) *Research with Children: Perspectives and Practices*, 2nd edition. London: Falmer Press/Routledge (pp. 276–290) [https://discovery.ucl.ac.uk/id/eprint/10070478/1/Alderson_children%20as%20researchers.pdf].

*** Chamberlain, L., Afroze, J., Cooper, V. and Collins, T. (2019) *Representing children's rights from discussion through to illustration and interpretation*. Milton Keynes: The Open University Children's Research Centre and Amnesty UK International [http://wels.open.ac.uk/sites/wels.open.ac.uk/files/files/The%20Open%20University%E2%80%99s%20Children%E2%80%99s%20Research%20Centre%20Report_%20FINAL_%20revised%20print%20version.pdf].

Notes

1 https://chartered.college/meet-the-team/
2 https://www.teachers.ab.ca/News%20Room/ata%20magazine/Volume%2087/Number%203/Articles/Pages/Teachers%20as%20Researchers.aspx
3 https://www.straitstimes.com/singapore/education/extraordinary-teachers
4 https://www.globalteacherprize.org/winners/ranjitsinh-disale-2020/
5 https://www.globalteacherprize.org/pt/not%C3%ADcias-e-blogs/these-are-the-10-best-teachers-in-the-world/
6 Ofsted is the national inspection body in England and Wales for all state-funded schools.

Evaluating PD

#EC #ML #SL #TE

Chapters 9 and 10 are reflective chapters: the first practically, the second theoretically focused. This chapter examines how professional development (PD) can be evaluated to capture whether it has been impactful or not. Budget holders often want to know what the value of funded PD has been, in terms of what has been garnered for the money spent, to account for their allocation of funds. However, how 'value for money' ought to be measured is intractable. Furthermore, it will be appreciated from evidence presented in this book that PD cannot always be bought. Whether PD has been effective needs a holistic evaluation approach (e.g. Guskey, 2000). We start with a cross-sector view. Then, using Guskey's seminal framework specific to PD in education contexts (Guskey, 2002), we illustrate approaches to evaluating PD across contexts and scales.

Monitoring and evaluation

Monitoring and evaluation are generic expectations of accountability for funded projects across many sectors. The set of actions developed by the National Council for Voluntary Organisations (Valentine et al., 2018) and shown in Figure 9.1 might be useful to those responsible for the implementation and evaluation of funded PD in your context.

While fuller exemplification of each stage is available in the webpages provided for this 'How to … develop a monitoring and evaluation framework' guide, to appreciate its expectations it is useful to unpack the language used. Outputs are defined as 'the goods, services or products' under focus – in our context, PD activity. This might be a training package which is presented to a group of learners. An Outcome is 'a single measurable change' such as the learners changing something in their teaching practice. Indicators are 'what we will measure' and might be an aspect of learner performance linked to that practice (Valentine et al., 2018).

When making judgements about PD, evaluators will need to look for evidence of what is considered quality and important. These judgements vary depending on your perspective and it is useful to consider participant, organisational, and learner (those for whom the participants are responsible) perspectives. Critical evaluation should not only look for intended and positive benefits but also unintended and negative consequences. It is possible for PD to

Figure 9.1 A monitoring and evaluation framework development plan

(1) Use a planning tool

⬇

(2) Describe your outputs

⬇

(3) Set output indicators

⬇

(4) Describe your outcomes

⬇

(5) Set outcome indicators

⬇

(6) Plan how to measure soft outcomes

⬇

(7) Test knowledge and awareness carefully

⬇

(8) Review and prioritise your outcome indicators

⬇

(9) Consider whether you need to evidence impact

⬇

(10) Plan your process monitoring

⬇

(11) Finish the framework by deciding on your information collection methods

Adapted from Valentine et al. (2018).

lead to changes in thinking and practice which could not have been anticipated, for example new relationships and new collaborative opportunities beyond the original scope of the PD. It is also possible for PD to cause educators to become risk-averse, for example fearful of deviating from 'teaching to the test' after completing examination preparation-focused PD. In the context specifically of educational PD, Guskey's five levels (L1–L5) for evaluating PD provide an enduring framework (Guskey, 2002) used to scaffold this chapter. Guskey's framework encourages evaluators to consider the following dimensions:

L1. Participants' reactions
L2. Participants' learning
L3. Organisational support and change
L4. Participants' use of new knowledge and skills
L5. Student learning outcomes

Participants' reactions and learning: a place for PDP

We start thinking about Guskey's L1 and L2 with a personal reflection (Vignette 22) of a school senior leader after completing a distance learning master's qualification, part-time over three years, whilst working.

> **Vignette 22: A personal approach to evaluating PD (Sarah Badger)**
>
> As an experienced senior leader in an independent school in the South East of England, I had aspirations to further my career as a headteacher. After a number of job interviews, it became clear that I needed to strengthen my applications and potential competence in the role with some further professional development that went beyond the scope of one-day courses. It therefore seemed a natural decision to take a master's degree in Educational Leadership and Management.
>
> In the context of a busy working life, it is easy to ignore the need to evaluate one's own personal and professional development, but the process offered at regular intervals throughout the master's course encouraged me to do just that. It didn't come naturally at first, and at times I was reluctant to engage with reflection as I felt that I needed to press on with the academic aspects of the course, for fear of falling behind. Over time, I began to see that the power of the personal development planning process for me lay in the overlaps between the three domains presented in the framework used during my course: academic, professional, and personal. For example, my reading on power and affective aspects of leadership, combined with my observation of leaders' actions, has deepened my understanding of the responsibility I have as a leader to act authentically. I have become more aware of the need to reflect on my own actions and to examine the influence they may have on others. This, to me, is a much deeper level of learning than would be possible through a purely academic approach.

This vignette illustrates how Sarah, as a professional school leader, used personal (and professional) development planning (PDP) to identify PD opportunities, as well as articulate benefits, whilst studying the course. As PDP has been a device used in this book to support your reading of the book, you may consider that engaging with the content of this book and the various activities presented in its chapters (reflection points, PDP activities, recommended reading) is a form of PD and/or a tool to evaluate your experiences of PD.

> **Reflection point 9:1**
>
> *Have you been using the PDP tables in the chapters? If not, what has prevented you? If you have, do you see this as PD?*

PDP should be cyclical. Its structure of identifying goals, planning actions, acting, reviewing, and replanning is akin to the action research cycles for practitioner research referred to in Chapter 8, acting both as PD and evidence-based evaluation of that PD.

Gathering evidence over time: Portfolios and e-portfolios

As the book has shown, discrete, funded PD activities do not account for all of PD. Broader definitions of PD are needed to evaluate more fully how expansive a learning environment is available to employees (Evans et al., 2006; Fuller et al., 2012) (as described in Chapter 2). An issue raised by Sarah in Vignette 22 and those evaluating PD provision in the UK (e.g. Opfer and Pedder, 2010) is the over-reliance on one-off events without building in plans for longer-term, sustainable impact (e.g. Fox and McCormick, 2009).

Reflection point 9:2

- *Have you been curating possible actions you might take from this book?*
- *Which of your actions as identified in your PDP (either from this book or in your wider professional life) would you prioritise to set such a cycle in motion?*

Portfolios are a useful tool for gathering evidence across learning and skill development opportunities, especially when extending beyond an assemblage of certificates and including personal reflection. Trainees or practitioners expected to keep a professional portfolio are encouraged to make regular entries, personally evaluating PD activity as well as practice. These are particularly associated with gathering evidence of competency by early career professionals (Fox et al., 2015), whether training teachers or healthcare professionals. Chartered professions, such as surveying and psychology, retain a requirement for such portfolios or diaries of reflection on PD to demonstrate good standing to their professional bodies. Whether teaching is a Chartered profession or not varies across time and geography. Whilst once the case in Scotland, this was disbanded, and the cases made for Chartering in Ireland have not been successful (Lynch et al., 2013). In the UK, whilst a Chartered College of Teaching was established in 2017 (https://chartered.college), membership is not a requirement for English teachers. A similar partial-profession Chartering is in place in the United States of America (National Board for Professional Teaching Standards: https://www.nbpts.org). Whilst portfolios are not established as a requirement in-service across teaching, ongoing evidence of reflection and CPD plays a role for many education professionals in career progression (Dinham and Scott, 2003).

In more recent times, electronic versions (e-portfolios) reflect the digital turn. These can be individually created using personal website or blogging platforms (http://teacherprofessionalism.weebly.com/tools-for-creating-eportfolios.html) or are provided during programme-wide or organisational-level training (such as at the time of writing this book Mahara and Microsoft OneNote). These can be designed to gather together evidence against professional standards, host and self-evaluate the associated PDP. In Wales, a national Professional

Development Passport (Education Workforce Council, n.d.) was launched for teachers, lecturers, and support staff in 2016 as a bilingual and online portfolio to record and evaluate their PD. However, this was not mandatory, and the National Assembly for Wales (2017) concluded that professional reflection was not sufficiently embedded in staff work practices to maximise its potential.

Reflection point 9:3

Do you keep a portfolio which evaluates your PD? If so, would you say you use it more for professional (evidence against professional standards), employability (skills development for career) or academic (increased knowledge and understanding) purposes?

As was highlighted in Chapter 5, simply offering a well-intentioned support structure for PD does not ensure staff buy-in. In this case, the potential for educator empowerment through self-management and self-evaluation of PD was limited by its perception as an additional workload burden and fears of it being used for their assessment as a performance management tool.

Organisational support and change

To evaluate PD strategically, it is useful to have a framework against which the consequences of PD can be measured. This is something the Welsh government is likely to be considering. At organisational level, leaders might set a vision for their school being a learning organisation (Moloi, 2010; Silins and Mulford, 2004) or knowledge-building organisation (Chen and Hong, 2016). In these situations, the learning of staff measured through identifiable new knowledge would be a key indicator. To reflect on Guskey's L3 and L4, the following case study offers an English primary school headteacher's approach to provision, and hence evaluation, of PD. This covers how she views organisational support and change, and how she looks for her staff's application of knowledge and skills, mapped against the dimensions of MacGilchrist and colleagues' (2004) 'Intelligent School'.

Case study 6: Self-evaluation against the dimensions of an intelligent school (Anna-Claire Norden)

School self-evaluation is a fundamental principle of school development which should, in my view, have a broad focus. As a school, we aspire for all our children to develop the skills, attributes, and knowledge to become lifelong learners from their varied starting points and for all our staff to be able to contribute effectively to this journey, which starts with being a learning role model.

In drawing on the intelligences identified by MacGilchrist et al. (2004), we gather information on our children's holistic growth, as well as our staff's holistic pedagogy, identifying the needs of individuals alongside common threads and patterns. Moreover, we look to be proactive rather than simply reactive, looking to what our children will need as learners and adults of tomorrow as well as today. Through this reflective process, professional development opportunities are carefully considered identifying those which are likely to have the greatest impact.

This process is cyclic and so, once the professional development opportunity has been completed, we move into the implementation phase introducing new strategies and ideas, or adjusting those we already have in place. This leads to gathering evidence of the effectiveness of any changes, and therefore the value of professional development, again through the lens of the nine intelligences.

In addition, the development of staff as professionals, as well as the education profession, breeds passion and encourages creativity. In encouraging staff to explore their interests and develop their skills and knowledge across a range of topics, the school benefits in a variety of ways, for example through new initiatives recommended or external experts introduced to us. Furthermore, while we strive for stability within our teams, we also recognise we may not always be able to offer opportunities for progression at the right time and have a duty to support education more widely in nurturing talent. It is therefore important to enable staff to grow beyond the priorities of the school.

Table 9.1 summarises how MacGilchrist's intelligences impacted on the headteacher's organisation-level decision-making.

The headteacher had come across this framework during master's study 20 years earlier and had been applying it through her leadership of school culture and support for staff ever since; first as a deputy headteacher and then headteacher in two schools. The impact of PD can be long standing and used to underpin vision, strategy, and implementation. However, in lower income countries, where PD for practitioners often relies on a few days' isolated training, such potential for long-term impact on staff or children is limited (Pearson et al., 2017).

Reflection point 9:4

Reflect on your organisation's processes for evaluating PD. How does this relate to the organisation's vision for PD?

Table 9.1 Explanations of how intelligences can be used to impact on decision-making

Intelligence	Explanation
Contextual	In understanding our place within the local and wider community, as well as the impact of changes within society, we support teachers in ensuring that our children's learning fits them for the life they will lead today and tomorrow by accessing a range of initiatives
Collegial	
	We explore CPD through internal coaching, school-to-school opportunities, local community expertise, and external courses from the various providers
Strategic	We are clear about our values and aims. These are revisited and reviewed regularly by all stakeholders, with school development being as proactive as possible whilst acknowledging and impacting on arising trends
Academic	In using the Campaign for Learning's 5Rs (Rod, 2008) and Carol Dweck's (e.g. 2016) Growth mindset, we promote the 'can do' factor (MacGilchrist et al., 2004) with staff learning being valued as much as that of the children. Staff model in their dialogue their own journeys for children to hear their personal evaluations, illustrating Responsibility as a core value underpinning a lifelong learner's attributes
Reflective	
Pedagogical	
Emotional	
	In reflecting, we look beyond data to ensure our curriculum, environments, and experiences enhance holistic growth for children and staff alike
Spiritual	We commit to a whole-school approach where staff in all roles are nurtured to support the development of all children to ensure our teaching and learning pushes boundaries and strives to equip our children and staff for today and the changing world of tomorrow

Some PD is offered by external providers. Practitioners expected to benefit from it are at a distance from those with the original vision for it. This is often the case with PD associated with curricular reform, which might be instigated at national, regional or local authority level. For example, a district coordinator in Western Canada delivered a PD programme to support the implementation of a new social studies curriculum in elementary schools (Gibson and Brooks, 2012). Five years later, a local university evaluated the impact of this by contacting the 67 teachers who had completed the initial PD in the district's eight schools. Just under half agreed to complete a questionnaire and a few teachers agreed to be interviewed or accepted a classroom visit. Disappointingly for the coordinator, the study reported a 'lack of congruence between the curriculum as envisioned by designers and lived in classrooms' (2012: 21). This was attributed to a lack of: follow-up by the PD provider, in-school leadership of the implementation in tune with the PD, and appreciation of how change affects individuals differently. Even though this PD involved three half-day workshops over the period of a year, with inter-workshop activity, it still could not be assumed to transfer into school contexts. PD is worthwhile evaluating over time and drawing on teachers' in-practice reactions and experiences to inform future PD provision. In this case, the coordinator was advised to develop sustained support, including modelling, coaching, and facilitating collaborative work in the school settings (as illustrated in Figure 1.1 in Chapter 1).

Evaluating impact on participants' use of PD for pupil outcomes

Guskey's framework has been used to evaluate collaborative forms of PD such as lesson study (as covered in Chapter 8). A university-based lesson study project team (Godfrey et al., 2019) used a literature review to identify the anticipated outcomes which might be expected from lesson study in their context. To capture participant reflections on their learning (Guskey's L1 and L2), the Lambeth Connecting Knowledge project funded by the London Schools Excellence Fund used surveys across 33 participating schools. One survey captured 78 teachers' attitudes towards and enjoyment of lesson study as PD (Guskey's L1). A second survey captured 72 teachers' baseline and final self-evaluations of their professional learning (Guskey's L2). The project sought 'to establish the logical chain between teacher learning and pupil outcomes' (Godfrey et al., 2019: 333). To capture evidence of organisational support and change (Guskey's L3), the team carried out interviews with leaders and teachers who were not directly involved and held a focus group of teachers who had been leading lesson study groups. They asked 53 teachers to complete impact assessments relating to over 160 pupils which both covered their own changes in knowledge and skills as well as evidence of changes to pupil performance. Observational evidence from 66 teachers and 221 pupils and review of pupil attainment, against targets set by the teachers at the start of the year, completed the dataset of evidence for impact (Guskey's L4 and L5).

Such designs demonstrate that self-report is an important source of evidence for evaluating PD. However, as PD is scaled up and externally funded, it often involves external evaluation and looking at broader datasets.

Reflection point 9:5

How would you evidence change in your (or as a leader, others') thinking and practice?

External evaluation of PD: national and international examples

Building on an evaluation of the education welfare system in 2003, the Welsh Assembly Government identified PD by school-based staff and other education welfare professionals in local authorities as needed to solve concerning pupil attendance rates (Reid et al., 2007). PD was put in place across Wales and a National Behaviour and Attendance Review Report commissioned to evaluate its impact (Reid, 2011a, 2011b). The strategy was ambitious and inclusive. It started with a group reviewing workshop-generated evidence from across

Wales before a set of iterative workshops, including 121 practitioners and a range of stakeholders. These working groups discussed evidence presented through a carousel of activities. This included the emerging analysis of one group being challenged by a subsequent group. One of the sources of evidence discussed was children's views collected across 22 Welsh local authorities (Reid et al., 2010). The key issues generated from these workshops fed into further working groups set up of 62 similarly diverse practitioners through a similar iterative process. Their remit was to identify possible solutions as the basis for staff PD, which extended to include the teacher training curriculum. By the time of the next focus on teacher PD needs in Wales (National Assembly for Wales, 2017), instigated in part by an OECD report highlighting the limited career progression and PD opportunities for teachers in Wales (OECD, 2014), pupil attendance and behaviour were no longer a focus. This might indicate some measure of previous success. An absence of need for PD and reprioritisation of needs to other initial teacher training and in-service PD areas are potential factors to consider when evaluating PD. However, their absence might also reflect a change in national agendas. The long-term view of the impact of PD around pupil attendance in Wales is difficult to ascertain. As identified in Chapter 3, a crisis can change priorities. The COVID-19 pandemic again put Welsh pupils' attendance into the spotlight (Sibieta, 2020). Whilst Wales (and Northern Ireland) fared well in pupil attendance rates following short lockdowns, start of year attendance and regional variations across Wales saw lower than other UK rates. PD therefore needs to be sustained and systematic.

Sustained investment in PD can come from long-term, funded projects. All five of Guskey's (2002) levels of evaluation are encapsulated in the sustained research and development work of an international project in Bangladesh (https://eiabd.com/publications/research-publications.html), which has been in place for over ten years at the time of writing this book.

Vignette 23: Evaluating the 'value for money' of a PD intervention – an international example (Tom Power)

The schools component of English in Action (EIA) was widely judged to be one of the most successful large-scale teacher development projects in low-to-middle income countries, reaching 43,000 primary teachers, 11,000 secondary teachers, and over 7 million schoolchildren across Bangladesh. The project was initiated by the Government of Bangladesh, to significantly improve the number of people able to communicate in the English language – at levels that would enable them to participate in social and economic activities. It was funded by UKAid and managed by Cambridge Education. The Open University was technical lead for the schools component.

Research, monitoring, and evaluation (RME) was integral to each phase of EIA (McCormick and Mathew, 2019), from needs identification and context mapping to pilot studies, impact evaluation, and institutionalisation.

The evaluation framework used mixed methods to study three main aspects relating to the learning and teaching of English language: *perceptions, practices*, and *proficiency*. These were designed to show the extent to which the programme influenced how teachers and students perceived English language teaching, what actually happened in the classroom, and subsequent changes in learning outcomes. Alongside at-scale quantitative methods, qualitative studies provided explanatory insights, explored changing conditions and approaches to implementation, and gave teachers a voice within the research. Triangulation was enhanced through monitoring data from teacher self-reporting and regular ongoing observations by government education officers or project field officers.

The challenges included working within and developing existing research capacity, such as working with Dhaka University to strengthen postgraduate training of early career researchers through participation in EIA classroom observations studies. Over the course of the ten-year programme, RME also had to respond to developments in donor thinking on evaluation, shifting from a baseline-endline methodology to a quasi-experimental approach (Power et al., 2017) – with donors and policy-makers particularly interested in quantitative evidence of impact on learning.

You might have noted in Vignette 23 the reference to 'RME'. In addition to the 'monitoring' and 'evaluation' expectations noted earlier in the chapter as commonplace for large, funded initiatives, there is an increasing move to include a strong evidence-base to underpin the evaluations. Hence 'research' is being added to many previously development-focused projects.

Reflection point 9:6

Having read this chapter, how would you evaluate the 'value for money' of any PD you have had funded (or have funded for others)?

In conclusion

Lessons learned from different forms and scales of PD evaluation include some useful takeaways. At a personal level, illustrated by Sarah in Vignette 22 and further exemplified in Chapter 11 by former Open University Master's in Education students, personal evaluation is highly impactful in stimulating changes in thinking and practice. A process of PDP can help professionals identify and articulate their learning and skills development in ways which can be used personally in terms of job satisfaction, academically in terms of greater understanding, and/or professionally in terms of career development. At an organisational level, leadership and a vision for the expectations of PD can lead to it being embedded, as illustrated in Case study 6. This vision can provide a framework in which PD can be evaluated against agreed and shared values. Once PD is disconnected from the setting in which it is provided, it becomes not only more complex to deliver but also to evaluate. The importance of partnerships, collaborative work, and ongoing PD has been illustrated. Getting feedback from the different levels identified by Guskey (2002) ensures that a range of stakeholders' (educators', educational leaders', and learners') perspectives on the PD can be triangulated.

Using Wales as an example of a national context for evaluating education workforce PD, the importance of context and political agendas is highlighted in prioritising funding. As highlighted in Chapter 4, the advantage of a national spotlight means that the recommendations are more likely to be funded. The larger the scale, such as international PD projects, the more explicit research, monitoring, and evaluation need to be and for this to be negotiated with funders and local partners. The benefits of the initiative can be claimed, not only to justify the significant funds spent, but also to recognise and value the work of all those involved in working towards educational improvements.

Personal Development Planning Table 9 Focus: Professional

Question	What can I do?	What do I need from others?
	Short-term action	Medium-term action
1. Have you been using PDP?	If you have not been using PDP, consider how this might fit in with and complement your current ways of working. If you use PDP, reflect on how well it captures evaluations of PD	Ask others how they capture their ongoing reflections on PD and whether they recognise that they are doing so through a form of PDP
2. What evidence do you draw on to evaluate your PD?	Identify the last PD opportunity you had (not necessarily funded) and list the forms of evidence which might capture any impact from this	Ask your line manager their opinion on what would be useful evidence to evaluate your recent PD
3. Do you now have a vision for what constitutes effective PD?	Read the seven characteristics of effective PD (Darling-Hammond et al., 2017) and evaluate your access to such PD over the last six months	Plan to review your PD opportunities in your next formal performance appraisal or mentoring review meeting

NB: Recommended Open Access Readings are highlighted below, using asterisks as follows: *Leaders and Teacher Educators, **Practitioners, ***Early Career Professionals.

Recommended reading

* Valentine, D., Willis, H.P., Metcalfe, C. and Barratt, M. (2018) *How to develop a monitoring and evaluation framework*. London: National Council for Voluntary Organisations [https://knowhow.ncvo.org.uk/how-to/how-to-develop-a-monitoring-and-evaluation-framework]. This framework will help get a sense of the language of monitoring and evaluation used across sectors.

** This chapter has shown that it is helpful to have clarity about expectations for PD. The following review of 35 rigorous empirical international studies on teacher PD identifies seven characteristics of effective PD which could be used to evaluate your access and experience of PD: Darling-Hammond, L., Hyler, M.E. and Gardner, M. with Espinoza, D. (2017) *Effective teacher professional development*. Palo Alto, CA: Learning Policy Institute [https://learningpolicyinstitute.org/sites/default/files/product-files/Effective_Teacher_Professional_Development_REPORT.pdf].

*** Emily, a practitioner blogger, has recommended her favourite examples of teaching portfolios, with links to some of the e-portfolio tools they used at: https://mytech-classroom.com/teaching-portfolio-examples/

10 PD, agency, and identity

#EC #ML #SL #TE

Why think about ideas such as agency and identity?

Throughout this book, we have explored how leaders have a key role in creating conditions that support professional development (PD). Each theme has offered examples of 'top-down' PD as well as PD driven by the educators themselves or co-created with learners from the 'bottom up'. As we have seen, PD, although a personal activity, can lead to organisational change building on individual and collective knowledge and relationships (Ellis, 2007). For these reasons, the ways in which educator and learner identities are reflected in PD are crucial to its success. PD has more impact on practice when educators have the agency to act upon their new understandings. This chapter reflects on what it means to be a professional educator: Who an educator thinks they are and who they relate to (their identity)? How they think they can develop their practice and hence the profession more generally (their agency)?

In some cases, we have presented inspiring stories of educators in challenging circumstances finding new ways to access and create PD: each requiring agency to do so. Although unique, key themes of values, identity, agency, and context have featured in every story. Here we focus on identity and agency to highlight ways in which they underpin PD and can be developed through PD with educators and learners.

PD and identity

The relationship between educator identity and PD has been considered in different ways in previous chapters. Professional identity is fluid and educators may view their role very differently depending on their history and context (Hargreaves, 2000, 2019). They may see themselves as an individual with their own priorities. Their identity might be much more firmly connected to the mission and culture of their school or educational organisation, or some combination of these and other influences. PD can contribute to the development of individual identity, as can the opportunities educators have to act in their current context (Frost, 2006). PD is also received differently depending on individual identities and how educators see themselves (Biesta and Tedder, 2007; Biesta et al., 2015).

Reflection point 10:1

- *How would you describe your identity as an educator?*
- *What factors influence your identity?*
- *How might this impact on your PD*

Valuing identities in PD

A key thread running through this book is the importance of creating PD that values educators' personal and professional identities as well as the identities of the learners they work with. This might be through creating networks of educators from marginalised groups, or ensuring that PD is adapted to reflect and value linguistic and cultural diversity.

Recognising the linguistic diversity of educators and learners is practically relevant but also inclusive for educators' identities. This can support their connection to the PD on offer. For example, in designing The Open University PGCE in Wales (Vignette 13, Chapter 4), pre-service teacher development was made available in Welsh and English, and included opportunities for student teachers' language learning, as well as pedagogy relevant to the bilingual contexts in which teachers were working. Whilst 'translanguaging' is advocated as a strategy to include all learners (Duarte and Günther-van der Meij, 2020; see Chapter 7), it is equally important for the educators as they experience PD. Work with the Meadow Lake Tribal Council in Canada involved developing PD for early childhood educators that included local language, values, and spirituality. However, in Kenya, Ng'asike (2019) reports linguistic imperialism, where English is used as the dominant language in classrooms and educator PD, thereby excluding local languages (Chapter 6). One solution, as seen in the TESS India resources for teachers and teacher educators, is to translate PD into local languages. However, it is equally important to adapt PD materials to reflect 'geographies, curriculum, resources available, and local cultural and institutional practices' (Case study 2, Chapter 5) (Wolfenden and Adinolfi, 2019).

Many examples in the book highlight that, as well as being linguistically inclusive, PD can connect with educators' identities by considering their backgrounds, the influence of local worldviews (Ncube, 2010), local knowledge and ways of learning (e.g. Vignette 16, Chapter 6). One way to achieve this is to co-create or adapt PD with local educators and avoid attempting to import PD schemes and systems without careful evaluation of their cultural and contextual relevance and connection to the educators' prior experiences (e.g. Vignette 18, Chapter 6). As Hallinger and Kulophas (2019) point out, much research and guidance for PD originates from the Global North, with a strong American influence which may not be relevant for all contexts and can alienate educators who cannot make connections with their own identities and philosophies of education. To overcome this, PD should establish channels for participants to exchange their experiences around a particular issue (Symeou and Karagiorgi, 2018). Leaders need to think about how educators from marginalised groups (e.g. LGBTQ+ educators, educators of colour, with learning differences, or from a non-traditional educational route) may be supported during PD. Discussions with individuals may need to take place before PD commences, as they should not be expected to act as expert representatives for any particular group, or contribute their own personal experiences unless they are comfortable to do so. However, as covered in Chapters 7 and 8, they should be supported to share their unique perspectives without fear of criticism (Donahue, 2018; Sitter and Nusbaum, 2018).

Reflection point 10:2

- *How do you feel PD supports your individual identity?*
- *What else would support it?*
- *How could you tackle fear of criticism?*

Overcoming threats to identity from PD

Depending on individual educators' identities, PD can be viewed as a positive motivator and support system. However, change through PD can also be perceived as a threat or potential criticism (Schilling, 2012). A good example of this is through collaborative PD either within one educational organisation or across a cluster of similar institutions such as a Multi-Academy Trust of schools. When PD stems from a school-improvement goal and requires observation of other colleagues or scrutiny of practice, individuals may fear change and criticism which threaten their professional identity. PD that includes a focus on observations of practice requires very careful handling. If there is too much focus on observations or these are conducted by colleagues where there is an unequal power dynamic, PD can result in a cycle of 'judgementoring', where critical feedback and targets are given to individual educators without consideration of positive elements or a plan for support (Hobson and Malderez, 2013). Externally mandated PD may need to be adapted by leaders within an organisation to better respond to the individual identities of educators (Vignette 2, Chapter 1).

If collaborative PD, even with an institutional improvement goal, can consider individual identities and support educators to assimilate new practices in line with their professional identity, this can result in powerful and sustained change. Examples throughout this book indicate that PD which incorporates explicit activities designed to encourage educators to reflect on their professional role (rather than an aspect of practice in isolation) will help to reduce fear of change and lead to greater long-term impact (Vignette 5, Chapter 2).

An example of this is the work of Cremin et al. (2014). Teachers from primary schools in England were introduced to new ways of encouraging reading for pleasure with their pupils. Over a year, they noticed and discussed their own reading habits, read and reflected on their responses to children's texts, and shared these with one another and children in their classes. They also researched and documented changes in children's reading behaviours as a result. The PD, which was collaborative and across a network of schools, prompted dialogue and reflection, thereby enabling the teachers to notice their classroom practices and slowly change these. More importantly, their own understanding of what it meant to be a reader and to teach reading changed, which changed their teacher identities. PD that influences professional identity and leads to sustained changes includes explicit activities where educators reflect on their own personal or professional identity, and identity as learners. Critical pedagogy seminars, mentor/peer support through dialogue and reframing, and educator networks are some of the ways of doing this shared in previous chapters (Kohli et al., 2021; Nicholson and Kroll, 2015; Vescio et al., 2009). Bringing educators together to reflect on their identities and experiences can support their agency and stimulate new proactive ways of changing practices driven by educators themselves.

Picking up on the theme of PD having potential to support equity (Chapter 7), powerful approaches can be through celebrating personal identity journeys within networks and organisations. In Wales, increased funds have been set aside for inclusive approaches within initial teacher education, awards such as honouring the first black headteacher, and a prize for teachers or schools supporting diversity and inclusion (BBC, 2021). The Welsh policy context includes changes to the school curriculum, but a lack of time, resources, competence, knowledge, and confidence has been evidenced, recommending that higher education providers as well as school staff receive appropriate training (Williams, 2021).

This need for PD to address what was originally termed an 'attainment gap' by ethnicity between black and white students across all types of institutions has been reworded to an 'awarding gap', shifting the emphasis from a deficit model to recognise how structural inequalities continue (Universities UK, 2019). Baroness Amos's report aimed at higher education institutions calls for mandatory training for educators in higher education. Analysing evidence on what is causing the gaps can help in planning to close these gaps through long-term institutional change. The UK's HE Race Equality Charter (AdvanceHE, 2020) is a framework where applicants use self-assessment data and action plans to improve success of staff and students. It recognises that BAME staff and students 'are not a homogenous group and complexity needs to be considered in analysing data and that individuals have multiple identities'.

Identity, digital identity, and PD

A professional's view of their agency and identity is important to the PD choices they make, their proactivity, their reflexivity, and the actions they take following PD. This includes how they view themselves in relation to the two dominant paradigms of teacher identity: as craftsperson or professional scholar (Stone, 2020). Whilst some educators may be more interested in making small-scale changes to their practice, others are keen to engage with research, innovation, and even lead new types of PD for other educators. Supporting educators to develop research literacy and engage in research may enable them to feel empowered to change their own and others' practices and to seek new ways of doing things. Digital communication, social media, and virtual learning platforms offer more opportunities for educators to select their own PD and engage with others in ways over which they have more agency.

However, as covered in Vignette 8, Chapter 2, social media is not embedded in current in-service or pre-service PD but is often engaged with by individual professionals and trainees. A doctoral study carried out with pre-service teachers in Greece explored how social media were used for academic purposes on their own initiative (Kontopoulou, 2019). Data obtained from 36 pre-service teachers' interviews and social media diaries across three different training providers showed how they used an array of social media to 'survive' their teacher education courses and how this related to their sense of identities whilst students. This was not just helping them as an individual student but also developing a sense of belonging with other students. They used groups closed to teachers and the public, such as Facebook, to grow their networks, compare perspectives on the course, share study techniques, discuss tricky concepts, and reassure one another when revising for exams.

They also used social media to prepare for their transition into their future profession. Whilst studying on their course, they used social media to keep abreast of wider news in the teaching profession, identified PD opportunities which extended their course, explored possible specialisation routes, and gathered pedagogical ideas for future use.

Participants were proactively exploring their future identities as teachers by growing their networks and engaging with loose assemblages of people (sets; see Table 8.1, Chapter 8) that consisted of their peers and future colleagues. These activities not only supported them in completing their course and succeeding in it, but also laid the ground for progressing confidently into the profession.

However, it should be noted that social media, although a freely available tool for PD, are not a neutral space. This partly explains the behaviours of teachers in Kontopoulou's (2019) study who did not post in the forums of the more experienced teachers for fear of being judged and potentially losing respect before they had even joined the profession. Pre-service teachers also talked about the need for closed spaces to be able to talk, for example about their teachers, in ways they would not want them to hear. Both open and closed spaces are needed for PD, especially for more personal and more reflective discussions.

Agency and context

When teachers are active agents in developing their professionalism (Sloan, 2006; Turnbull, 2005), they can be viewed as activists (Sachs, 2016) or agents of change (Frost et al., 2018). This empowerment is critical to the development of education as a profession. However, there is evidence that external context affects educators' capacity to exert this potential agency.

There are two main schools of thought about how agency relates to context, which can be presented as alternative questions. On the one hand, how can teachers progress their self-determined personal goals to develop practice without being constrained by their context (Frost, 2006)? This view assumes an educator has capacity to act, that their agency is innately held, and they just need to find ways to pursue this. On the other hand, we can ask how agency results from an educator's actions within the context they find themselves in and whether they have resources available to act (Biesta and Tedder, 2007)?

Both views emphasise that leaders have an important role in creating conditions for educators to develop agency. There have been illustrations and exploration of the advantages and disadvantages of bottom-up and top-down approaches to leadership of PD. In Uganda, teaching students were constrained by the rigid format and focus of their training on subject knowledge and felt that they could not act to overcome this (Buckler, 2020; Vignette 17, Chapter 6). Whilst volunteers in Afghanistan were supported by an NGO to create on online library of teaching resources (Vignette 10, Chapter 3). In each case, leadership of PD shaped the context.

Reflection point 10:3

- *What is your view of agency and why do you feel this way?*
- *In what ways do you feel you have the potential to make changes driven by what you value?*
- *How can you find ways to make the changes you believe are worth making?*
- *In what ways is your capacity to make changes shaped by the context either by enabling or constraining you?*

When we talk about context, this is not just the physical place but also digital space, a national policy context, or systems in an educational organisation. This book has shown how, especially in contemporary times, there are opportunities for educators to explore and expand their professional identity through networks beyond any individual establishment and work beyond boundaries. As Kontopoulou's (2019) study in Greece outlines, this can happen even before teachers join the profession.

Collaborative agency and identity

A key strand of this book has been to present a case for PD as a collaborative rather than solitary activity. This has been explored through different ways of thinking about teacher communities and how they might develop practice together through inquiry (Chapter 8). One example of this in the UK relates to how a vision developed into the collective practice development of teachers across a local authority in England and beyond, into international networked PD activity. This changed the identity of teachers from learners to educators and leaders of PD.

The HertsCam Network (https://www.hertscam.org.uk/) is an independent, teacher-led, not-for-profit organisation, whose stated aims are to support educational transformation through support for teacher leadership. It was not conceived as such but, as the aspirations of those involved grow, the collective decision was made to reify their collective identity. Starting as a school–university partnership in the 1990s, it became increasingly independent and, since 2013, HertsCam's operation and governance have been entirely in the hands of schools and teachers. Its core programmes are an Educator-Led Development Work (ELDW) programme (https://www.hertscam.org.uk/what-is-eldp.html), a master's course (https://www.hertscam.org.uk/the-hertscam-med.html), a Networking programme and an International Teacher Leadership (ITL) initiative (http://www.internationalteacherleadership.org/) involving 20 countries around the world in linked teacher leadership programmes. This sustained activity grew from the vision (Frost, 2018) that teachers should be supported in being agents of change in their settings, through supporting them in inquiry focused on driving practice change. Any educator, whatever their formal role in the local authority of Hertfordshire, in any educational setting, is offered the opportunity to show leadership by being given opportunities on one of these programmes. The first cohort of teachers completing the teacher-taught two-year master's programme, with their supervisory team, published a book about the tangible impacts on their practice (Frost et al., 2018). Gillot and Rose's (2018) chapter entitled 'reversing the roles of teacher and student' captures the identity shifts which went on in this network, as teachers shifted to become learners and then on to educators of their former peers on the MA. These leadership identities transformed the network into an organisation (Frost, 2018). It is therefore possible to link individual agency and identity with collective agency and identity, using PD as a vehicle.

Identity development as development of the profession

Individual educators, policy-makers, and leaders all have a role to play in the process of ensuring that PD connects meaningfully to educators and leads to sustained change. Barriers and challenges may stem from national expectations or organisational constraints, but leaders can draw on their local communities to provide an environment which contextualises the PD and links the PD needs of the educators to the needs of the learners for which they are responsible. An example from Sierra Leone illustrates how teacher identity can be developed in marginalised rural women, so much so that they become role models to encourage further recruitment into the profession. In response to the shortage of female teachers and unequal distribution of teachers in rural areas in Sierra Leone, linked to girls dropping out of school, often at puberty and in a context of rural poverty, early pregnancies, and gender-based violence, a programme has been developed to offer local work experience in schools and Teacher Training College study at a distance. The programme concluded that 'it takes a village to raise a teacher ...' (Crisp et al., 2017). The model developed by the Open University and a component of the Girls' Access to Education programme, funded by UK Aid, has so far supported 750 young women through a bursary, tutor support, bespoke self-study open materials, revision camps, and mentoring. Becoming a teacher represents a significant personal identity shift for these women, leading them to be perceived differently in their villages. One participant explained: 'My life was in the market selling ... now they call me madam'.

In conclusion

Professional development or development of the profession is most impactful when it is informed by the voice of learners, whether through research or co-creation (Pence et al., 2010; Rix et al., 2020; Soni et al., 2020). In our work with students at the Open University we strive to develop our practice through student-led work and co-creation, including student-led mentoring and coaching networks with MA Education students and alumni. It is then fitting that in their role as education professionals and learners they offer us Chapter 11 for this book, reflecting on the key themes of PD covered in this book.

Personal Development Planning Table 10 Focus: Academic and Professional

Question	What can I do?	What do I need from others?
	Short-term action	Medium-term action
1. How confident am I in my understanding of educator identity and agency?	Write your own definitions/explanations of these terms in a few sentences and why they might be important in your work	Talk to other leaders in your organisation about identity and agency in PD and their understandings of these concepts
2. Where can I go to find out more about developing educator agency and identity through PD?	Select a text from the recommended reading Open Access resources below that you would like to follow up	Look back to some of the vignettes and chapters mentioned here and list any key authors or projects to follow up
3. How can I use my understanding of identity and agency to inform PD?	Note down some strategies for supporting agency and identity offered in this chapter	Review your next planned PD activity or your strategy for the year with colleagues and look at where these might be incorporated

NB: Recommended Open Access Readings are highlighted below, using asterisks as follows: *Leaders and Teacher Educators, **Practitioners, ***Early Career Professionals.

Recommended reading

* Universities UK (2019) *Black, Asian and Minority Ethnic student attainment at UK universities: #closingthegap* [bame-student-attainment-uk-universities-case-studies .pdf].
* Williams, C. (2021) *Black, Asian and Minority Ethnic communities, contributions and Cynefin in the New Curriculum Working Group*, Final Report [black-asian-minority-ethnic-communities-contributions-cynefin-new-curriculum-working-group-final-report.pdf].
** Frost, D., Ball, S., Hill, V. and Lightfoot, S. (eds.) (2018) *Teachers as Agents of Change.* Letchworth Garden City: HertsCam Network [https://www.hertscam.org.uk/uploads/2/5/9/7/25979128/green_e-book.pdf]. Select a chapter which interests you from this practitioner-authored book and reflect on the identities and agency articulated.
*** Kontopoulou, K. (2019) *Pre-service teachers' use of social media for academic purposes*. Doctoral dissertation, University of Leicester [https://ethos.bl.uk/OrderDetails .do?uin=uk.bl.ethos.778389].

Harnessing your learning about PD

#EC #ML #SL #TE

As you complete your reading of this book, you may have seen this as an opportunity to reflect on your experience of and hopes for PD, whether you are a recipient of or leader of PD. We hope the book is a chance to consider your agency as a professional, whatever your formal role in employment, in terms of your PD.

This book has provided the opportunity to reflect on the ideas introduced in Chapter 1 and the conceptual framework for PD presented as Figure 1.1. The diagram that is Figure 1.1 offers a view of how PD could be thought of as sitting within national and local contexts of education, from national reforms to local

Figure 11.1 An adaptation of a conceptual framework for educator PD (developed from Figure 1.1)

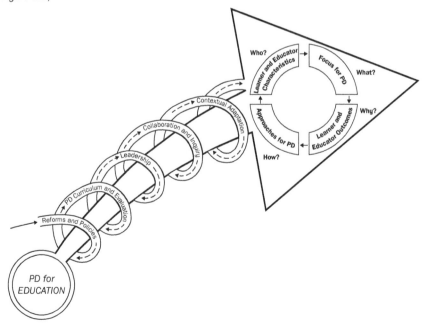

decisions. Figure 11.1 offers an extension of this thinking by specifically focusing on PD in education.

National reforms need to be adopted into practice at local level, as illustrated in this book. For the policies to be articulated and embedded, there are implications for PD. This involves making clear what the curriculum for PD is that results from the principles (or indeed dictates) of educational reform and how this will be evaluated. It also requires leadership at local level, whether formal or informal, to put into place the opportunities for such PD. This book has advocated that, whilst these might be individual, in the case of self-evaluation of practice and engagement in inquiry, collaboration is the most fruitful way forwards.

The final arrowhead of considerations for PD represented in Figure 11.1 captures practical questions individuals might ask of their PD needs. These are framed as the 'who', 'what', 'how', and 'why' of going about improving educational provision.

To address these questions, individuals need to engage in a process of critical reflection which holds up current practice against their personal professional values. In doing so, individuals can claim their agency to personalise PD. This might be in response to the educational challenges which present themselves. It might be through being inspired to close a perceived practice–values gap. Becoming aware of rifts between rhetoric and reality can create the motivation to call for and occupy spaces for learning through doing, learning through inquiry, and collective learning. Such activity connects with the development of professional identity both individually and collectively, hence reinvigorating the calls for an agentic profession by Judith Sachs (2000, 2016).

Examples of learning through doing and inquiry are seen in the following vignettes offered by practitioners and recent MA Education graduates at The Open University. Each vignette captures responses to a professional story in the context of the wider themes explored throughout this book. Each of Vignettes 24–27 is followed by author comments to help bring together the takeaway messages for the reader.

Vignette 24: Charlotte's reflections on career development

As a professional within an ever-developing profession, healthcare, to be able to maintain the quality of my practice, I am heavily reliant on personal reflection and additional learning, to achieve my goals in enhancing my professional identity and autonomy. I have learnt that:

- PD needs to be individual to my own goals as I can recognise my needs more readily than my employer, making PD a bottom-up perspective and more personal.

- A bottom-up perspective on PD also requires me to continuously reflect on the work I am undertaking, how changes are being implemented, and how I am going to adapt.
- Understanding my own strengths and weaknesses means developing my skills further to be able to cope with upcoming changes and consider support I will need. By recognising my strengths, I may be able to become an advocate for the changes and help others with learning or support. This approach has certainly helped me understand the need for changes and made me more adaptable.

PD has enabled me to work outside of my initial 'comfort zone'. When I qualified as a radiographer, not only did we have to complete PD as a requisite for practice, but as this role was consistently developing, it required further education to support new evidence-based practices. To advance in the profession, undertaking PD was essential, but there were times when I felt that the PD was basic and generic and didn't advance my personal goals as readily as I would have liked. I became very passionate about PD and took the opportunity to focus my skills on education, leading me to change the focus of my career and take on a lecturing role, providing me with flexibility to explore deeper PD opportunities, and focus on professional identity. PD, in this instance, has not only impacted my own professional career, but has given me additional confidence in my own abilities to work outside of my comfort zone and still be a successful practitioner.

I undertook a Master's in Education with The Open University and became a PDP coach. When I began working alongside these fellow students, I recognised the importance of collaboration within PD, learning about PD from a variety of perspectives, and the needs and goals of others, which were often different from my own. The collaboration helped us support each other in our own PD journeys, providing an abundance of ideas to improve our own learning or working with each other to explore new techniques for development.

These were then skills that I utilised within my profession, inviting my students to work collaboratively together when reflecting on their own practices, allowing them to build the same PD skills that we had embedded and enjoyed as PDP coaches.

Charlotte's reflections show how her thinking shifted from an individual to collaborative mindset, which included considering PD to benefit all. She has looked beyond her own workplace to learn from and respect different needs at different career stages. She seems to have relished taking ownership of her own development and identifies a variety of methods, looking beyond her own workplace for PD. This demonstrates leadership in PD and has helped her make a career shift as part of her developing identity as a practitioner.

Vignette 25: Elizabeth's reflections on culturally relevant PD and PD for equity

I worked simultaneously in two different educational contexts and studied for a master's:

- As a primary school teacher, PD centred around how other people saw me, how I was assessed – inspections, observations, judgments drawn from the opinions of those who were higher up in the hierarchy of leadership and experience.
- As a tutor at a college of music, PD was something much more flexible and interactive. My reflections involved watching how my practice and identity changed and developed in regard to where I was.

Travelling in one West African country and participating in a conference for teachers, I was startled by both similarities and differences. Some aspects of teaching PD transcended language, cultural and economic barriers, and made me feel like I was working alongside my colleagues at home – for example, discussions of pedagogy, the importance of oracy. Other issues were not as prominent in this different context, and some things that I had taken for granted were significant considerations, such as access to resources from crayons to books.

Taking on the master's qualification was itself an act of PD prompted by my context. I put myself back in the learner position adjusting to an unfamiliar context (of a virtual learning environment). Through interacting online, I was challenged about the ways in which my classroom was an 'insider' culture. For example, I taught a mixed-age class spanning several educational years and realised there were implicit habits I had absorbed into my idea of 'normality'. When children came into my class from another background – from a different school, entirely different country, language background or cultural context – then my own experiences in PD helped me to be more aware of assuming familiarity and the implicit barriers.

Most significantly for me, my PD opportunities brought me into contact with people with different backgrounds, different cultures, and different lived experiences. Until I started my studies with The Open University, my work was in a relatively insular background, with people with experiences similar to my own. I suppose that's one of the risks of regional-specific and institutional-specific PD. On the master's, interacting with different perspectives, alongside teachers from different subjects, age groups, institutions, and countries – and some who weren't teachers – gave me an opportunity to learn from experiences I wouldn't have met myself. On comparing the diversity of perspectives I was encountering, I began to recognise some of the assumptions that were constraining me. Ultimately, these conversations were part of informing changes we made as a primary school to our assessment practices.

Overlapping experiences developed my practice. My PD from the primary school informed my experiences deciding to teach children with SEN at the College of Music. My PD from an institutional background enabled me to source materials and adapt them for our needs as a community of music teachers – in a way, we were creating our own PD as we discovered our need for it.

Elizabeth's reflections, like those of Charlotte, present a story of agency and collaboration. She also demonstrates that PD can mean moving beyond everyday assumptions and asking questions about practice. The global contacts and perspectives she gained from visits and study outside her workplace seem to have been a catalyst to practical changes she could make when she went back to look again at needs in her local context, to evaluate practices and share these for change.

Vignette 26: Anne's reflections on PD through inquiry

PD through inquiry is fascinating. I have always sought out published research, even in the early part of my career when a particularly influential tutor at teaching college nurtured much debate around the philosophy of education. When my experience and my instinct were telling me one thing, but obstacles were placed in the way (to an action or change I sought), I looked for ways to overcome them. Published research, with its academic weighting and peer reviews, emboldens me to try a little harder, push a little farther, and to keep seeking 'truth'.

Through master's level study, I have:

- Become more critical of the research, less likely to follow an idea just because it resonates with my beliefs. I do examine the counter-arguments now!
- Shared published research with other colleagues. It has been particularly wonderful working with two other colleagues who were also studying.
- Nurtured further inquiry through this environment and the support of the management team.
- Generated evidence through inquiry as part of my PD (recorded lessons, children's learning, informal observations and feedback).

I have always found it hard to 'sell myself' but am gradually seeing PD as a way to affirm the positive steps I take to improve and grow and how those steps benefit not only myself, but more importantly the children I learn alongside, as well as the institution within which we learn.

Whilst there is still a great emphasis on quantitative data (particularly attainment scores), I am heartened by the growing number of requests for qualitative evidence from awarding bodies. Actively seeking children's voices to justify and evidence quality PD is a very positive shift.

Like Elizabeth, Anne seems to have brought colleagues with her on her discovery of the benefits of research, study, re-evaluating the role of data, and inquiry as a form of evolving PD. She seeks out rigorous studies she considers offer a credible evidence base for re-evaluating practice and welcomes critical perspectives as a form of problem-solving. She also sees child and learner participation as a valid part of the inquiry process.

Vignette 27: Susannah's personal reflections on evaluating PD

Within previous primary education teaching jobs, PD at a whole-staff level was evaluated by senior leadership in relation to the perceived needs of the school, then a member of staff completing external training and feeding back ideas, with most staff lacking any agency regarding these choices. These brief PD opportunities can be insightful but they tend to lack depth and may seem irrelevant to staff.

At individual level, PD is often evaluated during the appraisal system when discussions take place regarding the impact of any training or observation opportunities from the previous academic year and what further PD may be useful to help meet targets set. These evaluations continue to be influenced heavily by school priorities set at a leadership level, thus agency continues to be limited.

Personally, I have found that the most effective evaluations of PD have been self-evaluations, especially after leaving a long-term post for supply teaching. I was able to:

- Identify areas of interest that excited or intrigued me about teaching, alongside elements where I felt less confident.
- Have full agency to seek my own opportunities for development, testing out relevant ideas and considering how useful these had been in developing my understanding or practice, using a process that I would now identify as PDP.

I have continued to regularly evaluate my own PD in this way, finding this more rewarding than the structured, limited opportunities within a workplace, as it has allowed me to reflect on the impact of my PD relative to my own professional identity. I believe that worthwhile evaluations of PD should capture relevance to individuals and form part of a personal development journal or log that can be used to support professional discussions with current and future colleagues and employers.

In my current further education setting, self-evaluation is encouraged with access to teaching and learning coaches alongside the traditional appraisal process. As teachers, we are passing on PDP to our childcare and education students, hopefully starting them off on their own rewarding journeys.

Susannah's reflections about the constraints of top-down PD, as opposed to the freer possibilities of self-evaluation, are relevant not only to her own confidence but also to the development of the next generation of educators. It seems she is well aware of the bigger national reforms impacting on practice, but that keeping a space for her own reflections and observations is an important way to enact agency for discussing her career, her knowledge, and building on her experience.

In conclusion

As we write this book, societies internationally are in crisis as educationalists respond to the impact of coronavirus and conflict their roles as professionals. Charlotte, Elizabeth, Anne, and Susannah's personal reflections offer some final thoughts regarding the key themes that might enable you to harness professional development for your own benefit or for others with whom you work. In particular, the importance of self-directed or 'volitional' PD and opportunities to think more critically about taken-for-granted practice and assumptions.

From their perspectives, personal motivation for PD has been important. They chose to seek out PD related to their own needs and interests and as a result found this volitional PD to be particularly engaging and impactful. In contrast, they suggest that 'top-down' PD that is mandated and devised by leaders seemed less relevant and engaging. Even top-down evaluation appears to offer less meaningful insight than self-evaluation, which, Susannah argues, helped her to identify what kind of PD she needed. Ultimately, they found PD to be significant when it addressed practical challenges they were facing and, more importantly, broadened their understanding and practices as educators for the benefit of the learners in their care.

Although they do not offer specific examples of PD responding to crisis situations, it seems likely that, when confronted with a crisis, educators like Charlotte, Elizabeth, Anne, and Susannah would apply this volitional PD approach, looking for opportunities to connect with others and develop understanding and practice that could support them. However, we cannot assume that all educators will respond in this way, and proactively seek or create PD opportunities when challenges present themselves. Sometimes there will also be large-scale top-down mandates for PD that need to be addressed at local levels. Perhaps what these reflections highlight is that, as leaders of PD in any circumstance, we must consider how we can harness educator needs and interests to ensure that the volitional aspect remains.

Charlotte, Elizabeth, Anne, and Susannah agree that their most successful experiences of PD enabled them to question taken-for-granted assumptions about education and learners. This resulted in a shift to their own professional identities and even career pathways. These educators emphasise that PD created connections with others outside of their usual sphere. Broadening their horizons through collaboration and discussion with other educators was a vital part of PD and was equally powerful from a distance and via online, asynchronous channels. They also mention developing their own skills of practitioner inquiry and learning to read published research with a critical eye as essential parts of the transformative shift that they recount.

The insightful reflections from educators offered in this chapter show us that there is reason to be optimistic about the power of PD and the potential benefits for educators and learners, even in very challenging circumstances. Throughout the book, there are inspirational examples of educators connecting, innovating, and developing PD for their own contexts with limited resources. We hope that the toolkit you have had opportunity to engage with through the chapters offers you direction and practical strategies to harness PD for yourself and other educators. Good luck!

Bibliography

Aaen, J. (2015) Making sense of Facebook: A mixed methods approach to analysing online student groups, *Seminar.net – International Journal of Media, Technology and Lifelong Learning*, 11 (1): 1–7.

Academy of Singapore Teachers (n.d.) *Networked learning communities* [https://academyofsingaporeteachers.moe.edu.sg/professional-excellence/networked-learning-communities].

Adagiri, S.O. (2014) *A comparative study of teachers' continuing professional development (CPD) in Nigeria and England: A study of primary schools in Abuja and Portsmouth.* Doctoral dissertation, University of Portsmouth [https://researchportal.port.ac.uk/en/studentTheses/a-comparative-study-of-teachers-continuing-professional-developme].

Addae-Kyeremeh, E. (2020) Teachers' access to and use of evidence, in A. Fox and V. Poultney (eds.) *Professional Learning Communities and Teacher Enquiry: Evidence-based Teaching for Enquiring Teachers.* St. Albans: Critical Publishing (pp. 80–92).

AdvanceHE (2020) *HE Race Equality Charter* [https://www.advance-he.ac.uk/equality-charters/race-equality-charter].

Agbenyega, J.S. (2018) Examining early childhood education system in Ghana: How can Bourdieuian theorisation support a transformational approach to pedagogy?, in M. Fleer and B. van Oers (eds.) *International Handbook of Early Childhood Education*, Vol. I. Dordrecht: Springer (pp. 673–690).

Akayuure, P. and Ali, C.A. (2016) Incorporating indigenous *Bukre* game into mathematics lessons: A teaching experiment, *Researchjournali's Journal of Mathematics*, 3 (1): 1–15.

Akayuure, P. and Nabie, J.M. (2021) Using Indigenous games to demystify probability theorem in Ghanaian classrooms: Mathematical analysis of Ampe. *World Academy of Science, Engineering and Technology International Journal of Educational and Pedagogical Sciences*, 15 (3) [https://publications.waset.org/abstracts/133895/using-indigenous-games-to-demystify-probability-theorem-in-ghanaian-classrooms-mathematical-analysis-of-ampe].

Akiba, M. and LeTendre, G.K. (2017) *International Handbook of Teacher Quality and Policy.* London: Routledge.

Akinbote, O. (2009) Problems of teacher education for primary schools in Nigeria: Beyond curriculum design and implementation, *International Journal of African and African-American Studies*, 6 (2): 64–71.

Akyeampong, K. (2019) *Improving Teaching and Learning.* A Knowledge and Innovation Exchange (KIX) Discussion Paper. Washington, DC: Global Partnership for Education.

Akyeampong, K., Lussier, K., Pryor, J. and Westbrook, J. (2013) Improving teaching and learning of basic maths and reading in Africa: Does teacher preparation count?, *International Journal of Educational Development*, 33: 272–282.

Alderson, P. (2012) Children as researchers: Participation rights and research methods, in P. Christensen and A. James (eds.) *Research with Children: Perspectives and Practices*, 2nd edition. London: Falmer Press/Routledge (pp. 276–290) [https://discovery.ucl.ac.uk/id/eprint/10070478/1/Alderson_children%20as%20researchers.pdf].

Alexander, R.J. (2020) *A Dialogic Teaching Companion*. London: Routledge.

Allan, L. (2020) Teachers are holding our families together during the coronavirus pandemic, *Goodhousekeeping.com*, 4 May [https://www.goodhousekeeping.com/life/parenting/a32362127/teacher-appreciation-during-pandemic/].

Alvesson, M. and Sandberg, J. (2013) *Constructing Research Questions: Doing Interesting Research*. Los Angeles, CA: Sage.

Amaral, E., Campos, H.H., Friedman, S., Morahan, P.S., Araujo, M.N.T., Carvalho, P.M. et al. (2012) An educational international partnership responding to local needs: Process evaluation of the Brazil FAIMER Regional Institute, *Education for Health*, 25 (2): 116–123.

Anderson, B. and Simpson, M. (2012) History and heritage in distance education, *Journal of Open, Flexible and Distance Learning*, 16 (2): 1–10.

Aronson, B., Meyers, L. and Winn, V. (2020) 'Lies my teacher [educator] still tells': Using critical race counternarratives to disrupt whiteness in teacher education, *The Teacher Educator*, 55 (3): 300–322.

Arthur-Kelly, M., Sutherland, D., Lyons, G., Macfarlane, S. and Foreman, P. (2013). Reflections on enhancing pre-service teacher education programmes to support inclusion: Perspectives from New Zealand and Australia, *European Journal of Special Needs Education*, 28 (2): 217–233.

Association for School and College Leaders (ASCL) (2016) *Social Networking, Social Media and Email: Protecting your professional reputation*. Guidance Paper. Leicester: ASCL.

Aubusson, P., Ewing, R. and Hoban, G.F. (2009) *Action Learning in Schools: Reframing Teachers' Professional Learning and Development*. London: Routledge.

Avornyo, E.A. (2018) *Investigating play and learning in the Ghanaian early years' classroom: A mixed methods study*. Doctoral thesis, University of Cambridge.

Baker, B., Graham, S. and Williams, S. (2003) Teaching under a glass ceiling: A study of gender equity in federal education career fields, *Advancing Women in Leadership Journal*, 13 [http://advancingwomen.com/awl/spring2003/BAKER~1.HTML].

Baker, G. (2020) Leading professional learning communities: Opportunities and challenges, in A. Fox and V. Poultney (eds.) *Professional Learning Communities and Teacher Enquiry: Evidence-based Teaching for Enquiring Teachers*. St. Albans: Critical Publishing (pp. 70–79).

Ball, J. and Pence, A. (2006) *Supporting Indigenous Children's Development: Community–University Partnerships*. Vancouver, BC: UBC Press.

Ball, S. (2012) *Global Education Inc.: New Policy Networks and the Neo-liberal Imaginary*. London: Routledge.

Banegas, D.L. (2020) Online teacher education in times of Covid-19 [blog post], *BERA blog*, 15 May [https://www.bera.ac.uk/blog/online-teacher-education-in-times-of-covid-19].

Baraniuk, R.G. (2007) Challenges and opportunities for the open education movement: A Connexions case study, in T. Iiyoshi and M.S.V. Kumar (eds.) *Opening Up Education: The Collective Advancement of Education through Open Technology, Open Content, and Open Knowledge*. Cambridge, MA: MIT Press (pp. 229–246).

Barnes, M. (2021) Creating 'advantageous' spaces for migrant and refugee youth in regional areas: A local approach, *Discourse: Studies in the Cultural Politics of Education*, 42 (3): 456–470.

Bart's Training and Support Alliance (BTSA) (2021) *School to school support*. London: BTSA [https://tinyurl.com/xfapwnan].

Baxter, J. (2021) *Post pandemic leadership*. British Educational Research Association seminar, 27 April [https://www.bera.ac.uk/event/post-pandemic-leadership].

BBC (2021) Wales teachers: Extra cash offered to attract BAME staff, *BBC News*, 22 October [https://www.bbc.co.uk/news/uk-wales-59004309].

Behlol, M.G. and Cajkler, W. (2018) Practices, challenges and implications of teaching and assessment of cognitive skills in higher education, *Pakistan Journal of Education*, 35 (1): 113–140.

Behlol, M.G. and Dad, H. (2020) Educational migration as a brain drain: Curse or boon for Pakistani universities, *Journal of Research in Social Sciences*, 8 (1): 35–47.

Behlol, M.G., Dad, H. and Raja, S.A. (2014) Educational policies syndrome: Teacher education programmes and teacher recruitment practices in Pakistan, *Journal of Research in Social Sciences*, 1 (1): 52–58.

Behlol, M.G., Akbar, R.A. and Shahid, M. (2017a) Capacity building of school councils: A study of government primary schools in district Bhakkar, *Bulletin of Education and Research*, 39 (1): 17–32.

Behlol, M.G., Fox, A. and Davis, S. (2017b) *An approach to developing methods of teaching in the B.Ed. Curriculum (British Council Knowledge Exchange Project)*. Presentation to the international conference on 'Promoting Inquiry-Informed Practice: Bridging the Gap between Theory & Practice for Participants of Pre-Service Teacher Education Program', Fatima Jinnah Women University, Islamabad, Pakistan, 16–18 May.

Behlol, M.G., Akbar, R.A. and Dad, H. (2019) Investigating secondary school effectiveness: Peer–teacher relationship and pedagogical practices, *Bulletin of Education and Research*, 41 (1): 43–55.

Belli, C. (2018) An exploration into how the impact of interventions for pupils with special educational needs can be sustainable and support long term progress, *Support for Learning*, 33 (1): 5–22.

Bennett, R.E. (2011) Formative assessment: A critical review, *Assessment in Education: Principles, Policy and Practice*, 18 (1): 5–25.

Berry, B., Airhart, K.M. and Byrd, P.A. (2016) Microcredentials: Teacher learning transformed, *Phi Delta Kappan*, 98 (3): 34–40.

Bhopal, K. and Rhamie, J. (2014) Initial teacher training: Understanding 'race', diversity and inclusion, *Race, Ethnicity and Education*, 17 (3): 304–325.

Biesta, G.J. (2007) Why 'what works' won't work: Evidence-based practice and the democratic deficit in educational research, *Educational Theory*, 57 (1): 1–22.

Biesta, G.J. (2010) Why 'what works' still won't work: From evidence-based education to value-based education, *Studies in Philosophy and Education*, 29 (5): 491–503 [https://orbilu.uni.lu/bitstream/10993/7820/1/116%20PUB%20What%20works%20SPED%202010.pdf].

Biesta, G. and Tedder, M. (2007) Agency and learning in the lifecourse: Towards an ecological perspective, *Studies in the Education of Adults*, 39 (2): 132–149.

Biesta, G., Priestley, M. and Robinson, S. (2015) The role of beliefs in teacher agency, *Teachers and Teaching, Theory and Practice*, 21 (6): 624–640 [https://doi.org/10.1080/13540602.2015.1044325].

Biraimah, K.L. (2016) Moving beyond a destructive past to a decolonised and inclusive future: The role of 'ubuntu'-style education in providing culturally relevant pedagogy for Namibia, *International Review of Education*, 62 (1): 45–62.

Black, P. (2015) Formative assessment – an optimistic but incomplete vision, *Assessment in Education: Principles, Policy and Practice*, 22 (1): 161–177.

Black, P. and Wiliam, D. (1998a) *Inside the black box: Raising standards through classroom assessment*. London: King's College, London School of Education.

Black, P. and Wiliam, D. (1998b) Inside the black box: Raising standards through classroom assessment, *Phi Delta Kappan*, 80 (2): 139–148.

Black, P. and Wiliam, D. (2003) In praise of educational research: Formative assessment, *British Educational Research Journal*, 29 (5): 623–637.

Black, P., Harrison, C., Lee, C., Marshall, B. and Wiliam, D. (2003) *Assessment for Learning: Putting It into Practice*. Maidenhead: Open University Press.

Black, P., Harrison, C., Hodgen, J. and Marshall, B. (2005) The dissemination of formative assessment: A lesson from, or about, evaluation, *Research Intelligence*, 92 (1): 14–15.

Black, P., McCormick, R., James, M. and Pedder, D. (2006) Learning how to learn and assessment for learning: A theoretical inquiry, *Research Papers in Education*, 21 (1): 119–132.

Bloom, B.S. (1969) Some theoretical issues relating to educational evaluation, in R.W. Tyler (ed.) *Educational Evaluation: New Roles, New Means*. The 63rd Handbook of the National Society for the Study of Education, Part 2. Chicago, IL: University of Chicago Press (pp. 26–50).

Bolam, R., McMahon, A., Stoll, L., Thomas, S. and Wallace, M. (2005) *Creating and sustaining effective professional learning communities*. Research Report RR637. London: Department for Education and Skills [https://dera.ioe.ac.uk/5622/1/RR637.pdf].

Bondy, E., Ross, D., Adams, A., Nowak, R., Brownell, M., Hoppey, D. et al. (2007) Personal epistemologies and learning to teach, *Teacher Education and Special Education*, 30 (2): 67–82.

Botha, E.M. (2012) Turning the tide: Creating Professional Learning Communities (PLC) to improve teaching practice and learning in South African public schools, *Africa Education Review*, 9 (2): 395–411.

Boylan, M. (2016) Enabling adaptive system leadership: Teachers leading professional development, *Educational Management Administration and Leadership*, 46 (1): 86–106.

Boylan, M. and Woolsey, I. (2015) Teacher education for social justice: Mapping identity spaces, *Teaching and Teacher Education*, 46 (1): 62–71.

Bozkurt, A., Akgun-Ozbek, E., Yilmazel, S., Erdogdu, E., Ucar, H., Guler, E. et al. (2015) Trends in distance education research: A content analysis of journals 2009–2013, *International Review of Research in Open and Distributed Learning*, 16 (1): 330–363.

Brighouse, T. and Moon, B. (2020) Like the Open University we now need an Open School for the whole country, *The Guardian*, 12 May [https://www.theguardian.com/education/2020/may/12/like-the-open-university-we-now-need-an-open-school-for-the-whole-country].

British Educational Research Association (BERA) (2014) *Research and the teaching profession: Building the capacity for a self-improving education system*. Final report of the BERA-RSA Inquiry into the role of research in teacher education [https://www.thersa.org/globalassets/pdfs/bera-rsa-research-teaching-profession-full-report-for-web-2.pdf].

British Pathé (1962) *'School Of The Air': Lessons broadcast to Outback* [video] [https://www.youtube.com/watch?v=WgZO7Ht_0M0].

Brown, A.W. (2017) Striving for social sensitivity: The impact of a social justice project on student teachers' understanding of pupils from socially disadvantaged backgrounds, *Pastoral Care in Education*, 35 (2): 77–87.

Browne, C., Wall, P., Batt, S. and Bennett, R. (2018) Understanding perceptions of nursing professional identity in students entering an Australian undergraduate nursing degree, *Nurse Education in Practice*, 9 (32): 90–96.

Bruff, D., McMahon, T., Goldberg, B. and Camps, H. (2014) *An introduction to evidence–based undergraduate STEM teaching*. Vanderbilt University: Coursera [https://www.coursera.org/course/stemteaching].

Brusca-Vega, R., Alexander, J. and Kamin, C. (2014) In support of access and inclusion: Joint professional development for science and special educators, *Global Education Review*, 1 (4): 37–42.

Bubb, S. and Jones, M.A. (2020) Learning from the COVID-19 home-schooling experience: Listening to pupils, parents/carers and teachers, *Improving Schools*, 23 (3): 209–222.

Buckler, A. (2020) Being and becoming in teacher education: Student-teachers' freedom to learn in a College of Education in Ghana, *Compare*, 50 (6): 844–864.

Buckler, A., Stutchbury, K., Kasule, G., Cullen, J. and Kaije, D. (2021) What prevents teacher educators from accessing professional development OER and MOOC? Storytelling and professional identity in Ugandan teacher colleges, *Journal of Learning for Development*, 8 (1): 10–26 [https://jl4d.org/index.php/ejl4d/article/view/493/602].

Burde, D. (2014) Humanitarian action and the neglect of education, in *Schools for Conflict or for Peace in Afghanistan*. New York: Columbia University Press (pp. 25–54).

Burger, U. and Trehan, K. (2018) Action learning in East Africa: New encounters or impossible challenges?, *Action Learning: Research and Practice*, 15 (2): 126–138.

Burn, K. and Mutton, T. (2015) A review of 'research-informed clinical practice' in Initial Teacher Education, *Oxford Review of Education*, 15 (2): 217–233.

Burnett, B. and Lampert, J. (2019) The Australian national exceptional teaching for disadvantaged schools programme: A reflection on its first 8 years, *Journal of Education for Teaching*, 45 (1): 31–46.

Burns, M. and Orne, P. (2020) *Will the COVID-19 pandemic speed a global embrace of online learning?* London: UKFIET [https://www.ukfiet.org/2021/will-the-covid-19-pandemic-speed-a-global-embrace-of-online-learning/].

Cain, T. (2015) Teachers' engagement with published research: Addressing the knowledge problem, *The Curriculum Journal*, 26 (3): 488–509.

Cain, T. (2017) Denial, opposition, rejection or dissent: Why do teachers contest research evidence?, *Research Papers in Education*, 32 (5): 611–625.

Cain, T. (2018) *Becoming a Research-informed School: Why? What? How?* London: Routledge.

Cambridge Dictionary (n.d.) *Evaluation.* Cambridge: University of Cambridge [https://dictionary.cambridge.org/dictionary/english/evaluation].

Cardozo, M.L. and Novelli, M. (2018) Education in emergencies: Tracing the emergence of a field, in A. Verger, H.K. Altinyelken and M. Novelli (eds.) *Global Education Policy and International Development: New Agendas, Issues and Policies*. New York: Bloomsbury Academic (pp. 233–254).

Carey, K. and Stefaniak, J. (2018) An exploration of the utility of digital badging in higher education settings, *Education Technology Research and Development*, 66 (1): 1211–1229.

Carnahan, C.R. (2006) Photovoice: Engaging children with autism and their teachers, *Teaching Exceptional Children*, 39 (2): 44–50.

Carrington, B. and Skelton, C. (2003) Re-thinking 'role models': Equal opportunities in teacher recruitment in England and Wales, *Journal of Education Policy*, 18 (3): 253–265.

Carter, A. (2015) *The Carter Review of Initial Teacher Training*. London: HMSO [https://www.gov.uk/government/publications/carter-review-of-initial-teacher-training].

Centre for Educational Research and Innovation (CERI) (2005) *What works* [https://www.oecd.org/education/ceri/centreforeducationalresearchandinnovationceri-whatworks.htm].

Cerna, L. (2019) *Refugee education: Integration models and practices in OECD countries*. OECD Education Working Paper No. 203 [https://www.oecd-ilibrary.org/

docserver/a3251a00-en.pdf?expires=1643388564&id=id&accname=guest&check
sum=26323235045C2CBA3E6972BACB99FB50].

Chamberlain, L. and Safford, K. (2019) *Learning assistants in Sierra Leone: Model, innovation, and impact.* 9th Pan-Commonwealth Forum on Open Learning – Innovations for Quality Education and Lifelong Learning (PCF9), 9–13 September, Edinburgh [http://oasis.col.org/bitstream/handle/11599/3389/PCF9_Papers_paper_79. pdf?sequence=1&isAllowed=y].

Chamberlain, L., Afroze, J., Cooper, V. and Collins, T. (2019) *Representing children's rights from discussion through to illustration and interpretation.* Milton Keynes: The Open University Children's Research Centre and Amnesty UK International [https://wels.open.ac.uk/sites/wels.open.ac.uk/files/files/The%20Open%20Universi- ty's%20Children's%20Research%20Centre%20Report_%20FINAL_%20revised%20 print%20version.pdf].

Chamberlain, L., Buckler, A. and Mkwananzi, F. (2021) Building a case for inclusive ways of knowing through a case study of a cross-cultural research project of out-of-school girls' aspirations in Zimbabwe: Practitioners' perspectives, in A. Fox, H. Busherand. C. Capewell (eds.) *Thinking Critically and Ethically about Research for Education: Engaging with People's Voices for Self-empowerment.* London: Routledge (pp. 27–39).

Chandler, K. (2021) *Researching online tuition: Narrative research into experiences of synchronous online tutorials* [https://kathychandler.org/].

Chang-Kredl, S. and Kingsley, S. (2014) Identity expectations in early childhood teacher education: Pre-service teachers' memories of prior experiences and reasons for entry into the profession, *Teaching and Teacher Education,* 43 (1): 27–36.

Chen, B. and Hong, H.-Y. (2016) Schools as knowledge-building organizations: Thirty years of design research, *Educational Psychologist,* 51 (2): 266–288.

Chen, L. (2020) A historical review of professional learning communities in China (1949– 2019): Some implications for collaborative teacher professional development, *Asia Pacific Journal of Education,* 40 (3): 373–385.

Chen, T. (2003) Recommendations for creating and maintaining effective networked learning communities: A review of the literature, *International Journal of Instruc- tional Media,* 30 (1): 35–40.

Children's Research Centre (CRC) (2021) Milton Keynes: The Open University [http:// wels.open.ac.uk/research/childrens-research-centre].

Christopherson, E. (2021) *These 10 Countries receive the most refugees.* Oslo: Norwegian Refugee Council [https://www.nrc.no/perspectives/2020/the-10-countries-that-receive- the-most-refugees/].

Clarke, M. and Drudy, S. (2006) Teaching for diversity, social justice and global aware- ness, *European Journal of Teacher Education,* 29 (3): 371–386.

Cochran-Smith, M. and Lytle, S.L. (1999) The teacher research movement: A decade later, *Educational Researcher,* 28 (7): 15–25.

Coffey, M., Sato, M. and Thiebault, M. (2005) Classroom assessment up close – and personal, *Teacher Development,* 9 (2): 169–184.

Collaborative Action Research Network-Action Learning: Action Research Association (CARN-ALARA) (2019) *The Collaborative Action Research Network* [https://carn- alara2019.org/about-carn].

Collins, M., Collins, G. and Butt, G. (2015) Social mobility or social reproduction? A case study of the attainment patterns of students according to their social background and ethnicity, *Educational Review (Birmingham),* 67 (2): 196–217.

Cordingley, P. (2009) *The impact of CPD and its role in leading staff and effective teams.* Nottingham: NSCL [http://www.inspiringleaders-elearning.co.uk/modules/ npqh_em/documents/npqh_em/lset/npqh_opinion_piece_the_impact_of_cpd.pdf].

Cremin, H., Mason, C. and Busher, H. (2011) Problematising pupil voice using visual methods: Findings from a study of engaged and disaffected pupils in an urban secondary school, *British Educational Research Journal*, 37 (4): 585–603.

Cremin, T., Mottram, M., Bearne, E. and Goodwin, L. (2008) Exploring teachers' knowledge of children's literature, *Cambridge Journal of Education*, 38 (4): 449–464.

Cremin, T., Mottram, M., Collins, F., Powell, S. and Safford, K. (2014) *Building Communities of Engaged Readers: Reading for Pleasure.* London: Routledge.

Cremin, T., Myhill, D., Eyres, I., Nash, T., Wilson, A. and Oliver, L. (2018) *Teachers as writers.* A report for Arts Council England on the value of writers' engagement with teachers to improve outcomes for all pupils [http://oro.open.ac.uk/53501/].

Cremin, T., Myhill, D., Eyres, I., Nash, T., Wilson, A. and Oliver, L. (2020) Teachers as writers: Learning together with others, *Literacy*, 54 (2): 49–59.

Creswell, J.W. (2014) *Research Design: Qualitative, Quantitative, and Mixed Methods Approaches*, 4th edition. Lincoln, NB: Sage.

Crisp, M., Safford, K. and Wolfenden, F. (2017) *It takes a village to raise a teacher: The Learning Assistant programme in Sierra Leone.* Report to PLAN International [http://oro.open.ac.uk/49603/1/Sierra%20Leone%20LA%20Research%20Report%20170517%20FINAL.PDF].

Cronenwett, L., Dracup, K., Grey, M., McCauley, L., Meleis, A. and Salmon M. (2011) The doctor of nursing practice: A national workforce perspective, *Nursing Outlook*, 59 (1): 9–17.

Crowley, C. (2017) Professional development as product implementation training, *Teaching and Teacher Education*, 67 (3): 477–486.

Cuenca, A. (2011) The role of legitimacy in student teaching: Learning to 'feel' like a teacher, *Teacher Education Quarterly*, 38 (2): 117–130.

Dados, N. and Connell, R. (2012) The Global South, *Contexts*, 11 (1): 12–13.

Dale, L., Fox, A., Loe, R., Richards, A., Sida-Nichols, K., Winkley, B. and Gaál, E. (2021) Personality traits linked to course withdrawal and retention for primary school teacher trainees, *Chartered College of Teaching: Impact 11*, https://impact.chartered.college/article/personality-traits-linked-course-withdrawal-retention-primary-school-teacher-trainees/

D'Antoni, S. (2009) Open educational resources: Reviewing initiatives and issues, *Open Learning: The Journal of Open, Distance and e-Learning*, 24 (1): 3–10 [https://www.tandfonline.com/doi/full/10.1080/02680510802625443].

Darling-Hammond, L., Hyler, M.E. and Gardner, M. with Espinoza, D. (2017) *Effective teacher professional development.* Palo Alto, CA: Learning Policy Institute [https://learningpolicyinstitute.org/sites/default/files/product-files/Effective_Teacher_Professional_Development_REPORT.pdf].

Da Silva, W.B., Amaro, R. and Mattar, J. (2019) Distance education and the Open University of Brazil: History, structure, and challenges, *International Review of Research in Open and Distributed Learning*, 20 (4): 99–115.

Daugherty, R., Black, P., Ecclestone, K., James, M. and Newton, P. (2008) Alternative perspectives on learning outcomes: Challenges for assessment, *The Curriculum Journal*, 19 (4): 243–254.

Day, C. and Sachs, J. (2004) Professionalism, performativity and empowerment: Discourses in the politics, policies and purposes of continuing professional development, in C. Day and J. Sachs (eds.) *International Handbook on the Continuing Professional Development of Teachers*. Milton Keynes: Open University Press (pp. 3–32).

De Laat, M. (2012) *Enabling professional development networks: How connected are you?* Netherlands: Open Universteit [https://avs.nl/sites/default/files/documenten/artikelen/12014/De%20Laat%20-%20Enabling%20professional%20development%20networks.pdf].

DeLuca, C., Klinger, D., Pyper, J. and Woods, J. (2015) Instructional rounds as a professional learning model for systemic implementation of assessment for learning, *Assessment in Education: Principles, Policy and Practice*, 22 (1): 122–139.

DeLuca, M., Tramontano, C. and Kett, M. (2014) *Including children with disabilities in primary school: The case of Mashonaland, Zimbabwe*. Working Paper Series 26. London: Leonard Cheshire Disability and Inclusive Development Centre, University College London [https://www.eenet.org.uk/resources/docs/WP26_IE_Zimbabwe.pdf].

Demie, F. (2005) Achievement of Black Caribbean pupils: Good practice in Lambeth schools, *British Educational Research Journal*, 31 (4): 481–508.

de Oliveira Andreotti, V., Stein, S., Ahenakew, C. and Hunt, D. (2015) Mapping interpretations of decolonization in the context of higher education, *Decolonization: Indigeneity, Education and Society*, 4 (1): 21–40.

Department for Education (DfE) (2014) *Cyberbullying: Advice for headteachers and school staff* [https://assets.publishing.service.gov.uk/government/uploads/system/uploads/attachment_data/file/374850/Cyberbullying_Advice_for_Headteachers_and_School_Staff_121114.pdf].

Department for Education (DfE) (2020) *Teaching school hubs* [https://www.gov.uk/guidance/teaching-school-hubs].

Department for Education (DfE) (2021) *Education staff wellbeing charter* [https://www.gov.uk/guidance/education-staff-wellbeing-charter#why-you-should-use-the-charter].

Department for Education and Skills (DfES) (2007) *Assessment for learning 8 schools project report. Secondary National Strategy for school improvement* [https://dera.ioe.ac.uk/7600/1/1f1ab286369a7ee24df53c863a72da97-1.pdf].

Dialogue and Argumentation for Cultural Literacy Learning in Schools (DIALLS) (2020) *DIALLS Student Manifesto* [https://dialls2020.eu/manifesto/#:~:text=The%20DIALLS%20Student%20Manifesto%20is%20a%20declaration%20—,towards%20each%20other%20and%20the%20planet%20we%20share].

Dinham, S. and Scott, C. (2003) Benefits to teachers of the professional learning portfolio: A case study, *Teacher Development*, 7 (2): 229–244.

Dixon, H.R., Hawe, E. and Parr, J. (2011) Enacting Assessment for Learning: The beliefs practice nexus, *Assessment in Education: Principles, Policy and Practice*, 18 (4): 365–379.

Dixson, A.D. (2018) 'What's going on?': A critical race theory perspective on Black Lives Matter and activism in education, *Urban Education*, 53 (2): 231–247.

Donahue, D. (2018) Service learning in higher education by, for and about LGBTQ people: Heterosexism and curriculum shadows, in D.E. Lund (ed.) *The Wiley International Handbook of Service-Learning for Social Justice*. Newark, NJ: Wiley (pp. 123–144).

Donitsa-Schmidt, S. and Ramot, R. (2020) Opportunities and challenges: Teacher education in Israel in the Covid-19 pandemic, *Journal of Education for Teaching*, 46 (4): 586–595.

Dover, A.G., Henning, N., Agarwal-Rangnath, R. and Dotson, E.K. (2018) It's heart work: Critical case studies, critical professional development, and fostering hope among social justice-oriented teacher educators, *Multicultural Perspectives*, 20 (4): 229–239.

Dover, A.G., Kressler, B. and Lozano, M. (2019) 'Learning our way through': Critical professional development for social justice in teacher education, *The New Educator*, 16 (1): 45–69.

Dron, J. and Anderson, T. (2014) *Teaching Crowds – Learning and Social Media*. Edmonton, AB: AU Press.

Duarte, J. and Günther-van der Meij, M. (2020) 'We learn together' – translanguaging within a holistic approach towards multilingualism in education, in J.A.

Panagiotopoulou, L. Rosen and J. Strzykala (eds.) *Inclusion, Education and Translanguaging*. Wiesbaden: Springer (pp. 125–144).

Duckworth, V. and Maxwell, B. (2015) Extending the mentor role in initial teacher education: Embracing social justice, *International Journal of Mentoring and Coaching in Education*, 4 (1): 4–20.

Dudley, P. (2012) Lesson study development in England: From school networks to national policy, *International Journal for Lesson and Learning Studies*, 1 (1): 85–100.

Dudley, P., Xu, H., Vermunt, J.D. and Lang, J. (2019) Empirical evidence of the impact of lesson study on students' achievement, teachers' professional learning and on institutional and system evolution, *European Journal of Education*, 54 (2): 202–217.

DuFour, R. and DuFour, R. (2012) *The School Leader's Guide to Professional Learning Communities at Work*. Bloomington, IN: Solution Tree Press.

DuFour, R. and Eaker, R. (1998) *Professional Learning Communities at Work: Best Practices for Enhancing Student Achievement*. Bloomington, IN: Solution Tree Press.

Dweck, C. (2016) What having a 'growth mindset' actually means, *Harvard Business Review*, 13: 213–226.

Dyjur, P. and Lindstrom, G. (2017) Perceptions and uses of digital badges for professional learning development in higher education, *TechTrends*, 61 (4): 386–392.

Dzamesi, F. and van Heerden, J. (2020) A professional development programme for implementing indigenous play-based pedagogy in kindergarten schools in Ghana, *South African Journal of Education*, 40 (3): 1–11.

Education Commission (2021) *Five ways geospatial analysis can help visualize and solve some of education's biggest challenges*. New York: The Education Commission [https://educationcommission.org/updates/five-ways-geospatial-analysis-can-help-visualize-and-solve-some-of-educations-biggest-challenges/].

Education Endowment Foundation (EEF) (2018) *Research champions: Ashford Teaching Alliance* [https://educationendowmentfoundation.org.uk/projects-and-evaluation/projects/research-champions].

Education Endowment Foundation (EEF) (n.d.) *The Research Schools Network* [https://researchschool.org.uk/].

Education and Training Foundation (2020) *New case studies illustrate transformational role of Professional Standards* [https://www.et-foundation.co.uk/news/new-case-studies-illustrate-transformational-role-of-professional-standards/].

Education Workforce Council, Wales (n.d.) *Professional Learning Passport (PLP)* [https://www.ewc.wales/site/index.php/en/professional-development/professional-learning-passport].

Ehrich, L.C., Hansford, B. and Tennent, L. (2004) Formal mentoring programs in education and other professions: A review of the literature, *Educational Administration Quarterly*, 40 (4): 518–540.

Einarsdóttir, J. (2007) Research with children: Methodological and ethical challenges, *European Early Childhood Education Research Journal*, 15 (2): 197–211.

Elçi, A. (2021) Academics' professional development needs and gains during COVID-19 distance education emergency transition in Turkey: Academics' professional development needs and gains, *International Journal of Curriculum and Instruction*, 13 (1): 343–358.

e-Learning for Kids (2014) *Manifesto* [https://youtu.be/qVlUVet5OQ0].

Elliott, J. (1991) *Action Research for Educational Change*. Milton Keynes: Open University Press.

Elliott, J. (2018) Buying in and selling out – the commodification of creativity in the classroom, *Changing English*, 25 (4): 396–409.

Ellis, S., Thompson, I., McNicholl, J. and Thomson, J. (2016) Student teachers' perceptions of the effects of poverty on learners' educational attainment and well-being: Perspectives from England and Scotland, *Journal of Education for Teaching*, 42 (4): 483–499.

Ellis, V. (2007) *Subject Knowledge and Teacher Education: The Development of Beginning Teachers' Thinking.* London: Continuum.

Elonga Mboyo, J.P. (2017) Reimagining Ubuntu in schools: A perspective from two primary school leaders in the Democratic Republic of Congo, *Educational Management, Administration and Leadership*, 47 (2): 206–223.

Elwood, J. and Murphy, P. (2015) Assessment systems as cultural scripts: A sociocultural theoretical lens on assessment practice and products, *Assessment in Education: Principles, Policy and Practice*, 22 (2): 182–192.

Emke, M. (2019) *Freelance language teachers' PD on ... and with ... and through Twitter*, Doctoral dissertation, The Open University [http://oro.open.ac.uk/60076/1/2019_Thesis_Martina_Emke_final.pdf].

Evans, K., Hodkinson, P., Rainbird, H. and Unwin, L. (2006) *Improving Workplace Learning.* London: Routledge.

Facer, K. and Thomas, L. (2012) Towards an area-based curriculum? Creating space for the city in schools, *International Journal of Educational Research*, 55 (1): 16–25.

Farrell, P. (1994) *Children with Emotional and Behavioural Difficulties: Strategies for Assessment and Intervention.* London: Falmer Press.

Fatima, F.M. and Behlol, M.G. (2018) *Mentoring prospective teachers at teaching practicum in B. Ed (Hons) 4 years program.* Proceedings of ADVED, 4th International Conference on Advances in Education and Social Sciences, 15–17 October, Istanbul, Turkey [www.ocerints.org/adved18_e-publication/papers/46.pdf].

Ferguson, R. and Sharples, M. (2014) Innovative pedagogy at massive scale: Teaching and learning in MOOCs. Open Learning and Teaching in Educational Communities: 9th European Conference on Technology Enhanced Learning, EC-TEL 2014. Dordrecht: Springer (pp. 98–111).

Fielding, M., Bragg, S., Craig, J., Cunningham, I., Eraut, M., Gillinson, S. et al. (2005) *Factors influencing the transfer of good practice.* Research Report RR615. Nottingham: DfES Publications [https://dera.ioe.ac.uk/21001/1/RR615.pdf].

Fiorentini, D., Bednarz, N. and Huang, R. (eds.) (2011) *International Approaches to PD for Mathematics Teachers.* Ottawa: University of Ottawa Press.

Fleer, M. (2015) Developing an assessment pedagogy: The tensions and struggles in re-theorising assessment from a cultural–historical perspective, *Assessment in Education: Principles, Policy and Practice*, 22 (2): 224–246.

Fleet, A., De Gioia, K. and Patterson, C. (2017) *Engaging with Educational Change: Voices of Practitioner Research.* London: Bloomsbury.

Florez Petour, M.T. (2015) Systems, ideologies and history: A three-dimensional absence in the study of assessment reform processes, *Assessment in Education: Principles, Policy and Practice*, 22 (1): 3–26.

Florian, L. and Beaton, M. (2018) Inclusive pedagogy in action: Getting it right for every child, *International Journal of Inclusive Education*, 22 (8): 870–884.

Forde, C. and Torrance, D. (2017) Social justice and leadership development, *Professional Development in Education*, 43 (1): 106–120.

Forrest, J., Lean, G. and Dunn, K. (2016) Challenging racism through schools: Teacher attitudes to cultural diversity and multicultural education in Sydney, Australia, *Race Ethnicity and Education*, 19 (3): 618–638.

Fox, A. (2021) *What are higher order (critical thinking) skills and approaches to developing them in HE and in schools?* Keynote Presentation to the 2-Day International

Virtual Workshop, Fatima Jinnah Women University, Rawalpindi, Pakistan, 19–20 January.

Fox, A. and Bird, T. (2017a) #any use? What do we know about how teachers and doctors learn through social media use?, *QWERTY – Open and Interdisciplinary Journal of Technology, Culture and Education*, 12 (2): 64–87.

Fox, A. and Bird, T. (2017b) The challenge to professionals of using social media: Teachers in England negotiating personal-professional identities, *Education and Information Technologies*, 22 (2): 647–675.

Fox, A. and McCormick, R. (2009) Events and professional learning: Studying educational practitioners, *Journal of Workplace Learning*, 21 (3): 198–218.

Fox, A. and Wilson, E. (2008) Viewing recently qualified teachers and their networks as a resource for a school, *Cambridge Journal of Education*, 12 (1): 97–99.

Fox, A. and Wilson, E. (2015) Networking and the development of professionals: ECTs building social capital, *Teaching and Teacher Education*, 47 (1): 93–107.

Fox, A., Sida-Nicholls, K. and Loe, R. (2021) Socio-mapping and the relational resilience of and for training teachers, in A. Fox, H. Busher and C. Capewell (eds.) *Thinking Critically and Ethically about Research for Education: Engaging with People's Voices for Self-empowerment*. London: Routledge (pp. 133–153).

Fox, D. (2021) Families praise Northumberland schools for going above and beyond during pandemic, *Northumberland Gazette*, 22 February [https://www.northumberlandgazette.co.uk/education/families-praise-northumberland-schools-for-going-above-and-beyond-during-pandemic-3142596].

Fox, R.K., Muccio, L.S., White, C.S. and Tian, J. (2015) Investigating advanced professional learning of early career and experienced teachers through program portfolios, *European Journal of Teacher Education*, 38 (2): 154–179.

Frost, D. (2006) The concept of 'agency' in leadership for learning, *Leading and Managing*, 12 (1): 19–28.

Frost, D. (2018) HertsCam: A teacher-led organisation to support teacher leadership, *International Journal of Teacher Leadership*, 9 (1): 79–100 [https://files.eric.ed.gov/fulltext/EJ1182712.pdf].

Frost, D., Ball, S., Hill, V. and Lightfoot, S. (eds.) (2018) *Teachers as Agents of Change*. Letchworth Garden City: HertsCam Network [https://www.hertscam.org.uk/uploads/2/5/9/7/25979128/green_e-book.pdf].

Fullan, M. (2007) *Leading in a Culture of Change*. Chicago, IL: Wiley.

Fuller, A and Unwin, A. (2004) Expansive learning environments: Integrating organisational and personal development, in A. Fuller, H. Rainbird and A. Munro (eds.) *Workplace Learning in Context*. London: Routledge (pp. 142–160).

Fuller, A., Unwin, L., Felstead, A., Jewson, N. and Kakavelakis, K. (2012) Creating and using knowledge: An analysis of the differentiated nature of workplace learning environments, in *The Knowledge Economy and Lifelong Learning*. Leiden: Brill Sense (pp. 191–206).

Furlong, J. (2015) *Teaching tomorrow's teachers: Options for the future of initial teacher education in Wales*. Oxford: University of Oxford [https://gov.wales/sites/default/files/publications/2018-03/teaching-tomorrow's-teachers.pdf].

Garcia, O. (2020) Singularity, complexities and contradictions: A commentary about translanguaging, social justice, and education, in J.A. Panagiotopoulou, L. Rosen and J. Strzykala (eds.) *Inclusion, Education and Translanguaging*. Wiesbaden: Springer (pp. 11–20).

Gardner, H., Clark, S., Mucinskas, D. and Magagna, S. (2019) *Harvard UWC Impact Study: Long methodology report*. Project Zero, Harvard University [https://drive.google.com/file/d/1_-Ll11cVIOe5FTQg362hPjmXfLAlCONJ/view?usp=sharing].

Garrison, D.R. (2009) Communities of inquiry in online learning, in *Encyclopaedia of Distance Learning*, 2nd edition. Hershey, PA: IGI Global (pp. 352–355).

Garrison, D.R., Anderson, T. and Archer, W. (2010) The first decade of the community of inquiry ramework: A retrospective, *Internet and Higher Education*, 13 (1): 5–9.

Gaved, M., Hanson, R. and Stutchbury, K. (2020) *Mobile offline networked learning for teacher Continuing Professional Development in Zambia*. Proceedings of mLearn2020: 19th World Conference on Mobile, Blended and Seamless Learning [http://oro.open.ac.uk/73404/1/Gaved-mLearn%202020-Extended%20Paper%20Submission-final.pdf].

Gay, G. (2013) Teaching to and through cultural diversity, *Curriculum Inquiry*, 43 (1): 48–70.

Gerde, H.K., Apol, L., Skibbe, L.E. and Bucyanna, C.M. (2020) Creating high-quality early childhood education in Rwanda: Teacher dispositions, child-centred play, and culturally relevant materials, *Early Child Development and Care*, 190 (15): 2437–2448.

Ghasia, M., Machumu, H. and Smet, E. (2019) Micro-credentials in higher education institutions: An exploratory study of its place in Tanzania, *International Journal of Education and Development using ICT*, 15 (1) [https://www.learntechlib.org/p/209746/].

Gibson, I., Clark, A., Dunnigan, H. and Cantali, D. (2021) Enabling positive change in primary school: Learner-led research in a Scottish context, *NASEN Journal: Support for Learning*, 37 (2): 278–295.

Gibson, S.E. and Brooks, C. (2012) Teachers' perspectives on the effectiveness of a locally planned professional development program for implementing new curriculum, *Teacher Development*, 16 (1): 1–23.

Giles, C. and Hargreaves, A. (2006) The sustainability of innovative schools as learning organizations and professional learning communities during standardized reform, *Educational Administration Quarterly*, 42 (1): 124–156.

Gill, E. (2021) 'They deserve a medal' – the teachers and schools praised by parents for support in pandemic, *Manchester Evening News*, 18 February [https://www.manchestereveningnews.co.uk/whats-on/family-kids-news/they-deserve-medal-teachers-schools-19847812].

Gillot, L. and Rose, P. (2018) Reversing the roles of teacher and student, in D. Frost (ed.) *Teachers as Agents of Change*. Letchworth Garden City: HertsCam Network (pp. 35–42) [https://www.hertscam.org.uk/uploads/2/5/9/7/25979128/green_e-book.pdf].

Godfrey, D., Seleznyov, S., Anders, J., Wollaston, W. and Barrera-Pedemonte, F. (2019) A developmental evaluation approach to lesson study: Exploring the impact of lesson study in London schools, *Professional Development in Education*, 45 (2): 325–340.

Goodwin, A.L. and Darity, K. (2019) Social justice teacher educators: What kind of knowing is needed?, *Journal of Education for Teaching*, 45 (1): 63–81.

Goodyear, V.A., Casey, A. and Kirk, D. (2014) Tweet me, message me, like me: Using social media to facilitate pedagogical change within an emerging community of practice, *Sport, Education and Society*, 19 (7): 927–943.

Gorard, S. and Smith, E. (2010) *Equity in Education: An International Comparison of Pupil Perspectives*. London: Palgrave.

Graff, N. (2011) An effective and agonizing way to learn: Backwards design and new teachers' preparation for planning curriculum, *Teacher Education Quarterly*, 38 (3): 151–168.

Gray, C. (2013) Bridging the teacher/researcher divide: Master's-level work in initial teacher education, *European Journal of Teacher Education*, 36 (1): 24–38.

Gregory, J. and Salmon, G. (2013) Professional development for online university teaching, *Distance Education*, 34 (3): 256–270.

Grint, K. (2008) Wicked problems and clumsy solutions: The role of leadership, *Clinical Leader*, 1 (2): 11–25.

Gronn, P. (2003) *The New Work of Educational Leaders*. London: Sage.

Groundwater-Smith, S. (2007) Student voice: Essential testimony for intelligent schools, in A. Campbell and S. Groundwater-Smith (eds.) *An Ethical Approach to Practitioner Research*. London: Routledge (pp. 129–144).

Groundwater-Smith, S. and Dodds, M. (2004) Critical practitioner inquiry: Towards professional communities of practice, in C. Day and J. Sachs (eds.) *International Handbook on the Continuing Professional Development of Teachers*. Milton Keynes: Open University Press (pp. 238–263).

Gunawardena, C.N. and McIsaac, M.S. (2004) Distance education, in D.H. Jonassen (ed.) *Handbook of Research in Educational Communications and Technology*, 2nd edition. Mahwah, NJ: Lawrence Erlbaum Associates (pp. 355–395).

Gurr, D. (2020) Educational leadership and the pandemic, *Academia Letters*, 29 [https://doi.org/10.20935/AL29].

Guskey, T.R. (2000) *Evaluating Professional Development*. Thousand Oaks, CA: Corwin Press.

Guskey, T.R. (2002) Does it make a difference? Evaluating professional development, *Educational Leadership*, 59 (6): 45–51.

Hadfield, M. and Jopling, M. (2016) Problematizing lesson study and its impacts: Studying a highly contextualised approach to professional learning, *Teaching and Teacher Education*, 60: 203–214.

Hagger, H. and McIntyre, D. (2006) *Learning Teaching from Teachers: Realising the Potential of School-based Teacher Education*. Maidenhead: Open University Press.

Haines, A. (2018) Dr Julian Tudor Hart – an appreciation, *Better Health For All* [blog post], 5 July [https://betterhealthforall.org/2018/07/05/dr-julian-tudor-hart-an-appreciation/].

Hallinger, P. (2016) Bringing context out of the shadows of leadership, *Educational Management, Administration and Leadership*, 46 (1): 5–24.

Hallinger, P. and Kulophas, D. (2019) The evolving knowledge base on leadership and teacher professional learning: A bibliometric analysis of the literature, 1960–2018, *Professional Development in Education*, 46 (4): 1–20.

Hammersley-Fletcher, L. and Lowe, M. (2006) Remodelling schools – experiences from within 'change teams', *Management in Education*, 20 (2): 16–19.

Hansford, B. and Ehrich, L.C. (2006) The principalship: How significant is mentoring?, *Journal of Educational Administration*, 44 (1): 36–52.

Hargreaves, A. (2000) Four ages of professionalism and professional learning, *Teachers and Teaching: Theory and Practice*, 6 (2): 151–182.

Hargreaves, A. (2019) Teacher collaboration: 30 years of research on its nature, forms, limitations and effects, *Teachers and Teaching: Theory and Practice*, 25 (5): 603–621.

Hargreaves, D.H. (2003) *Education Epidemic: Transforming Secondary Schools through Innovation Networks*. London: Demos [https://www.demos.co.uk/files/educationepidemic.pdf].

Hargreaves, D.H. (2014) A self-improving school system and its potential for reducing inequality, *Oxford Review of Education*, 40 (6): 696–714.

Hargreaves, D.H. (2019) *Beyond Schooling: An Anarchist Challenge*. London: Routledge.

Harjanto, I., Lie, A., Wihardini, D., Pryor, L. and Wilson, M. (2018) Community-based teacher professional development in remote areas in Indonesia, *Journal of Education for Teaching*, 44 (2): 212–231.

Harkness, S., Super, C.M., Barry, O., Zeitlin, M. and Long, J. (2009) Assessing the environment of children's learning: The developmental niche in Africa, in E.L Grigorenko (ed.) *Multicultural Psychoeducational Assessment*. Dordrecht: Springer (pp. 133–155).

Harmey, S. and Moss, G. (2020) *Learning loss versus learning disruption: Written evidence submitted by the International Literary Centre, UCL, Institute of Education to the Education Select Committee Inquiry into the impact of COVID-19 on education and children's services*, July. London: Institute of Education [https://discovery.ucl.ac.uk/id/eprint/10111094/].

Harris, A. and Jones, M. (2017) Leading educational change and improvement at-scale: Some inconvenient truths about system performance, *International Journal of Leadership in Education*, 20 (5): 632–641.

Harris, A. and Jones, M. (2020) COVID 19 – school leadership in disruptive times, *School Leadership and Management*, 40 (4): 243–247.

Harrison, C. (2005) Teachers developing assessment for learning: Mapping teacher change, *Teacher Development*, 9 (2): 255–264.

Hartshorne, R., Baumgartner, E., Kaplan-Rawoski, R., Mouza, C. and Ferdig, R.E. (2020) Special issue editorial: Preservice and inservice professional development during the COVID-19 pandemic, *Journal of Technology and Teacher Education*, 28 (2): 137–147.

Hendry, H. (2008) *'What if they don't understand?' A study of Primary PGCE trainees' developing pedagogy for children learning English as an additional language*. Unpublished Master's dissertation, Bishops Grosseteste University.

Hendry, H. (2016) *Becoming a teacher of early reading: An activity systems analysis of the journey from student to newly qualified teacher*. Doctoral dissertation, University of Leicester [https://ethos.bl.uk/OrderDetails.do?did=1&uin=uk.bl.ethos.696132].

Hendry, H. (2020) Becoming a teacher of early reading: Charting the knowledge and practices of pre-service and newly qualified teachers, *Literacy*, 54 (1): 58–69.

Her Majesty's Government (2010) *The Equality Act*. London: HMSO.

Herman, J., Osmundson, E., Dai, Y., Ringstaff, C. and Timms, M. (2015) Investigating the dynamics of formative assessment: Relationships between teacher knowledge, assessment practice and learning, *Assessment in Education: Principles, Policy and Practice*, 22 (3): 1–24.

Hill, M.F. (2011) 'Getting traction': Enablers and barriers to implementing Assessment for Learning in secondary schools, *Assessment in Education: Principles, Policy and Practice*, 18 (4): 347–364.

Hoare, L. (2012) Transnational student voices: Reflections on a second chance, *Journal of Studies in International Education*, 16 (3): 271–286.

Hobson, A. and Malderez, A. (2013) Judgementoring and other threats to realising the potential of school-based mentoring in teacher education, *International Journal of Mentoring and Coaching in Education*, 2 (2): 89–108.

Hobson, A.J., Giannakaki, M.-S. and Chambers, G.N. (2009) Who withdraws from initial teacher preparation programmes and why?, *Educational Research*, 51 (3): 321–340.

Hodson, E., Smith, K. and Brown, T. (2012) Reasserting theory in professionally based initial teacher education, *Teachers and Teaching: Theory and Practice*, 18 (2): 181–195.

Hofmann, R., Vrikki, M. and Evagorou, M. (2021) Engaging teachers in dialogic teaching as a way to promote cultural literacy learning: A reflection on teacher professional development, in F. Maine and M. Vrikki (eds.) *Dialogue for Intercultural Understanding: Placing Cultural Literacy at the Heart of Learning*. Cham: Springer (pp. 135–148).

Holmberg, B. (2005) *Theory and Practice of Distance Education*. London: Routledge.

Howard-Jones, P. (2014) Neuroscience and education: Myths and messages, *Nature*, 15: 817–824.

Hoy, W.K., Tarter, C.J. and Woolfolk Hoy, A. (2006) Academic optimism of schools: A force for student achievement, *American Educational Research Journal*, 43 (3): 425–446.

Hughes, G.D. (2012) Teacher retention: Teacher characteristics, school characteristics, organizational characteristics, and teacher efficacy, *Journal of Educational Research*, 105 (4): 245–255.

Hultberg, P., Calonge, D.S. and Kim, S.H. (2017) Education policy in South Korea: A contemporary model of human capital accumulation?, *Cogent Economics and Finance*, 5 (1): 1389804 [https://www.tandfonline.com/doi/full/10.1080/23322039.2017.1389804].

Institute for Fiscal Studies (IFS) (2018) *Improving ECD in rural Ghana: Baseline report*. IFS Idela-network.org [https://idela-network.org/wp-content/uploads/2018/08/Improving-ECD-in-rural-Ghana_Baseline-Report_IFS.pdf].

Institute for Fiscal Studies (2019) *Childcare and early years*. London: IFS [https://election2019.ifs.org.uk/childcare-and-early-years].

Isaacs, S., Roberts, N., Spencer-Smith, G. and Brink, S. (2019) Learning through play in Grade R classrooms: Measuring practitioners' confidence, knowledge and practice, *South African Journal of Childhood Education*, 9 (1): a704 [https://files.eric.ed.gov/fulltext/EJ1217481.pdf].

Iwaniec-Thompson, G. (2022) The identity trajectories of older academics: Workplace affordances and individual subjectivities, in B. Rienties (ed.) *Open World Learning*. London: Routledge.

Izadinia, M. (2016) Student teachers' and mentor teachers' perceptions and expectations of a mentoring relationship: Do they match or clash?, *Professional Development in Education*, 42 (3): 387–402.

Jackson, D. (2016) Re-conceptualising graduate employability: The importance of pre-professional identity, *Higher Education Research and Development*, 35 (5): 925–939.

Jackson, D. and Temperley, J. (2007) *From professional learning community to networked learning community. Professional learning communities: Divergence, depth and dilemmas*, London: Innovation Unit [http://www.innovationunit.org/wp-content/uploads/2017/04/From-professional-learning-community-to-networked-learning-community.pdf].

James, M.E. (2013) *Educational Assessment, Evaluation and Research: The Selected Works of Mary E. James*. London: Routledge.

James, M.E., Black, P., Carmichael, P., Conner, C., Dudley, P., Fox, A. et al. (2006) *Learning How to Learn: Tools for Schools*. TLRP Improving Practice Series, London: Routledge.

James, M.E., Black, P., Carmichael, P., Drummond, M.-J., Fox, A., Honour, L. et al. (2007) *Improving Learning How to Learn in Classrooms, Schools and Networks*. London: Routledge Falmer.

Jewitt, K. (2021) Key themes emerging from the qualitative pilot study, *Leading School Learning through Covid-19*, 30 April [https://www.open.ac.uk/projects/leading-online-learning/news/key-themes-emerging-qualitative-pilot-study].

Joiner, S. and Edwards, J. (2008) Novice teachers: Where are they going and why don't they stay?, *Journal of Cross-Disciplinary Perspectives in Education*, 1 (1): 36–43.

Jones, K. (2011) Central, local and individual continuing professional development (CPD) priorities: Changing policies of CPD in Wales, *Professional Development in Education*, 37 (5): 759–776.

J-PAL (2017–2018) *The effects of a play-based preschool learning program in rural Ghana* [https://www.povertyactionlab.org/evaluation/effects-play-based-preschool-learning-program-rural-ghana].

Kabay, S., Wolf, S. and Yoshikawa, H. (2017) 'So that his mind will open': Parental perceptions of early childhood education in Ghana, *International Journal of Educational
Development*, 57 (1): 44–53.

Kane, R.G. and Francis, A. (2013) Preparing teachers for professional learning: Is there a
future for teacher education in new teacher induction?, *Teacher Development*, 17 (3):
362–379.

Katz, S. and Earl, L. (2010) Learning about networked learning communities, *School
Effectiveness and School Improvement*, 21 (1): 27–51.

Keisu, B. and Ahlström, B. (2020) The silent voices: Pupil participation for gender equality and diversity, *Educational Research*, 62 (1): 1–17.

Kellett, M. (2005) *Children as active researchers: A new research paradigm for the 21st
century?* London: ESRC.

Kellett, M. (2011) Empowering children and young people as researchers: Overcoming
barriers and building capacity, *Child Indicators Research*, 4 (2): 205–219.

Kirkland, D.E. (2014) 'They look scared': Moving from service learning to learning to
serve in teacher education – a social justice perspective, *Equity and Excellence in
Education*, 47 (4): 580–603.

Kohli, R., Pizarro, M., Garcia, L.G., Kelly, L., Espinoza, M. and Cordova, J. (2021) Critical
professional development and the racial justice leadership possibilities of teachers of
colour in K-12 schools, *Professional Development in Education*, 47 (1): 89–101.

Kontopoulou, K. (2019) *Pre-service teachers' use of social media for academic purposes.*
Doctoral dissertation, University of Leicester [https://ethos.bl.uk/OrderDetails.
do?uin=uk.bl.ethos.778389].

Kulophas, D. and Hallinger, P. (2020) Leadership that matters: Creating cultures of academic optimism that support teacher learning in Thailand, *Journal of Educational
Administration*, 58 (6): 605–627.

Kwauk, C. (2021) *Why is girls' education important for climate action?* Brookings Institution [https://www.brookings.edu/blog/education-plus-development/2021/02/10/why-is-
girls-education-important-for-climate-action/].

Larssen, D.L.S., Cajkler, W., Mosvold, R., Bjuland, R., Helgevold, N., Fauskanger, J. et al.
(2018) A literature review of lesson study in initial teacher education, *International
Journal for Lesson and Learning Studies*, 7 (1): 8–22.

Lave, J. and Wenger, E. (1991) *Situated Learning: Legitimate Peripheral Participation.*
Cambridge: Cambridge University Press.

Law, P. (2015) Digital badging at The Open University: Recognition for informal learning,
Open Learning: The Journal of Open, Distance and e-Learning, 30 (3): 221–234.

Law, P. (2021) *Exploring the potential of micro-credentials and digital badging: Digital
credentials and free learning at the Open University.* Glasgow: Quality Assurance
Agency for Higher Education [https://www.enhancementthemes.ac.uk/docs/ethemes/
resilient-learning-communities/exploring-the-potential-of-micro-credentials-and-
digital-badging-digital-credentials-and-free-learning-at-the-open-university.pdf?
sfvrsn=30ccd881_6].

Le Cornu, R. (2013) Building early career teacher resilience: The role of relationships,
Australian Journal of Teacher Education, 38 (4): 1–16 [https://files.eric.ed.gov/
fulltext/EJ1013933.pdf].

Lee, C. and Wiliam, D. (2005) Studying changes in the practice of two teachers developing assessment for learning, *Teacher Development*, 9 (2): 265–283.

Lee, M. and Kim, J. (2016) The emerging landscape of school-based professional learning
communities in South Korean schools, *Asia Pacific Journal of Education*, 36 (2):
266–284.

Lee, Y.M., Holm, K., Florez, E., Glauser, M. and Haswell, E. (2013) The DNP: Knowledge and perceptions of students in an accelerated master's program in nursing, *Open Journal of Nursing*, 3 (1): 138–146.

Lieberman, A. (2007) Professional learning communities: A reflection, in L. Stoll and K.S. Lewis (eds.) *Professional Learning Communities: Divergence, Depth and Dilemmas*. Maidenhead: Open University Press (pp. 199–203).

Lieberman, A. and Miller, A. (2008) *Teachers in Professional Communities: Improving Teaching and Learning*, Columbia, OH: Teachers College Press.

Lisle-Johnson, T. and Kohli, R. (2020) Critical Black women educators: Resisting the racial and ideological marginality of K-12 teaching through critical professional development, *Theory into Practice*, 59 (4): 348–357.

Lister, K., Seale, J. and Douce, C. (2021) Mental health in distance learning: A taxonomy of barriers and enablers to student mental wellbeing, *Open Learning: The Journal of Open, Distance and e-Learning* [https://www.tandfonline.com/doi/full/10.1080/02680513.2021.1899907].

Lofthouse, R.M. (2018) Re-imagining mentoring as a dynamic hub in the transformation of initial teacher education, *International Journal of Mentoring and Coaching in Education*, 7 (3): 248–260.

Luehmann, A.L. and Tinelli, L. (2008) Teacher professional identity development with social networking technologies: Learning reform through blogging, *Educational Media International*, 45 (4): 323–333.

Lutomia, A.N., Sibeyo, D. and Lutomia, N.I. (2018) *Bulala* as an Ubuntu-inspired approach to enhancing organizational culture in rural Kenya, *Journal of Pan African Studies*, 11 (4): 102–120.

Lynch, R., Hennessy, J. and Gleeson, J. (2013) Acknowledging teacher professionalism in Ireland: The case for a Chartered Teacher initiative, *Irish Educational Studies*, 32 (4): 493–510.

Lyon, E.G. (2013) Conceptualizing and exemplifying science teachers' assessment expertise, *International Journal of Science Education*, 35 (7): 1208–1229.

Maaranen, K. (2009) Practitioner research as part of professional development in initial teacher education, *Teacher Development*, 13 (3): 219–237.

MacGilchrist, B., Reed, J. and Myers, K. (2004) *The Intelligent School*. London: Sage.

Maine, F., Cook, V. and Lähdesmäki, T. (2019) Reconceptualizing cultural literacy as a dialogic practice, *London Review of Education*, 17 (3): 384–393.

Mansfield, K.C. (2014) How listening to student voices informs and strengthens social justice research and practice, *Educational Administration Quarterly*, 50 (3): 392–430.

Marshall, B. and Drummond, M.-J. (2006) How teachers engage with Assessment for Learning: Lessons from the classroom, *Research Papers in Education*, 21 (2): 133–149.

Masood, F. and Behlol, M.G. (2017) Learning and practicing of innovative pedagogical skills of prospective teachers in teaching practicum at B.ED (Hons) elementary program, *Journal of Managerial Sciences*, 11 (3): 237–251.

Matias, C.E. (2016) 'Why do you make me hate myself?': Re-teaching Whiteness, abuse, and love in urban teacher education, *Teaching Education*, 27 (2): 194–211.

McCormick. R. (2010) The state of the nation in CPD: A literature review, *The Curriculum Journal*, 21: 395–412.

McCormick, R. and Mathew, R. (2019) Research, Monitoring and Evaluation (RME): Foundational cornerstone or luxury addition?, in I. Eyres, R. McCormick and T. Power (eds.) *Sustainable English Language Teacher Development at Scale: Lessons from Bangladesh*. London: Bloomsbury Academic (pp. 158–170).

McCormick, R., Banks, F., Morgan, B., Opfer, V.D., Pedder, D., Storey, A. et al. (2008) *Schools and continuing professional development in England – State of the Nation research study*. Report T34718. London: Training and Development Agency for Schools.

McGill, I. and Brockband, A. (2004) *The Action Learning Handbook*. London: Routledge Falmer.

McLaughlin, C. and Black-Hawkins, K. (2007) School–university partnerships for educational research: Understandings, models and complexities, *Journal of In-Service Education*, 30 (2): 265–284.

McLaughlin, C., Black-Hawkins, K. and McIntyre, D. (2004) *Researching teachers, researching schools, researching networks: A review of the literature*. Cambridge: University of Cambridge [https://www.educ.cam.ac.uk/research/programmes/super/ReviewOfLiterature.pdf].

McLaughlin, C., Black-Hawkins, K., McIntyre, D. and Townsend, A. (2007) *Networking Practitioner Research*. London: Routledge.

Mellom, P., Straubhaar, R., Balderas, C., Ariail, M. and Portes, P. (2018) They come with nothing, *Teaching and Teacher Education*, 71 (1): 91–107.

Menashy, F. and Zakharia, Z. (2020) Private engagement in refugee education and the promise of digital humanitarianism, *Oxford Review of Education*, 46 (3): 313–330.

Ministry of Human Resource Development (MHRD) (2020) *New Education Policy*. New Delhi: MHRD, Government of India.

Moloi, K.C. (2010) How can schools build learning organisations in difficult education contexts?, *South African Journal of Education*, 30 (4): 621–633.

Montacute, R. and Cullinane, C. (2021) *Learning in Lockdown*. Research Brief, Sutton Trust [https://www.suttontrust.com/our-research/learning-in-lockdown/].

Morris, A.K. and Hiebert, J. (2011) Creating shared instructional products: An alternative approach to improving teaching, *Educational Researcher*, 40 (1): 5–14.

Moss, G. (2009) The politics of literacy in the context of large-scale education reform, *Research Papers in Education*, 24 (2): 155–174.

Moss, G. (2013) Research, policy and knowledge flows in education: What counts in knowledge mobilisation?, *Contemporary Social Science*, 8 (3): 237–248.

Moss, G., Allen, R., Bradbury, A., Duncan, S., Harmey, S. and Levy, R. (2020) *Primary teachers' experience of the COVID-19 lockdown – eight key messages for policymakers going forward*. London: Institute of Education [https://discovery.ucl.ac.uk/id/eprint/10103669/1/Moss_DCDT%20Report%201%20Final.pdf].

Müller, L.-M. and Goldenberg, G. (2020) *Education in times of crisis: The potential implications of school closures for teachers and students*. London: Chartered College of Teaching, May [https://chartered.college/education-in-times-of-crisis-the-potential-implications-of-school-closures-for-teachers-and-students/].

Musgrave, J. and Payler, J. (2021) Proposing a model for promoting children's health in early childhood education and care settings, *Children and Society*, 35 (5): 766–783 [https://onlinelibrary.wiley.com/doi/full/10.1111/chso.12449].

Mutton, T., Burn, K. and Hagger, H. (2010) Making sense of learning to teach: Learners in context, *Research Papers in Education*, 25 (1): 73–91.

National Assembly for Wales (2017) *Report on the Teachers' Professional Learning and Education Inquiry*. Cardiff: Children, Young People and Education Committee, National Assembly for Wales Commission [https://senedd.wales/laid%20documents/cr-ld11338/cr-ld11338-e.pdf].

National Council for Educational Research and Training (NCERT) (2005) *National Curriculum Framework*. New Delhi: NCERT [https://ncert.nic.in/pdf/nc-framework/nf2005-english.pdf].

National Council for Teacher Education (NCTE) (2009) *National Curriculum Framework for Teacher Education: Preparing the humane teacher*. New Delhi: NCTE.

Nazarbayev Intellectual Schools (2012) *Handbook for Teacher In-service Training Programme for the Pedagogic Staff of the Republic of Kazakhstan*, 3rd edition. Astana: Nazarbayev Intellectual Schools, Center of Excellence Press.

Ncube, L.B. (2010) Ubuntu: A transformative leadership philosophy, *Journal of Leadership Studies*, 4 (3): 77–82.

Nelson, R., Spence-Thomas, K. and Taylor, C. (2015) *What makes great pedagogy and great professional development. Final report: Teaching schools R&D network national themes projects 2012–14* [https://core.ac.uk/download/pdf/74377321.pdf].

Newmann, F.M., King, M.B. and Youngs, P. (2000) PD that addresses school capacity: Lessons from urban elementary schools, *American Journal of Education*, 108 (4): 259–299.

Ng'asike, J.T. (2014) African early childhood development curriculum and pedagogy for Turkana nomadic pastoralist communities of Kenya, in R. Serpell and K. Marfo (eds.) Child Development in Africa: Views from inside, *New Directions for Child and Adolescent Development*, 146: 43–60.

Ng'asike, J.T. (2019) Indigenous knowledge practices for sustainable lifelong education in pastoralist communities of Kenya, *International Review of Education*, 65: 19–46.

Nicholson, J.M. and Kroll, L. (2015) Developing leadership for early childhood professionals through oral inquiry: Strengthening equity through making particulars visible in dilemmas of practice, *Early Child Development and Care*, 185 (1): 17–43.

Nishimura, T. (2014) Effective PD of teachers: A guide to actualizing inclusive schooling, *International Journal of Whole Schooling*, 10 (1): 19–42.

Nsamenang, A.B. (2009) Conceptualizing developmental assessment within Africa's cultural setting, in E.L. Grigorenko (ed.) *Multicultural Psychoeducational Assessment*. Dordrecht: Springer (pp. 95–131).

Nuttman-Schwartz, O. (2017) Rethinking professional identity in a globalized world, *Clinical Social Work Journal*, 45: 1–9.

Oates, L. and Hashimi, J. (2016) Localizing OER in Afghanistan: Developing a multilingual digital library for Afghan teachers, *Open Praxis*, 8 (2): 151–161.

O'Connor, P. and Takahashi, N. (2014) From caring *about* to caring *for*: Case studies of New Zealand and Japanese schools post disaster, *Pastoral Care in Education*, 32 (1): 42–53.

Oddy, J. (2021) Why equity-based thinking is key to decolonising education in emergencies [blog post], 3 February [https://medium.com/@jlojlo/why-equity-based-design-thinking-is-key-todecolonising-education-in-emergencies-82cb5b2ebea].

OECD (Organisation for Economic Cooperation and Development) (2014) *Improving schools in Wales*. Paris: OECD [https://www.oecd.org/education/policyreviewswales.htm].

OECD (Organisation for Economic Cooperation and Development) (2016) *Supporting teacher professionalism – Insights from TALIS 2013*. Paris: OECD [https://www.oecd.org/publications/supporting-teacher-professionalism-9789264248601-en.htm].

OECD (Organisation for Economic Cooperation and Development) (2021) *The state of school education 18 months into the pandemic* [https://www.oecd.org/education/state-of-school-education-one-year-into-COVID.htm].

OECD/CERI (Organisation for Economic Cooperation and Development/Centre for Educational Research and Innovation) (2008) *Learning in the 21st Century: Research, Innovation and Policy*. International Conference, 15–16 May [http://www.oecd.org/edu/ceri/oecdceriinternationalconferencelearningin the21stcenturyr esearchinnovationandpolicy15–16may2008.htm].

Olsen, B., Hannahan, P. and Arica, G.P.E. (2021) How do government decisionmakers identify and adopt innovations for scale? [blog post], 13 May [https://www.globalpartnership.org/blog/how-do-government-decisionmakers-identify-and-adopt-innovations-scale].

O'Grady, G. (2004) *Holistic assessment and problem based learning*. Oral presentation to the 5th Asia-Pacific Conference on PBL, 16–17 March [http://www.myrp.sg/ced/research/papers/holistic_assessment_and_pbl.pdf].

OpenLearn (2020) *Take your teaching online*. Free OpenLearn course [https://www.open.edu/openlearn/education-development/learning/how-can-you-take-your-teaching-online].

Opfer, V. and Pedder, D. (2010) Benefits, status and effectiveness of Continuous Professional Development for teachers in England, *The Curriculum Journal*, 21 (4): 413–431.

Opfer, V. and Pedder, D. (2011) The lost promise of teacher professional development in England, *European Journal of Teacher Education*, 34 (1): 3–24.

Outhwaite, D. (2021) England's teaching school 'super-hub' policy: Policy meets practice [blog post], *BERA blog*, 10 March [https://www.bera.ac.uk/blog/englands-teaching-school-super-hub-policy-policy-meets-practice].

Ovenden-Hope, T. and Passy, R. (2021) *Exploring Teacher Recruitment and Retention: Contextual Challenges from International Perspectives*. London: Routledge.

Padilla Rodriguez, B.C. (2014) *Instructional interactions and online course effectiveness at a large Mexican organisation*. Doctoral thesis, University of Leicester.

Panagiotopoulou, J.A. and Hammel, M.J. (2020) 'What shall we sing now, Amir?': Developing a voice through translanguaging pedagogy – an ethnographic research and professional training project in day-care centers and schools, in J.A. Panagiotopoulou, L. Rosen and J. Strzykala (eds.) *Inclusion, Education and Translanguaging: How to Promote Social Justice in (Teacher) Education*. Wiesbaden: Springer (pp. 203–218) [https://library.oapen.org/viewer/web/viewer.html?file=/bitstream/handle/20.500.12657/41724/2020_Book_InclusionEducationAndTranslang.pdf?sequence=1&isAllowed=y].

Pantić, N. and Florian, L. (2015) Developing teachers as agents of inclusion and social justice, *Education Inquiry*, 6 (3): 27311 [https://www.tandfonline.com/doi/full/10.3402/edui.v6.27311].

Papanastasiou, N. (2017) The practice of scalecraft: Scale, policy and the politics of the market in England's academy schools, *Environment and Planning A*, 49 (5): 1060–1079.

Papathoma, T. (2019) *MOOC educators: Who they are and how they learn*. Doctoral thesis, The Open University.

Pardales, M.J. and Girod, M. (2006) Community of inquiry: Its past and present future, *Educational Philosophy and Theory*, 38 (3): 299–309.

Parkin, D. and Brown G. (2020) *Creating socially distanced campuses and the HE Project*. Final Capstone Report [https://www.usaf.ac.za/wp-content/uploads/2020/07/Advance-HE_Social-Distance-Project_Final-Report_July-2020.pdf].

Parsons, S.A., Hutchinson, A.C., Hall, L.A., Parsons, A.W., Ives, S.T. and Leggett, A.B. (2019) U.S. teachers' perceptions of online professional development, *Teaching and Teacher Education*, 82 (1): 33–42.

Paul, R. and Tait, A. (2019) Editorial: Open universities: Past, present and future, *International Review of Research in Open and Distributed Learning*, 20 (4): i–viii.

Pazey, B.L. and Cole, H.A. (2013) The role of special education training in the development of socially just leaders, *Educational Administration Quarterly*, 49 (2): 243–271.

Pearce, S. (2014) Dealing with racist incidents: What do beginning teachers learn from schools?, *Race, Ethnicity and Education*, 17 (3): 388–406.

Pearson, E., Hendry, H., Rao, N., Aboud, F., Horton, C., Siraj, I. et al. (2017) *Reaching expert consensus on training different cadres in delivering early childhood development*. Technical Report. London: Department for International Development [https://www.gov.uk/research-for-development-outputs/reaching-expert-consensus-on-training-different-cadres-in-delivering-early-childhood-development].

Pedder, D. and Opfer, V.D. (2013) Professional learning orientations: Patterns of dissonance and alignment between teachers' values and practices, *Research Papers in Education*, 28 (5): 539–570.

Pence, A. and Benner, A. (2015) *Complexities, capacities, communities: Changing development narratives in early childhood education, care and development*. Victoria, BC: University of Victoria [https://dspace.library.uvic.ca:8443/handle/1828/7069].

Pence, A., Anglin, J. and Hunt-Jinnouchi, F. (2010) Institutional engagement with Indigenous communities: The First Nations Partnership Program and the use of a borderland space, *Ngoonjook: A Journal of Australian and Indigenous Issues*, 34 (1): 57–71.

Petersen, N. and Henning, E. (2018) Service learning and the practice of social justice and care, *Journal of Human Behavior in the Social Environment*, 28 (4): 436–448.

Petrie, C. (2020) *Spotlight: Quality education for all during COVID-19 crisis*. HundrED Research Report, April [https://hundred-cdn.s3.amazonaws.com/uploads/report/file/15/hundred_spotlight_covid-19_digital.pdf].

Philipsen, B., Tondeur, J., Roblin, N.P., Vanslambrouck, S. and Zhu, C. (2019) Improving teacher professional development for online and blended learning: A systematic meta-aggregative review, *Educational Technology Research and Development*, 67 (5): 1145–1174.

Phillipson, R. (1997) Realities and myths of linguistic imperialism, *Journal of Multilingual and Multicultural Development*, 18 (3): 238–248.

PIECCE (2020) *Overview: PIECCE programme framework and illustrative packs*, January [https://piecce.co.za/wp-content/uploads/2020/02/programme-framework-overview-product.pdf].

Pike, A. (2009) *Developing on line communities to support distance learning in secure environments*. 7th International Conference on Education and Information Systems, Technologies and Applications: EISTA 2009, Orlando, FL, 10–13 July [http://oro.open.ac.uk/24175/1/A-Pike-Developing_online_communities_to_support_DL_in_secure_environments.pdf].

Poekert, P.E., Swaffield, S., Demir, E.K. and Wright, S.A. (2020) Leadership for professional learning towards educational equity: A systematic literature review, *Professional Development in Education*, 46 (4): 541–562.

Porter, A.C. (2004) *Curriculum assessment*. Additional SCALE Research Publications and Products. Nashville, TN: Vanderbilt University.

Poultney, V. (2020) School–university partnerships: Contexts for inquiry, in A. Fox and V. Poultney (eds.) *Professional Learning Communities and Teacher Enquiry: Evidence-based Teaching for Enquiring Teachers*. St. Albans: Critical Publishing (pp. 29–42).

Power, T., McCormick, R. and Asbeek-Brusse, E. (2017) *A quasi-experimental study of the classroom practices of English language teachers and the English language proficiency of students, in primary and secondary schools in Bangladesh*. Dhaka, Bangladesh: English in Action (EIA) [http://oro.open.ac.uk/57059/].

Price-Kelly, H. (2020) *The scaling playbook: A practical guide for researchers*, Ottawa: International Development Research Centre [https://idl-bnc-idrc.dspacedirect.org/bitstream/handle/10625/58780/IDL-58780.pdf].

Quan-Baffour, K.P. and Romm, N.R.A. (2014) Ubuntu-inspired training of adult literacy teachers as a route to generating 'community' enterprises, *Journal of Literacy Research*, 46 (4): 455–474.

Ratnam-Lim, C.T.L. and Tan, K.H.K. (2015) Large-scale implementation of formative assessment practices in an examination-oriented culture, *Assessment in Education: Principles, policy and Practice*, 22 (1): 61–78 [https://www.researchgate.net/publication/271774029_Large-scale_implementation_of_formative_assessment_practices_in_an_examination-oriented_culture].

Ravitch, D. (2015) Are scripted lessons in for-profit schools 'an audacious answer' for poor kids in Africa and Asia? [blog post], *Diane Ravitch's blog*, 3 August [https://dianeravitch.net/2015/08/03/are-scripted-lessons-in-for-profit-school-an-audacious-answer-for-poor-kids-in-africa-and-asia/].

Reid, K. (2011a) The professional development needs of staff in Wales on behaviour management and attendance: Findings from the NBAR report, *Educational Studies*, 37 (1): 15–30.

Reid, K. (2011b) Tackling behaviour and attendance issues in schools in Wales: Implications for training and professional development, *Educational Studies*, 37 (1): 31–48.

Reid, K., Smith, R., Powell, R., Reakes, A. and Jones, G. (2007) An evaluation of the effectiveness of the education welfare service in Wales, *Research in Education*, 77 (1): 108–128.

Reid, K., Challoner, C., Lancett, A., Jones, G., Rhysiart, G.A. and Challoner, S. (2010) The views of primary pupils on school attendance at Key Stage 2 in Wales, *Educational Studies*, 36 (5): 465–479.

Research for Equitable Access and Learning Centre/Education SubSahara Africa (REAL/ESSA) (n.d.) *African Education Research Database* [https://essa-africa.org/AERD].

Rix, J., Parry, J. and Malibha-Pinchbeck, M. (2020) 'Building a better picture': Practitioners' views of using a listening approach with young disabled children, *Journal of Early Childhood Research*, 18 (1): 3–17.

Robertson, H.C. and Brott, P.E. (2013) Male veterans' perceptions of midlife career transition and life satisfaction: A study of military men transitioning to the teaching profession, *Adultspan Journal*, 12 (2): 66–79.

Rod, Dr (2008) The 5Rs of lifelong learning [blog post], *Dr Rod's English's Blog Post*, 16 March [https://drrodenglish.blogspot.com/2008/03/5rs-of-lifelong-learning.html].

Rooney, K. (2018) *Scripted lessons are creating zombie teachers*, *Teachwire.net*, 11 June [https://www.teachwire.net/news/scripted-lessons-are-creating-zombie-teachers].

Rowan, L., Bourke, T., L'Estrange, L., Lunn Brownlee, J., Ryan, M., Walker, S. et al. (2021) How does initial teacher education research frame the challenge of preparing future teachers for student diversity in schools? A systematic review of literature, *Review of Educational Research*, 91 (1): 112–158.

RSA (2010) *Area-based curriculum, engaging the local* [https://www.thersa.org/reports/area-based-curriculum-engaging-the-local].

Rubin, M., Cohen Konrad, S., Nimmagadda, J., Scheyett, A. and Dunn, K. (2018) Social work and interprofessional education: Integration, intersectionality, and institutional leadership, *Social Work Education*, 37 (1): 17–33.

Rudduck, J. (1988) Changing the world of the classroom by understanding it: A review of some aspects of the work of Lawrence Stenhouse, *Journal of Curriculum and Supervision*, 4 (1): 30–42.

Runhare, T. and Gordon, R. (2004) *The comprehensive review of gender issues in the education sector*. UNICEF/MoESC [https://www.unicef.org/evaldatabase/files/Gender_Review_REPORT_final.pdf.pdf].

Rutherford, C. (2013) Facebook as a source of informal teacher professional development, *E in Education*, 16 (1): 60–74 [https://ourspace.uregina.ca/handle/10294/3101].

Sachs, J. (2000) The activist professional, *Journal of Educational Change*, 1 (1): 77–94.

Sachs, J. (2016) Teacher professionalism: Why are we still talking about it?, *Teachers and Teaching: Theory and Practice*, 22 (4): 413–425.

Sahlberg, P. (2021) *Finnish Lessons 3.00: What Can the World Learn from Educational Change in Finland?*, 3rd edition. New York: Teachers College Press.

Saito, E. (2012) Key issues of lesson study in Japan and the United States: A literature review, *Professional Development in Education*, 38 (5): 777–789.

Salimzadeh, R., Saroyan, A. and Hall, N.C. (2017) Examining the factors impacting academics' psychological well-being: A review of research, *International Education Research*, 5 (1): 13–44 [https://www.researchgate.net/publication/322523679_Examining_the_Factors_Impacting_Academics%27_Psychological_Well-Being_A_Review_of_Research].

Sancar, R., Atal, D. and Deryakulu, D. (2021) A new framework for teachers' professional development, *Teaching and Teacher Education*, 101: 103305.

Saykili, A. (2018) Distance education: Definitions, generations and key concepts and future directions, *International Journal of Contemporary Educational Research*, 5 (1): 2–17.

Schilling, E. (2012) Non-linear careers: Desirability and coping, *Equality, Diversity and Inclusion International Journal*, 31 (8): 725–740 https://doi.org/10.1108/02610151211277590].

Schleicher, A. (2019) *PISA 2018: Insights and interpretations*. Paris: OECD [https://www.oecd.org/pisa/PISA%202018%20Insights%20and%20Interpretations%20FINAL%20PDF.pdf].

Schön, D.A. (1983) *The Reflective Practitioner*. New York: Basic Books.

Schön, D.A. (1987) *Educating the Reflective Practitioner: Toward a New Design for Teaching and Learning in the Professions*. San Francisco, CA: Jossey-Bass.

Sebba, J., Kent, P. and Tregenza, J. (2012) *Joint practice development: What does the evidence suggest are effective approaches*. Nottingham: National College of School Leadership (NCSL) [https://assets.publishing.service.gov.uk/government/uploads/system/uploads/attachment_data/file/335729/jpd-what-does-the-evidence-suggest-are-effective-approaches-long.pdf].

Senge, P.M. (1995) *Learning Organizations*. Cambridge: Gilmour Drummond Publishing.

Sengupta, E., Reshef, S. and Blessinger, P. (2019) Creating a borderless world of education for refugees, in E. Sengupta and P. Blessinger (eds.) *Language, Teaching, and Pedagogy for Refugee Education*. Bingley: Emerald Publishing (pp. 181–191).

Shanafelt, T., Ripp, J. and Trockel, M. (2020) Understanding and addressing sources of anxiety among health care professionals during the COVID-19 pandemic, *Journal of the American Medical Association*, 323 (21): 2133–2134.

Shanks, R. and Carver, M. (2021) New teachers' responses to Covid-19: Getting by or getting ahead? [blog post], *BERA blog*, 27 April [https://www.bera.ac.uk/blog/new-teachers-responses-to-covid-19-getting-by-or-getting-ahead].

Shepard, L.A. (2000) The role of assessment in a learning culture, *Educational Researcher*, 29 (7): 4–14.

Sherrington, T. and Caviglioli, O. (2020) *Teaching WalkThrus: Five-Step Guides to Instructional Coaching*, Woodbridge: John Catt Educational.

Sherrington, T. and Caviglioli, O. (2021) *Teaching WalkThrus 2: Five-Step Guides to Instructional Coaching*, Woodbridge: John Catt Educational.

Shulman, L.S. and Shuman, J.H. (2009) How and what teachers learn: A shifting perspective, *Journal of Education*, 189 (1/2): 1–8.

Sibieta, L. (2020) *School attendance rates across the UK since full reopening*. London: Education Policy Institute and Nuffield Foundation [https://dera.ioe.ac.uk/36814/1/UK-school-reopening-attendance-November_EPI.pdf].

Silins, H. and Mulford, B. (2004) Schools as learning organisations: Effects on teacher leadership and student outcomes, *School Effectiveness and School Improvement*, 15 (3/4): 443–466.

Sitter, K.C. and Nusbaum, E.A. (2018) Critical disability studies and community engagement, in D.E. Lund (ed.) *The Wiley International Handbook of Service-Learning for Social Justice*. Newark, NJ: Wiley (pp. 191–202).

Skelton, C. (2009) Failing to get men into primary teaching: A feminist critique, *Journal of Education Policy*, 24 (1): 39–54.

Sleeter, C.E. (2017) Critical race theory and the Whiteness of teacher education, *Urban Education*, 52 (2): 155–169.

Sleeter, C.E. and Owuor, J. (2011) Research on the impact of teacher preparation to teach diverse students: The research we have and the research we need, *Action in Teacher Education*, 33 (5/6): 524–536.

Sloan, K. (2006) Teacher identity and agency in school worlds: Beyond the all-good/all-bad discourse on accountability-explicit curriculum policies, *Curriculum Inquiry*, 36 (2): 119–152.

Smith, E. and Gorard, S. (2005) 'They don't give us back our marks': The role of formative feedback in student progress, *Assessment in Education: Principles, Policy and Practice*, 12 (1): 21–38.

Smith, H.J. and Lander, V. (2012) Collusion or collision: Effects of teacher ethnicity in the teaching of critical whiteness, *Race, Ethnicity and Education*, 15 (3): 331–351.

Soler, J. and Openshaw, R. (2007) 'To be or not to be?': The politics of teaching phonics in England and New Zealand, *Journal of Early Childhood Literacy*, 7 (3): 333–352.

Soni, A., Lynch, P., McLinden, M., Mbukwa-Ngwira, J., Mankhwazi, M., Jolley E. et al. (2020) Facilitating the participation of children with disabilities in early childhood development centres in Malawi: Developing a sustainable staff training programme, *Sustainability*, 12 (5): 2104 [https://www.mdpi.com/2071-1050/12/5/2104].

Sriprakash, A., Tikly, L. and Walker, S. (2020) The erasures of racism in education and international development: Re-reading the 'global learning crisis', *Compare: A Journal of Comparative and International Education*, 50 (5): 676–692.

Steedle, J., Kugelmass, H. and Nemeth, A. (2010) What do they measure? Comparing three learning outcome assessments, *Change: The Magazine of Higher Learning*, 42 (4): 33–37.

Stiggins, R. (2005) From formative assessment to assessment FOR learning: A path to success in standards-based schools, *Phi Delta Kappan*, 87 (4): 324–328.

Stigler, J.W. and Hiebert, J. (1999) *The Teaching Gap: Best Ideas from the World's Teachers for Improving Education in the Classroom*. New York: Simon & Schuster.

Stoll, L., Bolam, R., McMahon, A., Wallace, M. and Thomas, S. (2006) Professional learning communities: A review of the literature, *Journal of Educational Change*, 7: 221–258.

Stoll, L., Harris, A. and Handscomb, G. (2012) *Great professional development which leads to great pedagogy: Nine claims from research schools and academies*. Nottingham: National College for School Leadership [https://assets.publishing.service.gov.uk/government/uploads/system/uploads/attachment_data/file/335707/Great-professional-development-which-leads-to-great-pedagogy-nine-claims-from-research.pdf].

Stone, P. (2020) Reconceptualising teacher identity, in V. Bower (ed.) *Debates in Primary Education*. London: Routledge.

Stutchbury, K., Chamberlain, L. and Amos, S. (2019) *Supporting professional development through MOOCs: The TESSA experience*. Pan-Commonwealth Forum 9 (PCF9), 2019. Conference Proceedings. Commonwealth of Learning, Vancouver, Canada [http://oro.open.ac.uk/70263/1/70263.pdf].

Su, B., Bonk, C.J., Magjuka, R.J., Liu, X. and Lee, S. (2005) The importance of interaction in web-based education: A program-level case study of online MBA courses, *Journal of Interactive Online Learning*, 4 (1): 1–19.

Sutton Trust (2021) *Learning in lockdown*. Research Brief, January [www.suttontrust.com/wp-content/uploads/2021/01/Learning-in-Lockdown.pdf].

Swaffield, S. (2011) Getting to the heart of authentic Assessment for Learning, *Assessment in Education: Principles, Policy and Practice*, 18 (4): 433–449.

Swaffield, S. (2015) Support and challenge for school leaders: Headteachers' perceptions of school improvement partners, *Educational Management Administration and Leadership*, 43 (1): 61–76.

Swann, M., Peacock, A., Hart, S. and Drummond, M.J. (2012) *Creating Learning without Limits*. Maidenhead: Open University Press.

Symeou, L. and Karagiorgi, Y. (2018) Culturally aware but not yet ready to teach the 'others', *Journal for Multicultural Education*, 12 (4): 314–329.

Tait, A. (2008) What are open universities for?, *Open Learning: The Journal of Open, Distance and e-Learning*, 23 (2): 85–93 [https://www.tandfonline.com/doi/full/10.1080/02680510802051871].

Taylor, M. (2017) *Good work: The Taylor review of modern working practices*. London: Department for Business, Energy and Industrial Strategy, 11 July [https://www.gov.uk/government/publications/good-work-the-taylor-review-of-modern-working-practices].

Teacher Toolkit (2019) *A 9-point professional development plan for schools* [https://www.teachertoolkit.co.uk/2019/10/27/9-point-cpd/#:~:text=Problems%20with%20Professional%20Development%20There%20are%20several%20reasons,another%20lack%20of%20funding%20and%20lack%20of%20time].

Tefera, A.A., Powers, J.M. and Fischman, G.E. (2018) Intersectionality in education: A conceptual aspiration and research imperative, *Review of Research in Education*, 42 (1): vii–xvii.

Tejeda, C., Espinoza, M. and Gutierrez, K. (2003) Toward a decolonizing pedagogy: Social justice reconsidered', in P.P. Trifonas (ed.) *Pedagogies of Difference: Rethinking Education for Social Change*. London: Routledge (pp. 9–38).

The King's School (2015) *E-safety and social media policy*. Canterbury: The King's School https://silo.tips/download/e-safety-digital-media-policy.

Thomas, L. (2012) *Thinking about an area based curriculum: A guide for practitioners*. London: RSA [https://www.thersa.org/globalassets/pdfs/rsa_thinking-about-an-area-based-curriculum-a-guide-for-practitioners.pdf].

Thomas, L., Deaudelin, C., Desjardins, J. and Dezutter, O. (2011) Elementary teachers' formative evaluation practices in an era of curricular reform in Quebec, Canada, *Assessment in Education: Principles, Policy and Practice*, 18 (4): 381–398.

Thomas, L.S. (2012) *A Masters level teaching profession: A study of the rationale for the Masters level Postgraduate Certificate in Education, a Masters level teaching profession and the Masters in Teaching and Learning and the perceptions of key stakeholders in the English West Midlands*. Doctoral thesis, University of Birmingham.

Tigchelaar, A., Brouwer, N. and Korthagen, F. (2008) Crossing horizons: Continuity and change during second-career teachers' entry into teaching, *Teaching and Teacher Education*, 24 (6): 1530–1550.

Timberlake, M.T., Thomas, A.B. and Barret, B. (2017) The allure of simplicity: Scripted curricula and equity, *Teaching and Teacher Education*, 67 (1): 46–52.

Torrance, D., Forde, C., King, F. and Razzaq, J. (2021) What is the problem? A critical review of social justice leadership preparation and development, *Professional Development in Education*, 47 (1): 22–35.

Truong-White, H. and McLean, L. (2015) Digital storytelling for transformative global citizenship education, *Canadian Journal of Education/Revue Canadienne de l'Éducation*, 38 (2): 38.2.03.

Tucker, M. (2019) *Leading High-Performing School Systems: Lessons from the World's Best*. Alexandria, VA: ASCD.

Turnbull, M.D. (2005) Student teacher professional agency in the practicum, *Asia-Pacific Journal of Teacher Education*, 33 (2): 195–208.

UNESCO (2009) *National professional standards for teachers in Pakistan* [http://unesco.org.pk/education/teachereducation/files/National%20Professional%20Standards%20for%20Teachers.pdf].

UNESCO (2015) *Rethinking education: Towards a global common good?* Paris: UNESCO [http://unesdoc.unesco.org/images/0023/002325/232555e.pdf].

United Nations Children's Fund (UNICEF) (2020) *A new era for girls: Taking stock of 25 years of progress* [https://data.unicef.org/resources/a-new-era-for-girls-taking-stock-of-25-years-of-progress/].

United Nations High Commissioner for Refugees (UNHCR) (2020) *Coming together for refugee education report* [https://www.unhcr.org/uk/publications/education/5f4f9a2b4/coming-together-refugee-education-education-report-2020.html].

Universities UK (2019) *Black, Asian and Minority Ethnic student attainment at UK universities: #closingthegap* [bame-student-attainment-uk-universities-case-studies.pdf].

Valentine, D., Willis, H.P., Metcalfe, C. and Barratt, M. (2018) *How to develop a monitoring and evaluation framework*. London: National Council for Voluntary Organisations [https://knowhow.ncvo.org.uk/how-to/how-to-develop-a-monitoring-and-evaluation-framework].

Van der Heijden, H.R.M.A., Geldens, J.J., Beijaard, D. and Popeijus, H.L. (2015) Characteristics of teachers as change agents, *Teachers and Teaching: Theory and Practice*, 21 (6): 681–699.

Van der Riet, P., Rossiter, R., Kirby, D., Dluzewska, T. and Harmon, C. (2015) Piloting a stress management and mindfulness program for undergraduate nursing students: Student feedback and lessons learned, *Nurse Education Today*, 35 (1): 44–49.

van Schaik, P., Volman, M., Admiraal, W. and Schenke, W. (2018) Barriers and conditions for teachers' utilisation of academic knowledge, *International Journal of Educational Research*, 90 (1): 50–63.

Varkey Foundation (2018) *Making Ghanaian girls great!* [https://www.varkeyfoundation.org/what-we-do/programmes/making-ghanaian-girls-great].

Vass, G. (2017) Preparing for culturally responsive schooling: Initial teacher educators into the fray, *Journal of Teacher Education*, 68 (5): 451–462.

Vescio, V., Bondy, E. and Poekert, P.E. (2009) Preparing multicultural teacher educators: Toward a pedagogy of transformation, *Teacher Education Quarterly*, 36 (2): 5–24.

Victoria State Government (VSG) (2013) *Professional codes of conduct*. Victoria, Australia: VSG.

Vince, R. and Martin, L. (1993) Inside action learning: An exploration of the psychology and politics of the action learning model, *Management, Education and Development*, 24 (3): 205–215.

Walton, E. and Rusznyak, L. (2020) Cumulative knowledge-building for inclusive education in initial teacher education, *European Journal of Teacher Education*, 43 (1): 18–37.

Waters, M. (2020) *Learning to be a teacher for Wales: The induction of teachers into the profession*. Cardiff: Welsh Government [https://gov.wales/sites/default/files/publications/2020-11/learning-to-be-teacher-wales-induction-teachers-into-profession.pdf].

Welsh Government (2017) *Education in Wales: Our national mission. Action plan 2017–21* [https://gov.wales/sites/default/files/publications/2018-03/education-in-wales-our-national-mission.pdf].

Welsh Government (2021) *The National Strategy for Educational Research and Enquiry (NSERE): Vision document* [https://gov.wales/national-strategy-educational-research-and-enquiry-nsere-vision-document-html].

Weurlander, M., Soderberg, M., Scheja, M., Hult, H. and Wernerson, A. (2012) Exploring formative assessment as a tool for learning: Students' experiences of different methods of formative assessment, *Assessment and Evaluation in Higher Education*, 37 (6): 747–760.

White, P. (2013) Who's afraid of research questions? The neglect of research questions in the methods literature and a call for question-led methods teaching, *International Journal of Research and Method in Education*, 36 (3): 213–227.

White, S. (2021) Strengthening a research-rich teaching profession: An Australian study, *Teaching Education*, 32 (1): 47–62.

Wiles, F. (2013) Not easily put into a box: Constructing professional identity, *Social Work Education*, 32 (7): 854–866.

Wiley, D., Bliss, T.J. and McEwen, M. (2014) Open educational resources: A review of the literature, in J.M. Spector, M.D. Merrill, J. Elen and M.J. Bishop (eds.) *Handbook of Research on Educational Communications and Technology*, 4th edition. New York: Springer (pp. 781–789).

Wiliam, D., Lee, C., Harrison, C. and Black, P. (2004). Teachers developing assessment for learning: Impact on student achievement. *Assessment in education: principles, policy & practice*, 11 (1): 49–65.

Wilkins, C. and Comber, C. (2015) 'Elite' career-changers in the teaching profession, *British Educational Research Journal*, 41 (6): 1010–1030.

Willemse, T.M., Boei, F. and Pillen, M. (2016) Fostering teacher educators' professional development on practice-based research through communities of inquiry, *Vocations and Learning*, 9 (1): 85–110.

Williams, C. (2021) *Black, Asian and Minority Ethnic communities, contributions and Cynefin in the New Curriculum Working Group*, Final Report [black-asian-minority-ethnic-communities-contributions-cynefin-new-curriculum-working-group-final-report.pdf].

Wolfenden, F. (2008) *TESSA: An open educational resource site for teacher education in Africa*. eLearning Africa: 3rd International Conference on ICT for Development, Education and Training, 28–30 May, Accra, Ghana [http://www.elearning-africa.com].

Wolfenden, F. (2015) TESS-India OER: Collaborative practices to improve teacher education, *Indian Journal of Teacher Education*, 1 (3): 13–29.

Wolfenden, F. and Adinolfi, L. (2019) An exploration of agency in the localisation of open educational resources for teacher development, *Journal of Learning, Media and Technology*, 4 (3): 327–344.

Wolfenden, F., Adinolfi, L., Cross, S., Lee, C., Paranjpe, S. and Safford, K. (2017a) *Moving towards more participatory practice with Open Educational Resources: TESS-India academic review*. Milton Keynes: The Open University [http://oro.open.ac.uk/49631/].

Wolfenden, F., Auckloo, P., Buckler, A. and Cullen, J. (2017b) Teacher educators and OER in East Africa: Interrogating pedagogic change, in C. Hodgkinson-Williams and P.B. Arinto (eds.) *Adoption and Impact of OER in the Global South*. Cape Town: ROER4D (pp. 251–286).

Wong, S., Shapcott, R. and Parker, E. (2020) Graphic lives, visual stories: Reflections on practice, participation, and the potentials of creative engagement, *Autobiographical Studies*, 35 (2): 311–329.

Wood, P. (2012) Blogs as liminal space: Student teachers at the threshold, *Technology, Pedagogy and Education*, 21 (1): 85–99.

Woodward, C., Harrison, S. and Tope, C. (2020) *A positive outcome in the time of COVID-19 through the use of WhatsApp in Zimbabwe*, UKFIET, 29 July [https://www.ukfiet .org/2020/a-positive-outcome-in-the-time-of-covid-19-through-the-use-of-whatsapp-in-zimbabwe/].

World Bank. (2011). *Learning for all: Investing in people's knowledge and skills to promote development*. Washington, DC: International Bank for Reconstruction and Development/World Bank.

Xu, H. (2020) Lesson study as evidence-based teacher collaboration and inquiry, in A. Fox and V. Poultney (eds.) *Professional Learning Communities and Teacher Enquiry: Evidence-based Teaching for Enquiring Teachers*. St. Albans: Critical Publishing (pp. 55–69).

Xu, H. and Pedder, D. (2014) Lesson study: An international review of the research, in P. Dudley (ed.) *Lesson Study*. London: Routledge (pp. 29–58).

Zeichner, K.M., Tabachnick, B.R. and Densmore, K. (1987) Individual, institutional and cultural influences on the development of teachers' craft knowledge, in J. Calderhead (ed.) *Exploring Teachers' Thinking*. London: Cassell (pp. 21–59).

Index

Page numbers in italics are figures; with 't' are tables.